GEOLOGY
OF THE
LEWIS & CLARK TRAIL
IN NORTH DAKOTA

GEOLOGY

OF THE
LEWIS & CLARK TRAIL
IN NORTH DAKOTA

JOHN W. HOGANSON
AND EDWARD C. MURPHY

2003
Mountain Press Publishing Company
Missoula, Montana

First Printing, April 2003

Cover photo: *Exposures of the yellow-colored Bullion Creek formation along a Yellowstone River cutbank south of the confluence of the Missouri and Yellowstone Rivers. View is to the north from the Highway 200 Hjalmer Nelson Memorial Bridge.*
Inset photo on back cover: *Cannonball concretions in the Fox Hills sandstone just north of the mouth of the Cannonball River.*

Library of Congress Cataloging-in-Publication Data

Hoganson, John W.
  Geology of the Lewis and Clark Trail in North Dakota / John
W. Hoganson and Edward C. Murphy.
       p.   cm.
Includes bibliographical references and index.
  ISBN 0-87842-476-8 (pbk. : alk. paper)
  1. Geology—North Dakota. 2. Lewis and Clark National
Historic Trail.   I. Murphy, Edward C.   II. Title.
  QE149.H64 2003
  557.84—dc21

                                                      2003004812

PRINTED IN HONG KONG BY MANTEC PRODUCTION COMPANY

Mountain Press Publishing Company
P.O. Box 2399 • Missoula, Montana 59806
(406) 728-1900

To my children, Kelly and Josh, who have always been a source of inspiration for me, and their children, Macaulay, Zoey, Noah, Tierney, and Nikolas, future travelers of the Lewis and Clark Trail. —John

To my father who, having grown up next to the steel mills in South Buffalo, New York, appreciated the wide open spaces of North Dakota and was intrigued by the vast uncharted lands that lay before Lewis and Clark. He passed his interest in the expedition on to me, and I, in turn, hope to pass it along to my sons, Paul and Daniel, while we explore the Lewis and Clark Trail. —Ed

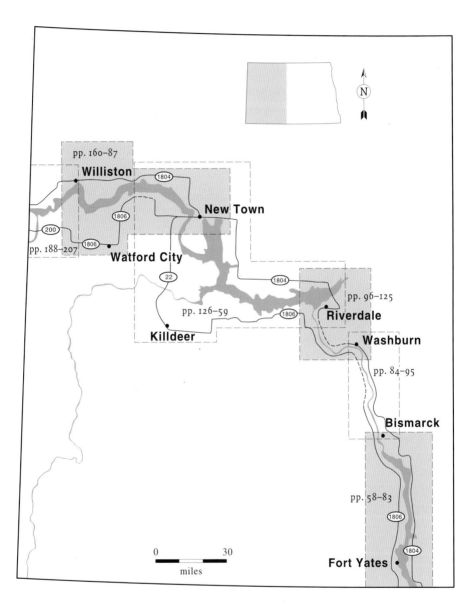

pp. 160–87

Williston

1804

New Town

1806

200

pp. 188–207

1806

Watford City

22

1804

pp. 126–59

1806

pp. 96–125

Riverdale

Killdeer

Washburn

pp. 84–95

Bismarck

pp. 58–83

1806

0   30

miles

1804

Fort Yates

CONTENTS

PREFACE

Neither of us are, in the true sense, Lewis and Clark scholars. We wrote this book because we believed it would be of interest to those traveling the Lewis and Clark Trail and to those who are just interested in the geology along the Missouri River. Between the two of us, we have more than forty years of experience studying the geology along the Missouri River and adjacent areas. As we researched Lewis and Clark's observations of geologic features, we were caught up in the intriguing story of the expedition and were amazed by its scientific accomplishments.

One of our mentors from the University of North Dakota, Professor Emeritus F. D. Holland, Jr., wrote that one of his historian friends had pointed out that "geologists would certainly not want historians running geological surveys and that, in like manner, scientists do not do the best job of writing history" (Holland, 1961). Aware of our shortcomings as historians, we proceeded on and wrote this account of the geology that Lewis and Clark observed as they passed through what we now call North Dakota. Any errors in historical fact presented herein should be attributed to us.

The Lewis and Clark Expedition spent more time in North Dakota— a total of 213 days—than in any other state during the 2 1/2-year-long journey that spanned a distance of 4,162 miles from St. Louis to the Pacific Ocean. They traveled about 362 river miles (one way) in North Dakota. The expedition entered North Dakota on October 14, 1804, and spent the winter of 1804-5 at Fort Mandan, a building they constructed near the thriving Mandan and Hidatsa villages near present-day Washburn. They resumed their journey on April 7, 1805, and crossed into Montana on April 27. Anxious to get back to St. Louis, their return trip through North Dakota took only 17 days (August 3 through August 20, 1806).

Lewis, Clark, and other expedition members were astute observers and recorders of information. Though they seldom theorized about origins of landforms or other geological phenomena, when they did, they made insightful comments. They made the first collection of rocks, minerals, and fossils in North Dakota for the purpose of scientific study, and they recorded the occurrence of potentially commercial natural resources such as lignite coal and Glauber's salt. Their observations about the beauty of the North Dakota landscape, the richness of the soil, and the clarity of the air fit well the preconceived view of many at the time that areas west of the Mississippi were gardens of Eden, "a fertile, well-watered area perfectly suited for occupancy by an agrarian people" (Allen, 1975).

Thanks to the journal entries and Clark's maps, there are several locations in North Dakota where one can literally stand in the spot where Lewis or Clark stood. Their campsites have been inundated by Lakes Oahe and Sakakawea or destroyed by floods, but in a few places along the noninundated stretches, the Missouri River is in the same approximate position that it was two hundred years ago. At these sites, it takes little imagination to envision the countryside as it must have appeared to Lewis and Clark.

Geologic features are visible from a number of roads that parallel the river and, if you have a boat, from the water. The U.S. Army Corps of Engineers manages land adjacent to Lakes Oahe and Sakakawea, but land adjacent to the Missouri River is generally privately owned. Please obtain permission from the appropriate source before leaving the roadways or venturing off the water.

We are grateful to a number of people and thank them for their support of this project. John P. Bluemle, North Dakota State Geologist, granted us permission to work on this book. John's book on the geology of North Dakota, *Face of North Dakota*, was a valuable tool in our research. In addition, his editorial suggestions greatly improved this manuscript.

We obtained the journal entries (verbatim) of Lewis and Clark and other expedition members from *The Journals of the Lewis and Clark Expedition*, a thirteen-volume compilation edited by Gary E. Moulton and published by the University of Nebraska Press. Moulton made a great effort to present as accurate and reliable an edition of the journals as possible, and his work is viewed as the primary Lewis and Clark journal source. We thank Gary for providing us additional information about the expedition.

In constructing our geologic maps, we modified the 1:500,000 scale geologic map of North Dakota by Lee Clayton and others (1980). Martin Plamondon II and Washington State University Press permitted us to incorporate Plamondon's rendition of Clark's map of the Missouri River into our geologic maps. Martin Plamondon's maps and text also provided much valuable information about Clark's mapping methods, the location of Lewis and Clark campsites, and other features.

Bob Bergantino of the Montana Bureau of Mines and Geology provided valuable insight into several topics associated with the expedition. Ken Karsmizki of the Columbia Gorge Discovery Center provided information on his quest to discover the site of Fort Mandan. Ray Wood, University of Missouri-Columbia, provided us information about maps that were available to and were carried by the Lewis and Clark Expedition. Earle Spamer and Rick McCourt of the Academy of Natural Sciences of Philadelphia shared information about geological specimens that the Lewis and Clark Expedition collected in North Dakota and are now part of the academy's collections. Earle graciously allowed one of us (Ed) to examine the specimens and provided images of the Lewis and Clark clinker specimens illustrated in this book. The Smithsonian National Museum of American History provided an image of Clark's compass, which we included in this book. Robert Cox and the American Philosophical Society Library provided the image of the Lewis and Clark journals collage. The National Park Service Independence National Historical Park Library gave us permission to use the Lewis and Clark portraits.

Larry Mensching and the Joslyn Art Museum gave us permission to use the Karl Bodmer images. Richard Sorensen and the Smithsonian American Art Museum gave us permission to use the George Catlin image. The State Historical Society of North Dakota allowed us to use the images by Andy Knutson and Ralph W. Smith and historical photographs. Bruce Erickson of the Science Museum of Minnesota provided us the Julie Martinez Paleocene habitat painting. Vern Erickson, Charles Fritz, Gary P. Miller, and Michael Haynes enthusiastically provided images of their Lewis and Clark paintings. Unless otherwise noted, the photographs in this book were taken by us. Jeffrey Olson of the National Park Service, Lewis and Clark National Historic Trail, provided a photograph and the North Dakota tourism Division of the Department of Commerce allowed use of a photograph by Will Kincaid.

Joanne Olson of the North Dakota Tourism Division of the Department of Commerce provided tourism statistics about recreational use of Lake Sakakawea. John Jacobs, of Basin Electric Power Cooperative, gave us information about the engineering of Lake Sakakawea's water intake systems. Charlie Jaszkowiak, from the Bismarck Water Treatment Plant, provided historical information about the water quality of the Missouri River at Bismarck. Todd Sando of the North Dakota State Water Commission supplied us with hydrological data for the Missouri River. Marilyn Hudson and Calvin Grinnell, of the Three Affiliated Tribes, provided insight into Mandan and Hidatsa lore and history. Cheryl Koulas, of the North Dakota Indian Affairs Commission, recommended terms to use when referring to Native peoples. Terry O'Halloran, Dorothy Cook, and Cindy Haakenson, of the Knife River Indian Villages National Historic Site, located artifacts and images for use in this book and allowed us to borrow and photograph them. Renee Boen, of the South Dakota State Historical Society Archaeological Research Center, provided us access to the "buffalo stone" from the Anton Rygh site. Several members of the State Historical Society of North Dakota provided information and assistance: Brian Austin, Jim Davis, Kathy Davison, Susan Dingle, Mark Halvorson, Shawn Holz, Paul Picha, Len Thorson, Sharon Silengo, Fern Swenson, Tim Reed, and Lottie Bailey. GIS specialists Elroy Kadrmas of the North Dakota Geological Survey and Rod Bassler of the North Dakota State Water Commission collaborated in generating the maps in this book. Ken Urlacher of the North Dakota Geological Survey created the line drawings. Linda Johnson, North Dakota Geological Survey administrative assistant, and Karen Gutenkunst, North Dakota Industrial Commission business manager, provided much valuable assistance. We gratefully acknowledge the cooperation of landowners in the Missouri River Valley. Special thanks to landowners Monte and Nancy Allen, Max Guenthner, and Orville Oster (Missouri River Lodge). Helen Volk-Schill, manager of the Lewis and Clark State Park, gave us access to the park during the off-season.

Jennifer Carey and James Lainsbury, our editors at Mountain Press Publishing Company, provided many insightful suggestions and ideas on how best to present information in this book and did an outstanding job of editing. It was a joy working with them. We are particularly thankful for partial funding for this project through a grant from the National Park Service Lewis and Clark National Historic Trail Challenge Cost Share Program administered by Richard Williams and our old friend Gerard Baker. The North Dakota Lewis and Clark Bicentennial Foundation, under direction of David Borlag, processed that funding. Our thanks to Noel Poe, former superintendent of the Theodore Roosevelt National Park, who provided us with encouragement. We extend special thanks to Merl Paaverud, Director of the State Historical Society of North Dakota, and Claudia Berg, Director of the Museum and Education Division of the State Historical Society of North Dakota, for recognizing this as a worthwhile project and for providing funding from the State Historical Society of North Dakota for completion of this book.

An Expedition
to the Northwest

Jefferson's Vision

In addition to being a statesman, Thomas Jefferson was a visionary and a promoter of science. He was a prominent figure during the eighteenth-century Age of Enlightenment, and this period in the development of American science is often called the Age of Jefferson. As an expansionist, Jefferson had a consuming interest in the exploration of the West even though he never traveled more than a few miles west of Monticello, Virginia. Much of his knowledge about western North America was gained through his extensive library, one of the best in America at that time. He amassed most of the library while in France from 1784 to 1789, where he succeeded Benjamin Franklin as U.S. Minister to France. His library of over 6,500 volumes later became the nucleus for the Library of Congress.

Jefferson realized that expansion of the United States to the West was necessary and inevitable, an idea later called Manifest Destiny. Recognizing the need to gain information about this essentially uncharted part of North America, he conceptualized a plan in 1793, while serving as vice president of the American Philosophical Society, to explore the region. The French biologist André Michaux was commissioned to travel up the Missouri River and across the mountains to the West Coast, essentially the same route that Lewis and Clark would explore ten years later. Many of the instructions that Jefferson gave Michaux were the same as those he gave to Meriwether Lewis in 1803. The Michaux Expedition never materialized because Michaux was found to be an agent of the French government. Jefferson made other attempts to organize expeditions to explore the West but was not able to do so until he became president of the United States in 1801.

President Jefferson was able to gain legislative and therefore financial support for the Lewis and Clark Expedition by promoting the project as a commercial, military, and political venture. In a secret message to

1

Congress on January 18, 1803, Jefferson asked for and was granted an appropriation of $2,500 "for the purpose of extending the external commerce of the United States" (Jackson, 1962). Lewis had estimated the cost of the expedition although it was known that this was a very low estimate; the final cost was over $30,000. The primary objectives of the expedition were to find a water passage to the West Coast, to potentially establish commercial ties with Native peoples living along the Missouri River, to assess areas for agriculture potential, and to identify natural resources. In fact, Jefferson, Lewis, Clark, and others often referred to the expedition as an "enterprise." The purchase of the area from the Mississippi River to the "crest of the Rocky Mountains" from France in the Louisiana Purchase of 1803, primarily to secure more agricultural land for the United States, is one of the most dramatic examples of territorial expansion in history and illustrates Jefferson's remarkable foresight. The Lewis and Clark Expedition was planned well before the purchase, and the expedition was already at the mouth of the Missouri River preparing to depart upriver when news of the Louisiana Purchase was released. This expedition began a tradition of federal government–sponsored scientific expeditions to the West that eventually resulted in the establishment of the United States Geological Survey.

From the beginning, Jefferson envisioned a major scientific component of the expedition. Jefferson's philosophy of science, including geology, was utilitarian, and he believed that geology was worthy of study only for the practical purpose of serving humankind. As stated in a letter to Dr. John P. Emmet in 1826, Jefferson thought that dwelling on the theoretical aspect of geology was not a worthy endeavor:

> To learn as far as observation has informed us . . . the ordinary arrangement of the different strata of minerals in the earth, to know from their habitual collocations, and proximities, where we find ore mineral; whether another, for which we are seeking, may be expected to be in its neighborhood, is useful. But the dreams about the modes of creation, enquiries whether our globe has been formed by the agency of fire or water, how many millions of years it has cost Vulcan or Neptune to produce what the fist of the Creator would effect by a single act of will, is too idle to be worth a single hour of any man's life. (BROWNE, 1944)

Jefferson also once wrote that he:

> could not see any practical importance in knowing whether the earth was six thousand or six million years old, and the different formations were of no consequence so long as they were not composed of coal, iron, or useful minerals. (BROWN, 1943)

It should be noted that Jefferson deviated from this utilitarian philosophy at times. An example would be his interest in theoretical paleontology. He speculated about the origin of fossils on mountaintops in his 1782 publication *Notes on the State of Virginia*, and he suggested, in his 1799 article on the ground sloth *Megalonyx*, that Ice Age mammals still existed in western North America.

He did recognize, however, the practical and commercial value of geology and included geological inquiry in the goals of the expedition. The directive to make geological observations was spelled out in Jefferson's June 20, 1803, letter to Meriwether Lewis (in which Jefferson, after consulting with eminent scientists and other knowledgeable leaders, gave specific instructions on what he expected the expedition to accomplish):

> Other objects worthy of notice will be . . .
>
> the soil & face of the country, its growth & vegetable productions, especially those not of the U.S.;
>
> the animals of the country generally, & especially those not know in the U.S.;
>
> the remains or accounts of any which may be deemed rare or extinct;
>
> the mineral productions of every kind; but more particularly metals, limestone, pit coal, & saltpetre; salines & mineral waters, noting the temperature of the last, & such circumstances as may indicate their character;
>
> volcanic appearances;
>
> climate, as characterized by the thermometer, by the proportion of rainy, cloudy, & clear days, by lightening, hail, snow, ice, by the access & recess of frost, by the winds prevailing at different seasons, the dates at which particular plants put forth or lose their flower, or leaf, times of appearances of particular birds, reptiles or insects.
>
> Altho' your route will be along the channel of the Missouri, yet you will endeavor to inform yourself, by enquiry, of the character & extent of the country watered by its branches, & especially on it's Southern side. (JACKSON, 1962)

Thomas Jefferson was not only one of the Founding Fathers of the United States, but he was also one of the early members of the American Philosophical Society, which Benjamin Franklin founded to bring together the leading scholars of the country. Jefferson was elected as a member of the society in 1780 at the same time as George Washington, John Adams, and James Madison. He was president of this society from 1797 to 1815 following the terms of George Washington and astronomer David Rittenhouse. Philadelphia, headquarters of the American Philosophical Society, became the center of science in the United States. Jefferson consulted many of the society members while drafting the instruction letter to Lewis. Several of the society members, including Jefferson and Franklin, frequented Europe and were acquaintances of European scientists, including the renowned French paleontologist Georges Cuvier. France was leading the world in the biological sciences, especially in its study of prehistoric animals. Jefferson and other members of the society were well aware of the prevailing theories about geology and paleontology, and these theories became the basis for many of the scientific goals of the Lewis and Clark Expedition.

The science of geology was in its infancy during the Age of Jefferson. Scientists were just beginning to employ empirical observations in establishing geological theory, and they were just starting to understand the geological processes affecting the earth. The formation of mountain ranges by global tectonic processes had not been conceived. There was very little information about the location, extent, and elevation of the Rocky Mountains other than the knowledge that they existed.

Quest for a Northwest Passage

The notion that a water route through the Rocky Mountains ("Stony" or "Shining" Mountains at the time) existed was prevalent during the time of the Lewis and Clark Expedition. The French Jesuit missionary Jacques Marquette, who discovered the Missouri River in 1673, was first to perceive the Missouri as an integral part of that route. The importance of finding such a route, as a conduit to enhance commerce, was paramount to the argument Jefferson used to obtain support for the Lewis and Clark Expedition. Geographic dogma of the time, although incorrect, supported the concept of a transcontinental waterway that would link the eastern part of the North American continent with the western part.

Scholars believed that mountains in the western part of the continent would be similar to those in the east: narrow with relatively low-elevation summits and passes and waterways through them. They also believed that rivers in western North America were navigable to their sources and that the headwaters of these rivers originated from a hypothetical pyramidal high ground, upland plateau, or a narrow mountain range—the "height-of-land" theory. This height-of-land was the drainage divide from which rivers either flowed to the Pacific Ocean or to the Atlantic Ocean. Jefferson and others thought that short portages would be enough to connect the east- and west-flowing rivers. They believed that such a connection was likely between the headwaters of the Missouri and Columbia Rivers—a Northwest Passage.

Maps of "Louisiana" available to Jefferson, Lewis, and Clark generally showed the Rocky Mountains as a single mountain chain extending from Canada to Mexico with gaps in the mountains to accommodate the waterways. The coastal mountain ranges in the Pacific Northwest were mostly unknown and did not appear on these maps. Even though the Lewis and Clark Expedition dispelled the notion of a Northwest Passage, we cannot emphasize enough the importance of the knowledge gained during the expedition about the geology of the northwest, particularly illustrated by Clark's map.

Hunt for Prehistoric Beasts

Jefferson was particularly interested in prehistoric animals. In 1782, in a letter to a friend, he stated, "I received in August your favor, wherein you give me hopes of being able to procure for me some of the big bones. . . . A specimen of each of several species of bones now to be found, is to me the most desirable objects in natural history" (Osborn, 1935). In 1782, in his *Notes on the State of Virginia*, Jefferson discussed the proposed theories to explain the occurrence of marine fossils entombed in rocks in mountains several thousand feet above sea level. In 1797, while vice president of the United States, he presented a paper at the American Philosophical Society describing the fossil remains of a huge, clawed animal found in a cave during excavation of saltpeter in western Virginia. He called the animal, *Megalonyx*, or "large claw," and was initially convinced the fossils were from a large cat. Jefferson's memoir describing *Megalonyx*, the only paleontological article published by Jefferson, appeared in 1799 in the *Transactions of the American Philosophical Society*. Caspar Wistar, also a member of the American Philosophical Society and a good friend of Jefferson's, suggested in an accompanying memoir that the bones were from a giant sloth. In 1804, Georges Cuvier confirmed this based on casts of some of the *Megalonyx* bones that Jefferson sent to Paris. In 1822, Anselme Desmarest, a French naturalist, named the prehistoric animal *Megalonyx jeffersoni* in Thomas Jefferson's honor.

Jefferson's 1797 American Philosophical Society presentation on *Megalonyx* marked the beginning of vertebrate paleontology in North America, and Jefferson has been referred to as the "father of American paleontology." Coincidentally, a claw from *Megalonyx jeffersoni* was found

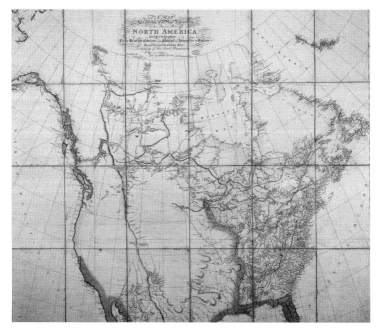

Aaron Arrowsmith's 1802 map shows the vast area of mostly uncharted land in western North America prior to the Lewis and Clark Expedition. Areas inside the green borders were not part of the United States at the time. —Map courtesy of the Library of Congress

Clark's historic expedition map. Clark compiled most of this map while the expedition camped at Fort Clatsop. It was redrawn by Samuel Lewis in 1814. The extent of knowledge gained by the expedition about the geography of the northwest can be appreciated by comparing this map to the 1802 Arrowsmith map. Clark's incredibly detailed map was the primary source of geographic information about western North America for several decades. —Map courtesy of the Library of Congress

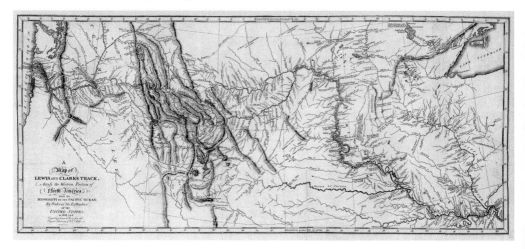

near one of Lewis and Clark's campsites in North Dakota nearly two hundred years after the expedition passed through the area.

Fossil discoveries in the eastern United States stimulated the American Philosophical Society to establish a committee to promote research on fossils and other natural history objects. One stated goal was to collect skeletons of mammoths and other prehistoric animals. Members of the society had collected "mammoth" fossils at Big Bone Lick in Kentucky near Cincinnati, Ohio, and at other locations in New York. At that time, the term "mammoth" referred to woolly mammoths and also to what was called the "North American incognitum." Some of these fossils and diagrams of the fossils were sent to Cuvier, who determined that many of the fossils were different than those of the woolly mammoth and placed them in a new genus that he referred to as *Mastodonte*, the American mastodon.

After the Lewis and Clark Expedition, Jefferson hired William Clark in 1807 to excavate "mammoth" fossils at Big Bone Lick. These bones were spread out on a floor at the White House where some of them were selected for the American Philosophical Society collection, some for Jefferson's museum at Monticello, some for display at the White House, and the remainder were sent to the National Institute of France. Cuvier identified most of these bones as mastodon, which confirmed his earlier interpretations.

As president, Jefferson provided government support for a mastodon excavation in New York led by the artist and naturalist Charles Willson Peale. A friend of Jefferson's and a member of the American Philosophical Society, Peale had established a museum in Philadelphia and wanted to restore a complete mastodon skeleton to exhibit in the museum. Enough bones were recovered from the excavation, with missing parts replaced by carved wood, to reconstruct the skeleton. The Peale Museum skeleton, the first skeleton of a prehistoric animal displayed in America, became a popular wonder, and the museum was referred to as the "Ninth Wonder of the World" (West, 1975). Public interest in large prehistoric animals developed similarly to the public's interest in dinosaurs today. Like today's commercialization of dinosaurs, products in Philadelphia were given names such as Mammoth Bread and Mammoth Cheese.

Jefferson, like many of his colleagues in the late 1700s, believed the pre-Darwinian orthodoxy of the absolute fixity of species. This scientific dogma viewed species as permanent and held that species do not become extinct. The discovery of the large prehistoric animal bones at Big Bone Lick and other localities, coupled with this philosophy, explains why Jefferson, in his letter of June 20, 1803, directed Lewis to record the animals or remains and accounts of animals that are thought to be rare or extinct. Jefferson speculated that some of the animals represented by fossils found in the eastern United States might still be living and roaming the American northwest. In his 1799 *Megalonyx* paper he wrote:

> In the present interior of our continent there is surely space and range enough for elephants and lions, if in that climate they could subsist; and for mammoths and megalonyxes who may subsist there. Our entire ignorance of the immense country to the West and North-west,

The skeleton of the Highgate Mastodon on display at the North Dakota Heritage Center in Bismarck is similar to the one exhibited at the Peale Museum in Philadelphia. The Peale museum closed around 1850 and its contents were scattered. This skeleton is 10 feet tall at the shoulder. —Courtesy of the State Historical Society of North Dakota (SHSND 88.240.1)

and of its contents, does not authorize us to say what it does not contain. . . . In fine, the bones exist: therefore the animal has existed. The movements of nature are in a never-ending circle. The animal species which have once put into a train of motion, is still probably moving in that train. For, if one link in nature's chain might be lost, another and another might be lost, till this whole system of things should vanish by piecemeal.

In a February 24, 1803, letter to the French naturalist Bernard Lacepede, Jefferson wrote this about the Lewis and Clark Expedition: "It is not improbable that this voyage of discovery will procure us further information of the Mammoth, & of the Megatherium" (Jackson, 1962).

The concept that prehistoric animals still existed in western North America was reinforced in Jefferson's mind by frontiersmen claiming to have encountered strange beasts in the wilderness and by a traditional Delaware Indian story that Jefferson told in his Notes on the State of Virginia (1782). During a visit by a delegation of warriors from the Delaware tribe, the governor of Virginia asked if they had heard of the large animals whose bones were found in salt deposits along the Ohio River. A Delaware spokesman related this story:

That in ancient times a herd of these large tremendous animals came to the Big-bone licks, and began an universal destruction of the bears, deer, elks, and buffaloes, and other animals, which had been created for the use of the Indians: that the Great Man above, looking down and seeing this, was so enraged that he seized his lightning, descended on the earth, seated himself on a neighboring mountain, on a rock, of which his seat and the print of his feet are still to be seen, and hurled his bolts among them till the whole were slaughtered, except the big large bull, who presented his forehead to the shafts, shook them off as they fell; but missing one at length, it wounded him in the side; whereon, springing round, he bounded over the Ohio, over the Wabash, the Illinois, and finally over the great lakes, where he is living at this day.

The fixity of species doctrine was rapidly falling out of favor in Europe, and evolutionary theory was beginning to be developed by Comte de Buffon, Erasmus Darwin, J. D. de Lamarck, and others. Georges Cuvier began writing a series of articles in 1799 that demonstrated that life on earth was dynamic and that many former inhabitants of earth had become extinct. In 1807, the Philadelphia biologist Benjamin Smith Barton, after reviewing Cuvier's work, proclaimed to members of the Linnaean Society in Philadelphia that it was now clear that "the continent of North America was formerly inhabited by several species of animals, which are now entirely unknown to us, except by their bones, and which, there is reason to believe, now no longer exist" (Greene, 1984).

The Captains

It seems evident to many, but not all, that Jefferson had Meriwether Lewis in mind to lead a transcontinental expedition when he hired Lewis to be his private secretary shortly after being elected president of the United States in 1801. Even if Jefferson had not hired Lewis with thoughts of putting him in charge of an expedition, he eventually came to believe that Lewis was the most qualified person for the job. In a February 27, 1803, letter to Benjamin Smith Barton, he stated that Lewis was skilled "in botany, natural history, mineralogy & astronomy, joined to the firmness of constitution and character, prudence, habits adapted to the woods, & a familiarity with the Indian manners and character, requisite for this undertaking" (Jackson, 1962).

Ronda (1998) observed that some, such as Jefferson's attorney general Levi Lincoln, questioned Lewis's appointment because of Lewis's "temperament and reputation for impetuousness" and his disposition "to court danger and perhaps even stand in harm's way." This uncer-

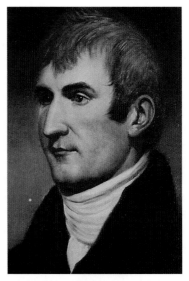

Portraits of William Clark (l., 1807–8) and Meriwether Lewis (r., 1807) painted by Charles Willson Peale.
—Art courtesy of Independence National Historical Park

tainty probably resulted from Ensign Meriwether Lewis's court-martial on November 1795 for insulting an officer while intoxicated. He pleaded not guilty and was exonerated of the charges.

Lewis, like Jefferson, was one of Virginia's gentry, and Jefferson had known Lewis when he was a child. Lewis was born in 1774, and after completing grammar school he joined the militia in 1794 during the Whiskey Rebellion. In 1795 he enlisted in the regular army. Captain Lewis was paymaster in the army and twenty-six years old when Jefferson appointed him his secretary in 1801. When Lewis was eighteen, he had applied for the job to lead the aborted expedition to the West that André Michaux was eventually chosen to lead. Apparently Jefferson thought Lewis was too young and inexperienced to lead an expedition at that time. Although Lewis had no formal training, he taught himself natural history and he was a woodsman. Jefferson listed one of Lewis's qualifications as "a talent for observation which had led him to an accurate knowledge of the plants and animals of his own country [Virginia]" (Cutright, 1969). Lewis gained training in the natural sciences and the use of instruments for surveying and determining latitude from Jefferson during his tenure as Jefferson's secretary from April 1801 to July 1803. Lewis also had access to Jefferson's comprehensive library during that time and likely spent considerable time reading about the western territory and the sciences. Lewis traveled extensively while in the army and learned military leadership, which proved to be an invaluable skill during the expedition.

Shortly after Congress appropriated funds for the expedition, Jefferson sent Lewis to Philadelphia for instruction from leading scientists to gain, according to Jefferson, "a greater familiarity with the technical language of the natural sciences, and a readiness in the astronomical observations necessary for the geography of his route" (Cutright, 1969). These scientists were colleagues of Jefferson and members of the American Philosophical Society.

In Lancaster, Pennsylvania, on his way to Philadelphia, Lewis obtained instruction on the use of instruments to establish longitude and latitude from the astronomer and mathematician Andrew Ellicott. He gained additional training in the use of the sextant and chronometer from another mathematician, Robert Patterson in Philadelphia. Although Lewis undoubtedly had already learned a great deal about geology and paleontology from Jefferson, Lewis spent time with the eminent anatomist and paleontologist Caspar Wistar while in Philadelphia. Lewis also visited with Charles Willson Peale at Peale's museum in Philadelphia, where many of the Lewis and Clark Expedition's natural history and ethnology collections would eventually be stored. Lewis also met with biologist and ethnologist Benjamin Smith Barton and the physician Benjamin Rush. This tutelage along with Lewis's keen observational skills served the expedition well. His detailed observations and specimen collections contributed greatly to scientific knowledge.

Although the expedition was initially intended to have one leader, Jefferson decided that a coleader was necessary in the event that Lewis became incapacitated. Jefferson left the selection of that person to Lewis. A military background, leadership qualities, and map-making skills were prerequisites for the position. Lewis asked William Clark, an army friend with considerable military experience and four years Lewis's senior, to colead the expedition. Clark, like Lewis, was from Albemarle County, Virginia. Jefferson knew the Clark family, whose residence was only a mile from the Jefferson plantation, and gladly sanctioned the coleadership appointment.

William Clark did not receive a formal education because the Clark family moved to the Kentucky wilderness when he was a young boy. Although he has often been viewed as the rugged, frontiersman coleader of the expedition in contrast to the intellectual Lewis, Clark did have an interest in history and the natural sciences and was self-educated in many subjects. His lack of formal education is rather dramatically emphasized in the spelling and grammar used in his expedition journal entries. Cutright (1969) called his spelling "picturesque," and Betts (1981) suggested that Clark was, "not only the master misspeller of them all, but also displayed dazzling virtuosity in his approach to punctuation, capitalization, and simple sentence structure." Betts also noted that Clark spelled *Sioux* twenty-seven different ways in his expedition journal entries. Clark, influenced by five brothers who fought in the Revolutionary War, joined the military at the age of nineteen where he learned leadership, engineering, and diplomatic skills primarily in campaigns against Native peoples in the Ohio Valley area. It was during this time, when Clark served under Major General "Mad" Anthony Wayne, that Clark and Meriwether Lewis became acquainted. After his court-martial trial, Lewis was transferred to an elite rifleman-sharpshooter company under Lieutenant William Clark's command. They became close friends during the eight months while in the same company, and that friendship solidified when Lewis became Jefferson's private secretary.

It is likely that Lewis taught Clark many of the skills he had learned during his time with Jefferson and the instructors in Philadelphia, including the use of the octant and other instruments. Because Clark's primary role in the expedition was to collect navigational data, survey the river, and make maps, his contributions to natural history and ethnology are generally understated. He was a keen observer and contributed greatly to the scientific objectives of the expedition, particularly during the times when Lewis was not recording information. Lewis either did not keep a daily journal until April 1805 or these journals have been lost. Therefore, Clark made most of the geological observations for the Missouri River valley south of Fort Mandan.

Serving as coleaders for twenty-eight months, it is remarkable that conflicts between them did not develop. Cutright (1969) suggested that perhaps they got along so well because of their different personalities: "Lewis was a dreamer, intent, fine-drawn, reserved, unwavering, generally humorless. Clark was warm, companionable, a good judge of men, an easy conversationalist—but inclined to keep a portion of his counsel to himself—and highly successful in meeting the demands of actual living."

Scientific Instruments, Books, and Maps

One of the primary objectives of the Lewis and Clark Expedition, stated in Jefferson's instruction letter to Lewis on June 20, 1803, was to conduct a detailed land survey of the route:

> Beginning at the mouth of the Missouri, you will take observations of latitude and longitude, at all remarkable points on the river, & especially at the mouths of rivers, at rapids, at islands, & other places & objects distinguished by such natural marks & characters of a durable kind, as that they may with certainty be recognized hereafter. The courses of the river between these points of observation may be supplied by the compass the log-line & by time, corrected by the observations themselves. The variations of the compass too, in different places, should be noticed.

> The interesting points of the portage between the heads of the Missouri, & of the water offering the best communication with the Pacific Ocean, should also be fixed by observations, & the course of that water to the ocean, in the same manner as that of the Missouri. (JACKSON, 1962)

It is probable that one of the reasons Lewis chose Clark as coleader was because of his knowledge of surveying. Private John Thompson, a professional surveyor before enlisting, undoubtedly assisted Clark in his surveying responsibilities. Observations made during surveying assisted Clark in the development of his incredibly detailed and accurate maps of the explored territory.

Jefferson was an experienced surveyor and, although not a cartographer, had constructed at least one map for public use. He knew the tools of the trade and their limitations in the frontier. For determining the distance between two points, the preferred surveying method was triangulation using a transit mounted on a tripod. This generally proved impractical, and Clark often chose to use a sighting compass mounted on a single leg or tripod to determine, but less accurately, the bearings of traverses. A surveying chain and measuring tape were used to determine the distance between two points. Jefferson thought that most distances would be measured while on water and recommended the use of the log line to determine the distances between two points. The log

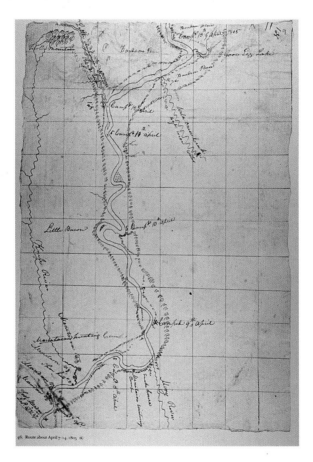

Clark's sketch map (Clark-Maximilian pictographic map, sheet 19) for the route traveled in North Dakota from April 7 through April 14, 1805. Fort Mandan and the Knife River Indian villages are shown in the lower left and the Killdeer Mountains ("Turtle Mountains") in the upper left. North is to the right.
—Map courtesy of the Joslyn Art Museum, Omaha, Nebraska

line was a cord of predetermined length with a wooden float attached to one end. It was used primarily to determine the speeds of ships at sea. The float was dropped into the water and the surveyor determined the amount of time it took the current to carry the float until the cord reached its end. This determined the speed of the river and the distance was calculated mathematically. As it turned out, the log line was not suited for determining accurate measurements of distances on rivers, and Plamondon (2000), who provides an excellent discussion of Clark's surveying techniques, estimated that Clark was 25 to 40 percent too long in determining distances between observation points.

The octant, sextant, chronometer, and several types of artificial horizons were used to determine longitude and latitude by celestial navigation. Longitude and latitude coordinates locate a place on the globe. In surveying, determination of longitude and latitude is critical to place bearings and distances in fixed positions. Determining latitude is relatively straightforward but establishing longitude is difficult and requires accurate instruments, experience using them, and detailed mathematical calculations. Jefferson was aware of this, and that is why Lewis, while training for the expedition, spent considerable time learning how to use celestial navigation instruments, and why the best instruments money could buy were sent on the expedition. Lewis received most of his training using these instruments from Ellicott during a two-week period. In a March 6, 1803, letter, Ellicott emphasized to Jefferson that Lewis needed "to acquire a facility, and dexterity, in making the observations" through practice (Jackson, 1962).

Most of the time Lewis and Clark took the celestial observations together. In order to take accurate measurements of latitude and longitude, the explorers needed an accurate timepiece (chronometer). The expedition's clock, an Arnold's watch purchased from watchmaker Thomas Parker, was one of the best available but was not designed to suffer the rigors of a trip into the frontier and was not waterproof. The accuracy of the clock also diminished through time because it was not always wound when it should have been. For many years, historians considered Lewis and Clark's data mostly useless for establishing longitude. However, Richard Preston (2000) and Robert Bergantino (cited in Preston) found that the longitudes they calculated from Lewis and Clark's data agreed quite well with actual longitude values. It seems that it was initial calculations of longitude from Lewis and Clark's data that were off, not necessarily the observations. Many of the instruments were purchased from Thomas Whitney, a maker of mathematical instruments in Philadelphia. Whitney also modified some of the instruments for use on the expedition.

The following is a list of scientific instruments from the Summary of Purchases for the expedition (Jackson, 1962). These articles were purchased in Philadelphia by Isreal Whelen, Purveyor of Public Supplies, for the expedition.

1 Spirit level [for surveying]	$4
1 Case platting instruments	$14
1 Two pole chain	$2
1 Pocket Compass plated	$5
1 Brass boat Compass	$1.50
3 Brass pocket Compasses	$7.50
1 Magnet [for "touching" the compass needles]	$1
1 Hadleys Quadrant with Tangt screw	$22
1 Metal Sextant	$90
Microscope to index of d	$7
Sett of slates in a case	$4
4 oz of Talc [for artificial horizon]	$1.25
1 Surveying Compass with extra needles	$23.50
1 Circular protractor & index [for map-making]	$8
1 Six In. Pocket Telescope	$7
1 Chronometer & Keys	$250.75
Log line reel & log ship	$1.95
Parrellel Glass for a Horison	$1

Lewis and Clark routinely made weather observations during the expedition. They recorded temperatures, cloud cover, and wind direction twice each day, at sunrise and at 4:00 P.M., and also observed other meteorological phenomena such as river level changes, wind strength, fog, rain, dew, hail, thunder, lightning, snow, snow depths, frost, humidity, northern lights, sundogs, and moondogs. They carried several thermometers but it is unclear where they were obtained. Bedini (1998) suggested that they were purchased in Philadelphia and must have been similar to the ones that Jefferson had described in a June 5, 1804, correspondence to Isaac Briggs: "The kind preferred is that on a lackered plate slid into a mahogany case with a glass sliding cover, these being best on exposure to the weather." Thermometer readings ceased on September 6, 1805, when the last of the thermometers broke.

Lewis took books on botany, zoology, and mineralogy on the expedition. They also had with them Aaron Arrowsmith's 1802 map of North

America, a copy of David Thompson's map of 1798, maps by George Vancouver and Alexander Mackenzie, and John Thomas Evans's detailed maps from northeast Nebraska to the Mandan villages in North Dakota (Bedini, 1990, and Wood, 1983b). The Evans maps were particularly useful to the expedition. Lewis also carried Mackenzie's account of his travels to the west coast of Canada, *Voyages from Montreal on the River St. Laurence, through the continent of North America to the Frozen and Pacific Ocean* (published in London in 1801).

The Journals

Jefferson stressed the importance of keeping detailed, daily journals of expedition observations and activities in his instruction letter to Lewis, and Lewis and Clark became, as Jackson (1978) observed, "the writingest explorers of their time." Jefferson wrote:

> Your observations are to be taken with great pains & accuracy, to be entered distinctly & intelligibly for others as well as yourself, to comprehend all the elements necessary. . .
>
> Several copies of these as well as of your other notes should be made at leisure times, & put into the care of the most trust-worthy of your attendants, to guard, by multiplying them, against the accidental losses to which they will be exposed. A further guard would be that one of these copies be on the paper of the birch, as less liable to injury from damp than common paper. (JACKSON, 1962)

Lewis and Clark, in detachment orders of May 26, 1804, also directed the sargents "each to keep a separate journal from day to day of all passing occurrences, and such other observations on the country &c as shall appear to them worthy of notice" (Cutright, 1969). Also, in a letter to Jefferson, Lewis wrote, "We have encouraged our men to keep journals, and seven of them do so, to whom in this respect we give every assistance in our power" (Jackson, 1962). Plamondon (2000) pointed out that at least eight members of the expedition kept journals. Five of the original journals—those by Meriwether Lewis, William Clark, Sergeant Charles Floyd Jr., Sergeant John Ordway, and Private Joseph Whitehouse—exist today. An extensively edited version of Sergeant Patrick Gass's journal was published in 1807, but the original Gass journal is missing. All of these journalists made entries in North Dakota except for Floyd, who died before the expedition reached this area. Only the Clark and Ordway journals have entries for every day of the journey. Many of the original Lewis and Clark journals are archived at the American Philosophical Society in Philadelphia.

Moulton (1986) provided an interesting and informative account of the journal-keeping methods of Lewis and Clark. One would expect that the journal entries were written on a daily basis and on the date of the entry. Moulton argues that this was not always the case and provides evidence that some entries could not have been made on the date indicated. Duplicate journals for certain times, particularly by Clark, also indicate that the entries were brought up to date and revised with more complete information at times when the journalists were at camp, such as at Fort Mandan in North Dakota, or during times of good weather. Field notebooks were kept at times, and that information was transferred into the primary journals when the opportunity arose. Apparently no journals were kept on birch bark as Jefferson recommended.

Lewis was inconsistent in his note taking, particularly during the early part of the expedition. The most conspicuous gap in Lewis's journal entries is from the onset of the expedition in May 1804 until the they departed Fort Mandan on April 7, 1805. During this time Lewis did, however, record natural history, astronomical, geological, and weather observations and, while at Fort Mandan, he wrote a summary of the rivers and creeks the expedition passed and the character of the country adjacent to the waterways. Moulton suggested that the captains may have been sharing writing responsibilities at that time wherein Lewis kept those kinds of records and Clark recorded daily activities. Lewis also kept notes for a few days at Fort Mandan while Clark was leading a hunting party away from the fort. Throughout the expedition, Lewis kept journal entries for only about four hundred days. This has led to speculation that some of Lewis's notes and other field notes are missing and perhaps might yet be found.

In contrast to Lewis, Clark kept both field notes and journal entries during the expedition's travels from the North Dakota–South Dakota border to the Mandan and Hidatsa villages. While at Fort Mandan, Clark often abandoned entering information into a field notebook in favor of direct entries into his journal. After departing Fort Mandan on April 7, 1805, both captains kept daily journals while in North Dakota. Both Lewis and Clark were keeping journals when they entered North Dakota on their return trip on August 3, 1806. Clark continued daily entries through August 20, when the expedition departed the state. Lewis's journal entries continue until August 12. He didn't write for the remainder of the expedition because he had been incapacitated by a gunshot wound. Pierre Cruzatte accidentally shot Lewis on August 11 near Williston, North Dakota.

Lewis and Clark used many abbreviations in their journals. Moulton (1986) provides a full account of the editorial procedures and symbols used in the journal entries in Volume 2 of *The Journals of the Lewis and Clark Expedition*. Following are a few common abbreviations that appear in the quotes we used.

MOULTON'S EDITORIAL SYMBOLS

[roman]   Word or phrase supplied or corrected by Moulton*

[*NB: italics*]   Nicholas Biddle's emendations or interlineations, as given by Moulton*

<roman>   Word or phrase deleted by the journal writer and restored by Moulton*

ABBREVIATIONS

&.c., &c	and so forth or etc.
pt.	point*
yds.	yards
abo.	above (typically referring to upriver)
mes.	miles*
S. S., Stad. Side, Stard. Side, S.	starboard (or right) side*
S.	at times means south
L. S., L. Side, Lard.	larboard (or left) side*
Lad.	left side
N. S.	north side
N.	north
NE	northeast
N. W.	northwest
S.	south
SE	southeast
S. W.	southwest

UNUSUAL WORDS

in fine	in conclusion
het	heated
dreans	drains, tributaries

*definitions by Moulton (1987)

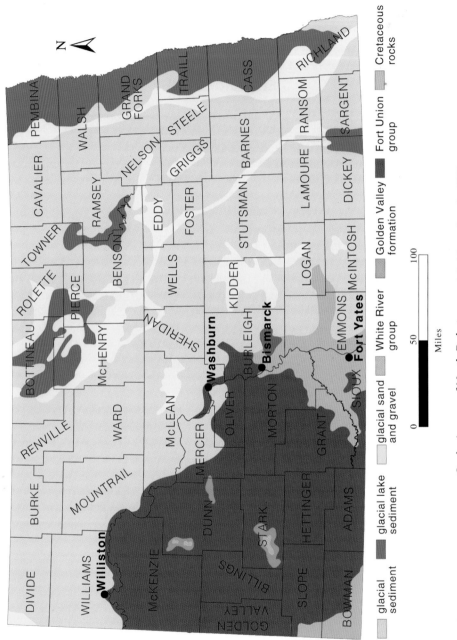

Geologic map of North Dakota. —Modified from Bluemle, 1977

glacial sediment

glacial lake sediment

glacial sand and gravel

White River group

Golden Valley formation

Fort Union group

Cretaceous rocks

0   50   100

Miles

N

General Geology

North Dakota, part of the stable interior of the North American continent, may not conjure up images of tumultuous geology, but if you follow the Missouri River from South Dakota to Montana, you'll see about 75 million years of geologic history recorded in the sedimentary rocks that form the river banks and bluffs. Sandstones, siltstones, and shale contain fossils of sharks that swam in shallow seas, dinosaurs that lived just prior to the great extinction event at the end of Cretaceous time, and giant trees that towered over crocodile-infested swamps. Later, continental glaciers changed the course of the Missouri River, and meltwater scoured channels across the glacial plains.

Active geologic processes along the modern river valley continue today, as they did two hundred years ago when Lewis and Clark passed through. The expedition encountered burning coal veins that cooked and even melted the overlying rock. They wove back and forth across the river, avoiding submerged sandbars and steep riverbanks that threatened to cave in. They even drank the muddy water of the scouring river, preferring it to the alkali springs that seeped from the coal-rich hillsides.

Before we delve into all the geologic features and processes that we can see at the surface, we'll discuss the buried foundation of North Dakota, the Williston Basin.

The Williston Basin

North Dakota occupies the central and eastern portion of the huge Williston Basin, an area of the North American continent that has been tectonically active since Precambrian time. The basin is a large bowl-shaped depression that encompasses an area of more than 300,000 square miles. It includes portions of North Dakota, South Dakota, Montana, and the Canadian provinces of Manitoba and Saskatchewan.

AGE	ERA	SYSTEM	FORMATION or GROUP		THICKNESS max. (feet)	DOMINANT LITHOLOGY
		QUATERNARY	alluvium, colluvium, and lacustrine		50	sand, silt, clay, and gravel
			COLEHARBOR		1,000	sand, silt, clay, till, and gravel
	CENOZOIC	TERTIARY		ARIKAREE	400	tuffaceous siltstone and carbonate
				WHITE RIVER	250	conglomerate, sand, silt, and clay
				GOLDEN VALLEY	215	silt, clay, sand, and lignite
			FORT UNION GROUP	SENTINEL BUTTE	650	silt, clay, sand, and lignite
				BULLION CREEK	650	silt, clay, sand, and lignite
				SLOPE	150	silt, clay, sand, and lignite
				CANNONBALL	400	mudstone and sandstone
65				LUDLOW	200	silt, clay, sand, and lignite
	MESOZOIC	CRETACEOUS	MONTANA GROUP	HELL CREEK	500	clay, sandstone, and shale
				FOX HILLS	400	sandstone and shale
				PIERRE	2,300	shale
			COLORADO GROUP	NIOBRARA	250	shale, calcareous
				CARLILE	400	shale
				GREENHORN	150	shale, calcareous
				BELLE FOURCHE	350	shale
			DAKOTA GROUP	MOWRY	180	shale
				NEWCASTLE	150	sandstone
				SKULL CREEK	140	shale
				INYAN KARA	450	sandstone and shale
		JURASSIC		SWIFT	700	mudstone
				RIERDON	100	shale and sandstone
				PIPER	625	limestone, shale, and anhydrite
		TRIASSIC		SPEARFISH	750	siltsone and salt
250		PERMIAN		MINNEKAHTA	40	limestone
				OPECHE	400	shale and siltstone
		PENNSYLVANIAN	MINNE-LUSA GROUP	BROOM CREEK	335	sandstone and dolomite
				AMSDEN	450	dolomite, sandstone, and shale
				TYLER	270	mudstone and sandstone
		MISSISSIPPIAN		BIG SNOWY	450	shale, sandstone, and limestone
				MADISON	2,000	limestone and anhydrite
	PALEOZOIC			BAKKEN	110	shale and siltstone
		DEVONIAN		THREE FORKS	240	shale, siltstone, and dolomite
				BIRDBEAR	125	dolomite
				DUPEROW	460	dolomite and limestone
				SOURIS RIVER	350	dolomite and limestone
				DAWSON BAY	185	dolomite and limestone
				PRAIRIE	650	limestone and anhydrite
				WINNIPEGOSIS	400	limestone and dolomite
		SILURIAN		INTERLAKE	1,100	dolomite
				STONEWALL	120	dolomite
				STONY MOUNTAIN	200	argillaceous limestone
				RED RIVER	700	limestone and dolomite
		ORDOVICIAN	WINNIPEG GROUP	ROUGHLOCK	90	calcareous shale and siltstone
				ICEBOX	145	shale
				BLACK ISLAND	170	sandstone
570		CAMBRIAN		DEADWOOD	1,000	limestone, shale, and sandstone
4500			PRECAMBRIAN ROCKS			

Generalized stratigraphic column of North Dakota. Crosshatched bar indicates position of the Cretaceous-Tertiary stratigraphic column on page 23. Age is in millions of years ago.

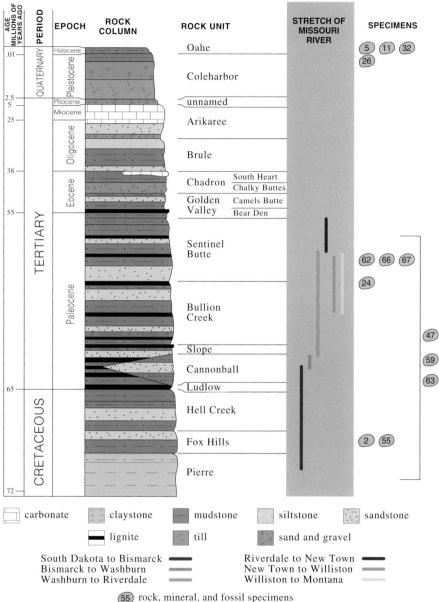

Cretaceous-Tertiary stratigraphic column of North Dakota. Color bars indicate the rock formations exposed along sections of the Missouri River. Numbers to the far right refer to rock, mineral, and fossil specimens collected by Lewis and Clark and described on pages 214–15. Clinker specimens 62 and 67, in the Academy of Natural Sciences of Philadelphia, are illustrated on page 216.

Since about 500 million years ago, the Williston Basin has mostly been subsiding, and more than 16,000 feet of Paleozoic, Mesozoic, and Cenozoic sedimentary rocks have accumulated at its center near Williston, North Dakota. At the eastern edge of the basin, along North Dakota's eastern border, the depth to the underlying Precambrian crystalline rocks is only about 300 feet. During most of this time, shallow oceans inundated North Dakota, and the sediments deposited in these marine and shoreline environments were rich in organic material derived from the organisms living in the oceans. Fossils in rock cores extracted from oil wells provide us with information about changes in marine life through time, oceanic conditions, and climate. Some of the organic material was the source for petroleum that is found at various stratigraphic levels within these Paleozoic and Mesozoic rocks. The Williston Basin is an important source of petroleum reserves for the United States.

Late Cretaceous Seas

The oldest rocks exposed at the surface in North Dakota are Cretaceous in age, about 90 million years old. From 90 to 70 million years ago, shallow inland seas of the Western Interior Seaway covered the entire state and most of the midcontinent of North America. At times, these subtropical to warm temperate seas connected the Arctic Ocean with the Gulf of Mexico, splitting the North American continent in two. Some of the sediments deposited in these oceans, now called the Pierre and Fox Hills formations, were the first rocks encountered by Meriwether Lewis and William Clark when they entered North Dakota. They are exposed along the Missouri River from the South Dakota border to Huff, North Dakota. The Pierre formation consists almost entirely of gray shale deposited in the deeper portion of the inland sea. Brown sandstone and mudstone of the Fox Hills formation were deposited in shallow marine and brackish waters along the shore of the seaway. Abundant fossils of the organisms that inhabited these Cretaceous seas are entombed in these rocks: cephalopods, snails, clams, corals, sharks, bony fish, and large marine reptiles, including mosasaurs, plesiosaurs, and marine turtles.

About 68 million years ago, the Western Interior Seaway began to retreat and a huge, Mississippi Delta–size wedge of sediment formed in western North Dakota. Rivers and streams flowing from the west deposited sediments in and adjacent to this shrunken, shallow sea. Now called the Hell Creek formation, these deposits consist of gray sandstone, siltstone, mudstone, and swelling claystone. About a dozen different species of dinosaurs, including *Triceratops* and *Tyrannosaurus rex*, inhabited this delta in North Dakota, and their remains are preserved in these rocks. Several kinds of turtles, crocodiles, alligators, crocodile-like champsosaurs, freshwater fish, snails and clams, and small rodent-size mammals coexisted with the dinosaurs. Fossil leaves and pollen of numerous plants found in the Hell Creek formation in North Dakota indicate that the climate was probably warm and temperate. Even though the Lewis and Clark Expedition passed exposures of the Hell Creek formation near Huff, they did not report seeing any large fossil bones.

Position of the Western Interior Seaway during deposition of the Pierre shale about 75 million years ago during Cretaceous time. Note that North Dakota was entirely covered by the Western Interior Seaway at that time. —From Roberts and Kirschbaum, 1995

Cretaceous-Tertiary Extinction Event

About 65 million years ago, one of the most severe biological catastrophes ever recorded on earth occurred. The last of the dinosaurs and many other animals and plants became extinct during this Cretaceous-Tertiary (K-T) boundary extinction event. The search for the answer to why the dinosaurs became extinct has made the Hell Creek formation one of the most studied rock formations in North America. The boundary and the extinction event are recorded in the Hell Creek exposures south of Bismarck and Mandan. In recent years, most scientists have accepted the theory that climate change, triggered by an asteroid impacting the earth, caused the extinction. The evidence for this impact comes from a layer a few inches thick that contains elements, such as iridium, common to asteroids but rare on earth. Scientists have found this layer from New Mexico to western North Dakota. In addition, mineral grains in this layer often contain fracture patterns created by high-intensity explosions or impacts. Scientists have yet to find this layer in the Hell Creek exposures along the Missouri River in North Dakota.

Tertiary Swamplands and Savannas

The extinction of dinosaurs, other animals, and plants marks the end of the Mesozoic Era, or the Age of Reptiles, and the beginning of the Cenozoic Era, or the Age of Mammals. Rock formations deposited about 65 to 50 million years ago during the Paleocene Epoch, the first epoch of the Cenozoic Era, are exposed in the bluffs of the Missouri River and buttes from just south of Bismarck-Mandan to the Montana border. These formations, from oldest to youngest, are the Ludlow, Cannonball, Slope, Bullion Creek, and Sentinel Butte formations. Sandstones, siltstones, mudstones, claystones, and lignite are the dominant rock types in these formations. The Ludlow formation is so thin in the Missouri River valley, 50 feet or less, that it is seldom exposed.

Rocks of the Cannonball formation were deposited by the last ocean to cover North Dakota, the Cannonball Sea, about 60 million years ago. The Cannonball formation, which consists of 400 to 500 feet of sandstone and mudstone, is exposed along the Missouri River from Fort Lincoln to Washburn. Fossils found in exposures of the Cannonball formation along the Missouri River and its tributaries, such as the Heart River south of Mandan, provide an insight into life that inhabited this inland sea after the K-T boundary extinction. The large marine reptiles that lived in the Cretaceous seas no longer existed, and sharks and other fish that inhabited the Cannonball Sea were different than those that lived in the Cretaceous seas before the extinction event. The invertebrate animals—such as cephalopods, clams, snails, crabs, and lobster—were also different.

North Dakota's state fossil, Teredo petrified wood, is found in the Cannonball formation. The fossil is named for the *Teredo* genus (actually *Nototeredo*) of wormlike clams, called shipworms, that bored into driftwood along the shore of the Cannonball Sea and secreted calcium carbonate to line their tube-shaped living chambers. After burial the wood, riddled with tubes that often contained the clamshells, became petrified. People named these pests *shipworms* because they bore into the hulls of wooden ships. After 60 million years, shipworms still exist, creating problems in marine areas where there are wooden piers.

Teredo *petrified wood, North Dakota's state fossil, is driftwood that shipworms (clams) bored into to create living chambers as the wood floated in the Cannonball Sea about 60 million years ago. The specimen is cut and polished and 8 inches wide. It is on exhibit at the North Dakota Heritage Center in Bismarck.* —Courtesy of the State Historical Society of North Dakota (SHSND.12151)

Shark teeth, Carcharias taurus, *recovered from the Cannonball formation. Teeth are 1 inch long.*

After the Cannonball Sea receded, rivers and streams meandering across the subtle North Dakota terrain carried and deposited sediments derived from weathering of the rising Rocky Mountains. Lakes, ponds, and huge swamps existed in North Dakota at this time. The Slope formation overlies the Cannonball formation but is not well exposed along the Missouri River. An ancient, whitish soil, called the Rhame bed, caps the Slope formation. The Rhame bed often contains a 1- to 3-foot-thick siliceous layer, which is highly resistant to weathering, and blocks of this unit litter much of the surface of western North Dakota.

The Bullion Creek and Sentinel Butte formations, the rocks that Lewis, Clark, and other expedition journalists often wrote about on their journey from Fort Mandan to the Montana border, are the only bedrock formations exposed in the bluffs along that section of the Missouri River. These formations consist of mudstone, siltstone, sandstone, lignite, and occasionally volcanic ash. The sandstones were deposited in river and stream channels, and the mudstones and siltstones were deposited on floodplains or in lakes and ponds. The volcanic ash, altered to bentonitic or swelling clay in many places, was generally washed into lakes and ponds. Peat that accumulated in extensive swampy areas eventually became North Dakota's vast lignite coal reserves.

Fossils in the nonmarine rocks of Paleocene age dramatically document the new beginning of life after the K-T extinction. The faunas and

Fluvial sandstone in the Sentinel Butte formation capping Ragged Butte between Williston and Alexander. View is to the east.

floras had a much more modern aspect to them than those of Cretaceous time. Even though the dinosaurs were extinct, the main predators in the Paleocene swampy lowlands of North Dakota were still reptiles, but now they were crocodiles, alligators, and crocodile-like champsosaurs. Some of the crocodiles grew to lengths of 12 feet. Soft-shelled turtles, snapping turtles, lizards, and fish, including gars and pikes, that inhabited the freshwater environments during Paleocene time in North Dakota were similar to fish living in those kinds of environments today. Remains of shorebirds have also been found. Leaf, seed, and flower fossils and beautifully preserved petrified wood indicate that plants similar to ones that live in subtropical areas today, such as magnolia, bald cypress, and palm, grew in many areas of North Dakota. More than one hundred species of plants have been identified from fossils recovered from these rocks. Collectively, the plant and animal fossils indicate that North Dakota was a humid area with a subtropical climate similar to southern Florida today. Mammalian fossils are very sparse in these rocks and mostly consist of rodent-size animals and small primates. The largest mammals that lived in North Dakota during Paleocene time were only about as big as a black bear.

About 50 million years ago, the climate became cooler and drier. The swampy environments and the animals and plants that lived during the warmer and wetter Paleocene began to disappear from North Dakota. By about the end of Eocene time and into Oligocene time, from about 40 to 30 million years ago, the subtropical, swampy forests had given way to a drier, temperate climate in which a mostly treeless plain, or savanna, became established. Rivers and streams crossed the savanna, flowing from the west, and lakes occupied lowlands. Gravels and sandstones of the Chalky Buttes member of the Chadron formation were deposited in river channels. Large, active volcanoes in the Rocky Mountains produced volcanic ash, which was altered over time to the bentonitic claystone of the South Heart member of the Chadron formation. Freshwater limestones, deposited in lakes, are also found in the Chadron formation. The sandstones, siltstones, and mudstones of the Brule formation reflect deposition in rivers and on floodplains. Volcanic ash in the Brule formation, like the volcanic deposits in the Chadron formation, indicates greater volcanic activity in western North America than today.

Life during Eocene and Oligocene time in North Dakota was much different than in Paleocene time. The types and numbers of mammals dramatically increased as they adapted to life on the savanna. Many of the mammals that lived in North Dakota were members of families that still exist today, such as dogs, camels, deer, squirrels, and rhinoceroses. The most impressive of these mammals were the elephant-size brontotheres whose fossils have been recovered from the Chalky Buttes member of the Chadron formation and the rhinoceroses whose fossils have been found in the Brule formation. Large tortoises, some as large as the modern Galápagos turtles, lived near the rivers. Several species of fish, amphibians, turtles, and lizards lived in and near the lakes and rivers. Birds lived in North Dakota, too, but their fossils are seldom preserved and we know little about them. Plant fossils are seldom found in these rocks except for seeds of hackberry. Trees during this time were mostly restricted to riparian areas.

These Eocene and Oligocene rocks are preserved only in major buttes in western North Dakota and are not exposed in the bluffs along the Missouri River. The Killdeer Mountains are composed of these rocks and, even though Lewis and Clark did not visit them, Toussaint Charbonneau, the French Canadian fur trapper who fathered Sakakawea's son, probably did when he visited that area prior to the expedition.

The youngest bedrock exposed in North Dakota is the 25-million-year-old Arikaree formation of Miocene age. These rocks consist of siltstone that contains volcanic glass, sandstone, and limestone deposited in and near rivers, streams, and lakes. The Arikaree formation is exposed in the summit of the Killdeer Mountains and other isolated buttes in southwestern North Dakota. In Miocene time, the climate was arid and cool. Major ice sheets were forming in Antarctica. Most of North Dakota was a grassland and trees only grew along rivers and streams. Few fossils have been recovered from the Arikaree formation in North Dakota. Mammalian fossils include the remains of sheeplike oreodonts, deer, and a burrowing beaver.

The Great Ice Age

The last great Ice Age, which began about 1.6 million years ago, dramatically affected the geology and life of North Dakota. Glaciers, some several thousand feet thick, periodically advanced into North Dakota during cold periods. Most rivers in the state flowed north to Hudson Bay before glacial advances blocked their path and diverted them to the east and south. Numerous glaciers crossed North Dakota during early Pleistocene time, but erosion during ice-free periods removed most of the glacial deposits, leaving behind only large boulders called glacial erratics. Two of the early ice advances are differentiated by only the relative abundance of erratics. The interval of time between about 70,000 and 10,000 years ago is known as the Wisconsinan Age. Glacial episodes in North Dakota are generally divided into two main groups:

Pre-Wisconsinan and Wisconsinan. Little is known of the Pre-Wisconsinan and the Early Wisconsinan glaciations, but two or three glacial events are known to have occurred during the Wisconsinan. During the early part of the Wisconsinan, a pulse of glaciation occurred and ice withdrew about 40,000 years ago. The second major Wisconsinan glacial event occurred about 25,000 years ago and ice withdrew from North Dakota for the final time about 12,000 years ago.

During the last of the major glacial advances, ice sheets extended as far south as about the Missouri River, although during earlier times glaciers moved even farther south. The glaciers sculpted the landscape of most of North Dakota and created the rolling hills that the Lewis and Clark Expedition often referred to. As the climate began to warm, great volumes of meltwater entered the drainage systems, creating large meltwater channels that are visible today along the Lewis and Clark Trail. So much meltwater was produced that the large Glacial Lake Agassiz formed along the North Dakota–Minnesota border, the Red River valley, and a much larger area in Canada. The maximum depth of water in the lake near Fargo, North Dakota, was about 300 feet. Lake sediments are more than 100 feet thick in most areas of the Red River valley, which is one of the flattest and richest agricultural areas in the world.

When the glaciers melted, the sediment incorporated in the ice was deposited on the land surface in the form of glacial till, sediment of varying sizes ranging from clay to large boulders. Water flowing from the glaciers deposited outwash sands and gravels. The glaciers in North Dakota were often only about half ice; the rest was debris trapped in the ice. The glacial sediments in North Dakota, primarily deposited over the last 70,000 years, cover most of the northeastern three-fourths of the state and are 400 or more feet thick in some areas. Some of the erratics, transported from Canada, are huge—up to 20 feet in diameter—and range in composition from Precambrian igneous and metamorphic rocks to Paleozoic carbonates. Thousands of years of erosion, which removed smaller, softer material, concentrated these boulders at the surface in many areas. In several upland areas adjacent to the Missouri River, only glacial erratics remain as evidence that glaciers ever advanced through the area. Many of the large erratics are polished and have trenches worn around them, indicating that for thousands of years bison, and now cattle, used them for rubbing stones. Most of the area the Lewis and Clark Expedition traveled through in North Dakota is covered in a veneer of glacial deposits; the men noted the presence of these large boulders but did not speculate on their origin.

Glacial lobes advanced south across North Dakota several times during the Pleistocene. Precambrian to middle Paleozoic rocks are brown, Cretaceous and Tertiary rocks are tan, glacial ice is white, glacial sediment is green, mounded glacial sediment is green with dots, and glacial lakes are blue. —Modified from Bluemle, 1988.

2 million years ago

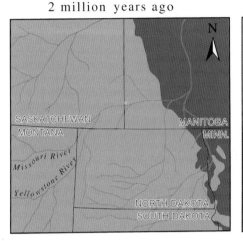

2 million years ago waterways flowed north to Hudson Bay.

600,000 years ago

600,000 years ago ice advanced south into North Dakota forcing rivers to flow southeast.

13,000 years ago

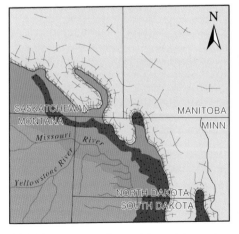

13,000 years ago the melting, thinner ice sheet could not flow over high areas so the ice front developed lobes.

11,000 years ago

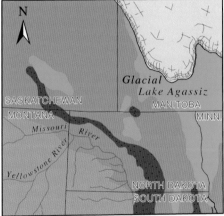

11,000 years ago meltwater filled low areas, forming meltwater rivers and enormous glacial lakes.

Sequence of Glacial Events Affecting Major Rivers in Western North Dakota

PRE-WISCONSINAN

2 million years ago	Yellowstone, Missouri, and Little Missouri Rivers flow north to Hudson Bay.
1.6 million years ago	The last great Ice Age begins.
1 million years ago	The Yellowstone River diverted through Charbonneau Creek.
1 million to 60,000 years ago	The Missouri River follows various routes into central North Dakota and then southward.
600,000 years ago	The Little Missouri River diverted east near North Unit of Theodore Roosevelt National Park and the Missouri River diverted southeastward.
Dates Unknown	Advance 2–Verone: (Pre-Wisconsinan or Early Wisconsinan) Drainage from the west enters North Dakota through Bennie Pierre channel and flows into the Killdeer–Shields channel.

EARLY WISCONSINAN

60,000 years ago	Missouri River in the Killdeer-Shields channel. The Killdeer-Shields system drained roughly the same area as the upper Missouri River does today but with ten times the channel size.
60,000 years ago	Missouri River flows through New Town Sag.
40,000 years ago?	Goodman Creek valley forms as glacier retreats from the Killdeer-Shields position. The Missouri River (and possibly the Little Missouri River) diverted into Goodman Creek.
Dates Unknown	Renner Trench forms and is overridden–older than Antelope Valley but possibly not much older.
Dates Unknown	Antelope Valley forms.

MIDDLE TO LATE WISCONSINAN

14,000 years ago	Glacial Lakes Crow Flies High and McKenzie form. Missouri River diverted from New Town Sag and assumes its current path.
12,000 years ago	Last glacial ice melts from North Dakota.

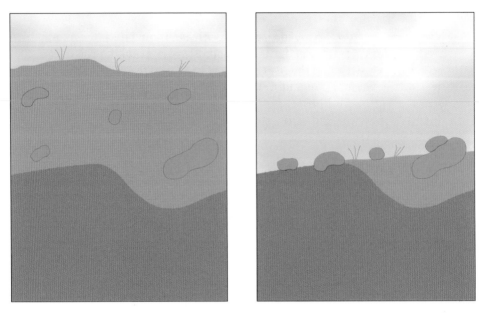

Erosion of glacial till (green) concentrates resistant boulders, called erratics (gray), at the surface. Fort Union strata is brown.

Bison used this large glacial erratic as a rubbing stone, probably for thousands of years. Note the depression worn around it.

Fossils of Ice Age animals have been found in glacial deposits in North Dakota, particularly in glacial sediments capping the bluffs along the Missouri River, glacial outwash channels eroded into the Paleocene bedrock exposed along the river, and in glacial lake beach-ridge deposits. Large mammals, including mammoths, mastodons, giant bison, ground sloths, and horses, inhabited this area but became extinct during or near the end of the Ice Age. Between about 13,000 to 8,500 years ago, after the glaciers had retreated into Canada, the cool and moist climate in many areas of North Dakota supported spruce-aspen forests. These forests contained bogs in which remains of plants and animals became entombed. These fossils indicate that small mammals, frogs, several kinds of fish, insects, crustaceans, mollusks, and many kinds of plants lived here. Deposits along the Missouri River also contain the artifacts of the first humans that lived in North Dakota about 11,000 years ago.

Prairie Development

Between about 8,500 to 4,500 years ago, North Dakota's climate became warmer and drier, and the spruce-aspen forests disappeared and prairie habitats developed. The climatic drying also decreased vegetation cover and increased wind erosion. Windblown silt, called loess, covers many areas of North Dakota. The prevailing northwesterly winds eroded sand and silt from the river valleys and deposited these sediments on the uplands adjacent to the eastern edge of the valleys. In most of these areas, the windblown sediment is less than 3 feet thick and slightly modifies, if at all, the land surface it was deposited on. In some areas, however, the windblown material has been preserved in dunes that reach heights of 30 feet and dominate the landscape. By about 4,000 years ago, North Dakota's present-day climate patterns, flora, and fauna were well established. Modern forests, primarily cottonwood trees, are confined to river valleys; humans have planted almost all trees you might see growing on the prairie.

Economic Resources

Petroleum. The first oil discovered in the North Dakota portion of the Williston Basin was in 1951 near Tioga in Williams County, although people had been producing natural gas in southwestern North Dakota since the 1920s. Since the initial discovery, petroleum has been found at several stratigraphic levels in Paleozoic and Mesozoic rocks. Oil companies have drilled more than 13,000 oil and gas wells in North Dakota and produced more than 1.3 billion barrels of oil. In 2001, North Dakota was ranked eighth among states in annual oil production. Most of the petroleum is recovered from carbonate marine rocks and almost 60 percent of this production is from the Madison group of Mississippian age. Most production is associated with two major structural features in North Dakota, the Nesson and Cedar Creek Anticlines. Other than these areas, most oil in North Dakota is found in subtle stratigraphic traps.

Petroleum and lignite coal fields in western North Dakota.

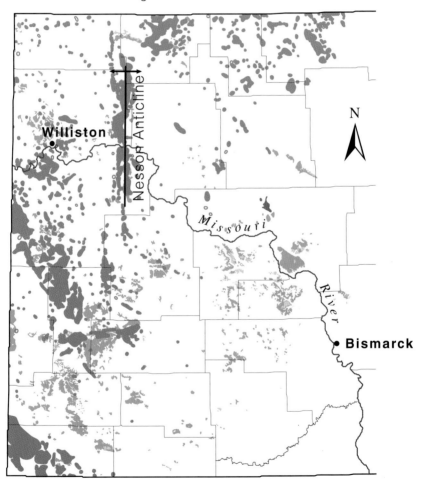

 petroleum fields   mined areas
economic coal deposits

Lignite Coal. Elevated temperatures and pressures within the earth convert buried peat into coal. Deposits of lignite, which is an intermediate form between peat and higher grades of coal, underlie approximately 32,000 square miles of western and central North Dakota. In eastern North Dakota, lignite-bearing rocks were either not deposited due to the presence of the Cannonball Sea or they were deposited in thin layers that were subsequently removed by erosion. Lignite seams are present at the surface throughout much of western and central North Dakota, particularly along the bluffs of the Missouri River from Washburn to the Montana border. Drilling has detected lignite beds to depths of greater than 1,800 feet.

The recorded history of coal mining in North Dakota extends back to 1873 when a small mine was operated at Sims, north of Almont in Morton County. The U.S. Seventh Calvary, under command of Lt. Colonel George A. Custer, provided the miners with protection but the workings were temporarily abandoned after several attacks by Sioux war parties. These small, early mines were called *wagon mines* because miners shoveled coal from the outcrop face directly into a farmer's wagon.

By the 1890s, large-scale mining began, much of it underground. About a half dozen areas became important mining centers, including three towns adjacent to the Missouri River: Washburn, Wilton, and Williston. By the early 1900s, three other towns close to the river—Beulah, Hazen, and Garrison—had also become important mining centers. From the 1880s to the 1920s, the number of active coal mines grew to almost two hundred, and annual coal production steadily increased but did not exceed 1 million tons until 1922. In 1939, 306 mines were operating in North Dakota and over half of these were surface mines. The advent of the steam shovel increased the profitability of surface mining. Large, electric-powered draglines began replacing steam shovels in the mid-1940s, and the last underground mine in North Dakota closed in 1967. By 1980, the number of mines operating in the state had dropped to a dozen. Currently, mining only occurs near Beulah, Center, Underwood, Williston, and Gascoyne. Despite the low number of mines now operating in the state, mine production in 2000 was approximately 31 million tons, only 1 million tons short of the record set in 1994.

North Dakota contains the world's largest reserve of lignite. A recently completed study identified 25.1 billion tons of economically strippable reserves. At the current rate of mining, it would take 835 years to exhaust North Dakota's reserves of lignite.

North Dakota's comprehensive mine reclamation laws, which require the land to be restored to its original contour, went into effect in the 1970s. Prior to that time, spoils from strip mines were left where they were discarded. Coal pillars left standing to support the mine roofs were routinely robbed of coal as underground mines were abandoned. The collapse of underground mines was identified as a problem in North Dakota as early as the 1920s. To date, more than $9 million has been spent filling sinkholes and injecting grout to stabilize old underground mines where their collapse threatens roads and dwellings. The North Dakota Public Service Commission has estimated that the total cost to deal with abandoned mines will be close to $22 million. In the 1980s, scientists debated whether or not to level all the old spoil ridges at the abandoned mines, but the idea was discarded because vegetation had re-established itself in some of the old mine areas and many of them had become wildlife sanctuaries.

Lignite is relatively expensive to transport because of its high water content (about 37 percent). That is why virtually all of the lignite mined in North Dakota is consumed in coal-fired electric generating plants in the state. About 25 percent of the electricity is used in North Dakota with the remainder going to Minnesota through large transmission lines.

Three journal entries from the Lewis and Clark Expedition describe the quality of the coal that they encountered in North Dakota. Only one of the entries could be described as a positive endorsement of lignite as fuel. The journalists' impressions were probably influenced by their familiarity with anthracite and bituminous coal in the East, which burn hotter than lignite. In addition, expedition members may have mistakenly identified a number of dark brown to black, organic-rich beds—ancient soil horizons—in sediments younger than the Fort Union strata as lignite. The journal entries don't indicate that they burned lignite for fuel, but the explorers did perform at least two test burns. (Apparently the people residing in the Knife River Indian villages did not burn lignite for fuel either.) Wood was plentiful along the Missouri River and was much better suited for evening campfires.

Clinker. Clinker is sedimentary rock that is baked by heat generated from burning coal. Since the establishment of grassland savannas about 40 million years ago, prairie fires have been ignited by lightning, possibly spontaneous combustion, and later by humans. In areas where lignite is exposed at the surface, these fires have ignited the lignite, creating burning coal veins. North Dakota's clinker deposits are generally found in nonmarine Paleocene rocks that contain lignite. We know lignite in Paleocene rocks burned prior to 25 million years ago because Miocene conglomerates contain clinker fragments. Clinker is also found in glacial deposits and in younger sands and gravel.

When a lignite bed burns, the heat of combustion bakes the overlying rock, most often producing hues of red, orange, and purple. The

A large dragline strips the overburden off a lignite bed at the Falkirk Mine north of Washburn. The lignite is burned to produce electricity at the adjacent Coal Creek Power Station.

Clinker forms when burning coal seams bake the overlying sedimentary rocks. Most layers of clinker are shades of red, but clinker can occur in a variety of colors including yellow, purple, gray, green, blue, and black.

color reflects the intensity of the heat and the chemistry, such as iron content, of the sedimentary rock. All types of rocks from sandstone to claystone can be baked in this manner to form clinker. The most intensively baked clinker is the rock immediately above the coal. In this layer, generally less that 3 feet thick, rocks often contain visible evidence of the intense heat. Melted glassy layers, at times resembling lava, and pumice, a lightweight rock containing froth vesicles, are typically present above the burning coal. Expedition members called these rocks "lava" or "pumice stone." Their use of these terms implies that, at least initially, they thought these rocks had a volcanic origin, but it is clear from the journals that before they left North Dakota they understood how clinker formed. North Dakotans often refer to clinker as "scoria," another misnomer of volcanic origin.

Rocks farther away from the burning coal bed are discolored but often retain their original sedimentary structures; fossils of leaves, other plants, and occasionally insects are beautifully preserved in this clinker. The lignite is generally entirely consumed when it burns. A 10-foot-thick lignite bed can be reduced to a few inches of ash. A burning 5- to 10-foot-thick coal bed can produce a 10- to 30-foot-thick layer of clinker.

When ignited, lignite beds can burn for many years. A seam burns both laterally along the outcrop face and also back into the hillside. As long as oxygen is present, the coal will continue to burn until the seam is consumed. The collapse of overlying baked material into the void created by the burning coal generally smothers the fire before it can move very far into the hillside. Clinker typically occurs along a line marking the old outcrop of lignite. Occasionally you can see burning coal veins in the Little Missouri National Grasslands in southwestern North Dakota. People often have to extinguish the burning lignite when the fire approaches oil well platforms or other structures.

Mandan and Hidatsa used the frothy, pumicelike variety of clinker as abrader tools. They also made gaming stones out of brightly colored clinker. In modern times, clinker has been an extremely important—though not particularly good—road surfacing material in western North Dakota where sand and gravel deposits are scarce. The durability of clinker is extremely variable, and much of it quickly breaks down to a cloud of dust. Many North Dakotans have had the unpleasant experience of having their tires cut to pieces by freshly crushed clinker after driving only a short distance on a recently surfaced country road. In outcrops, however, clinker is typically much more durable than the surrounding unbaked sedimentary rock. For that reason it is resistant to erosion and often forms the caprock on buttes and hills that protects the underlying rock. Because of its brittle nature, it tends to crack in response to stress brought on by the subtle shifting of the underlying soft sediment. Water moves easily through these cracks or joints, and the roots of trees and shrubs often seek them out to intercept the moisture. Rattlesnakes also enjoy these cool, dark cracks.

Clay. The Missouri River corridor in North Dakota is rich in clay, both in marine and nonmarine bedrock and in glacial and fluvial deposits. For thousands of years, Native peoples living along the Missouri River exploited this resource for making pottery and for other uses. The earliest pottery known from this area dates to 2,400 years ago. These people likely identified suitable clay sources near their villages, probably through trial and error. Several scientific studies currently underway are analyzing both pottery pieces and clay beds to determine the sources of the clay Native peoples used. The Lewis and Clark Expedition members used clay to fill chinks between logs when they constructed Fort Mandan in the fall of 1804.

Trees are a scarce commodity on the rolling prairie of North Dakota. The early pioneers quickly determined that the soft-wooded cottonwoods, which once grew in thick stands in the river bottoms, made poor building materials. As a result, brick plants, utilizing North Dakota clay, sprang up throughout the state in the late 1800s. In the Missouri River corridor, brick plants operated in Mandan, Bismarck, Wilton, and Williston. This industry was relatively short lived. By the early 1900s, most brick plants in the state had ceased operation due to various reasons including poor clay sources, inept management, and poor brick-making techniques. In the mid-1900s, clay was used from sites in Morton County to manufacture Rosemeade and University of North Dakota pottery, both collector's items. The Hebron Brick Company still operates near Hebron, west of Bismarck, and mines about 40,000 tons of clay per year to produce about 20 million bricks.

Sand and Gravel. Melting glacial ice fed a swollen Missouri River, enabling it to transport and deposit coarse sand and gravel, much of it originally carried to North Dakota from Canada by glaciers. You can see these gravel layers along the steep, poorly vegetated edges of terrace deposits along the Missouri River and its tributaries. Sand and gravel are sparse in western North Dakota, and these deposits along the Missouri River are a valuable commodity for the building industry. In 2000, the value of sand and gravel mined in North Dakota was $27.8 million, making it by far the most valuable nonfuel geologic resource in North Dakota. Urban sprawl in many areas of the Missouri River valley has made it difficult, impossible in some places, to mine many deposits. Some sand and gravel layers in the valley extend to depths of

The Golden Valley formation underlain by the Sentinel Butte formation near Grassy Butte in McKenzie County. The bright white layer is the lower member of the Golden Valley formation. This kaolinite (clay-rich) layer is mined by the Hebron Brick Company in Morton County.

more than 100 feet. Although too deep to mine, these deposits are important aquifers and provide water for domestic and industrial use.

Salt. Saline seeps are often present where groundwater surfaces in western North Dakota. The groundwater evaporates and leaves a white crust of salt that consists primarily of sodium sulfate. The salt builds up in the soil to the point that only salt-tolerant plants can survive. Fallow-field farming exacerbates this problem; if vegetation is not plowed under, its roots take up the groundwater before it has the opportunity to evaporate, leaving salt.

Sodium sulfate-rich water has been evaporating and concentrating salt in North Dakota for about 10,000 years. Playa lakes in northwestern North Dakota contain layers of crystalline sodium sulfate, know as Glauber's salt. These layers, up to 50 feet thick, are found in organic-rich lake deposits that are up to 90 feet thick. In the past fifty years, people have made three unsuccessful attempts to commercially process this salt in northwestern North Dakota. Lewis and Clark carried Glauber's salt with them for medicinal purposes, primarily to use as a laxative. They recognized thin layers of the salt while traveling through North Dakota.

Alternating lenses of well sorted sand within a layer of gravel in a pit near Williston. Glacial till caps the glacial outwash deposits at this site. Three-foot pick for scale.

Crystalline Glauber's salt from playa lake deposits in North Dakota. Penny is for scale.

The Missouri River

⌒≈⌒

On their return voyage, Lewis and Clark were surprised by how much the river had changed in the Fort Yates area after only twenty-two months. In its natural state, the upper Missouri is a dynamic, migrating river that cuts back and forth across its floodplain. Yearly spring floods carve new channels and abandon old ones. For thousands of years prior to dam construction, this regular scouring and deposition shaped the valley and floodplain. Even greater changes happened during the Pleistocene Ice Age.

> I observe a great alteration in the Corrent course and appearance of this pt. of the Missouri. in places where there was Sand bars in the fall 1804 at this time the main Current passes, and where the current then passed is now a Sand bar— Sand bars which were then naked are now covered with willow Several feet high. the enteranc of Some of the Rivers & Creeks Changed owing to the mud thrown into them, and a layor of mud over Some of the bottoms of 8 inches thick.
>
> —CLARK, August 20, 1806

The Missouri River drains more than half a million square miles, capturing Rocky Mountain snowmelt from Colorado to Alberta. Where it enters North Dakota, it is already a big river with an average discharge of about 11,000 cubic feet per second. Though the river did not yield a water passageway to the Northwest, it provided a corridor for river travel farther west than any other river on the east side of Rockies.

In North Dakota, the Missouri River valley ranges in width from slightly less than 2 miles to over 6 miles, and the countryside adjacent to the river is quite variable. Near Fort Yates, gently sloping uplands rise about 150 feet above Lake Oahe. South of Bismarck, the river flows through a broad valley bounded by gently sloping uplands that terminate in escarpments about 300 feet above the river. Near Charlson, badlands extend for about 3 miles on either side of the relatively narrow river valley and rise 400 feet above Lake Sakakawea.

The river carved its valley through rolling, glaciated countryside. Lewis showed remarkably good geological insight in a note that was attached to a specimen of clinker sent from Fort Mandan on April 7, 1805, in which he briefly described the hills adjacent to the river: "These are merely the river Hills which are the banks only of a Valley formed by the Missouri, passing thro' a level plain—from the tops of these hills the country as far as the eye can reach is a level plain."

River terraces are flat or gently sloping surfaces along the sides of the river valley that mark previous floodplain positions. In general, the age of a terrace decreases with decreasing elevation: the highest river terrace is the oldest. Terrace preservation is extremely variable, ranging from well preserved to obscure or absent. Where they have inundated the valley, Lakes Oahe and Sakakawea obscure most of the lower terraces. In places, till overlies the upper terraces, indicating they are older than at least some of the Pleistocene ice advances. Terraces are best preserved along the stretch of river between Riverdale and Huff. It is difficult to correlate terraces that are located on opposite sides of the river or downriver because they seldom are matched sets. One side of the river may contain terraces 1 and 4 and the other side terraces 1, 2, and 3 or some other combination of levels. If a terrace was deposited within the last 50,000 years, radiocarbon dating of wood, charcoal, bone, shell, or organic soil material can sometimes be used to establish a terrace deposit's age.

Information from water wells and test holes has enabled geologists to define a 400- to 500-foot-deep, buried river channel in the northwestern corner of North Dakota. The ancestral Missouri River carved this channel when it flowed north, perhaps for millions of years, near the Montana–North Dakota border, eventually emptying into Hudson Bay. All of the streams in North Dakota flowed generally northward approximately 1.5 million years ago. Then sometime between 1.2 and 0.6 million years ago, during the Pleistocene Ice Age, advancing ice sheets blocked the northward flow of the rivers and streams, diverting many to the southeast to ultimately drain into the Gulf of Mexico. About 60,000 years ago, the Missouri River flowed through a southeast-trending channel at New Town, which is now called the New Town Sag or Van Hook Arm. Approximately 20,000 years ago the Missouri River abandoned the 19-mile-long, southeast-trending New Town Sag and occupied a longer stretch, a 27-mile-long loop, which is its present course.

Glacial ice dammed the Missouri River at least twice in Late Wisconsinan time, about 14,000 years ago. The ice dam near New Town that eventually diverted the Missouri River from the New Town Sag formed Glacial Lake Crow Flies High, and another dam near the South Dakota border formed Glacial Lake McKenzie. Scattered remnants of the sediments deposited in these glacial lakes are preserved along the sides of the Missouri River valley. Glacial Lake McKenzie occupied the Missouri River valley from the South Dakota line to Riverdale, eventually spilling over and flooding the adjacent lowlands to the west.

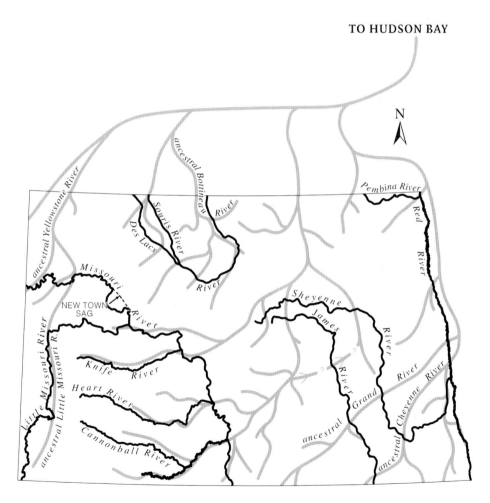

Preglacial drainages (gray) and present drainages (black) in North Dakota. The route of the Missouri River through the New Town Sag is shown. —Modified from Bluemle, 1988

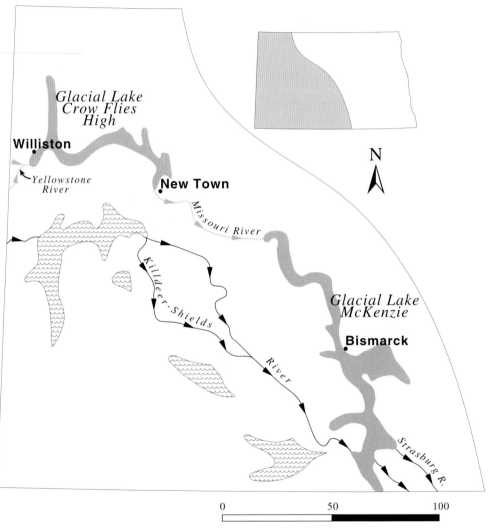

Ice-dammed glacial lakes in southwestern North Dakota during Wisconsinan time. The lake sediments in black are Early Wisconsinan in age (about 60,000 years old) and those in gray are Late Wisconsinan (about 14,000 years old).

—Modified from Clayton and others, 1980

Indigenous Peoples and Early Explorers

For hundreds of years, earthlodge villages, inhabited by the Mandan, Hidatsa, and Arikara, were situated adjacent to the Missouri River to take advantage of the aquatic life that lived in the river, the game that resided in the bottomlands or migrated through the area, and the fertile bottomland soil. These non-nomadic people subsisted by hunting and farming. Often, the villages consisted of two parts: a summer village on an adjacent upland or high river terrace where wind provided relief from insects and hot temperatures, and a winter village nestled in the bottomlands or lowermost terrace of the valley that provided protection from the harsh winter winds. Their gardens were on lower terraces, and they traded agricultural products to other tribes, including the nomadic Sioux, and white visitors to the region. It is often stated that the Lewis and Clark Expedition would probably not have survived the North Dakota winter of 1804–5 if it had not been for vegetables residents of the Knife River Indian villages provided them. Although the remnants of many of the summer villages remain, most of the winter villages were destroyed by the meandering Missouri River or inundated by Lakes Oahe and Sakakawea. The State Historical Society of North Dakota protects several of these historic sites and the National Park Service manages the Knife River Indian Villages National Historic Site.

Following the Lewis and Clark Expedition, several other early explorers traveled the Missouri River. In 1832, artist George Catlin traveled up the Missouri River on the *Yellow Stone*, the first steamboat to reach the mouth of the Yellowstone River. In 1833, the German explorer Prince Maximilian of Weid, accompanied by the Swiss artist Karl Bodmer, journeyed by the same steamboat through North Dakota on an expedition to the upper Missouri River basin. Together, the paintings of Bodmer and Catlin offered the first visual images of the area and Native residents encountered by Lewis and Clark.

Entrepreneurs built trading posts such as Fort Clark and Fort Union along the Missouri River in North Dakota in the early 1800s but abandoned them by the late 1800s. During this relatively brief but exciting period, gold and furs were sent downriver and staples such as powder, shot, salt, flour, blankets, trade beads, and hatchets traveled upriver.

The River as a Means of and Hindrance to Travel

Throughout historic time, the Missouri River has been both a hindrance to overland travel and a means of transportation. Swollen with snowmelt, runoff, and ice, the river posed a serious threat to humans and animals attempting to cross it in spring. In fall, river levels typically dropped very low, sometimes to the point that people and animals could wade across. Crossing the river was especially perilous in the early winter or spring when ice was forming or breaking up. Native peoples and migrating herds were generally forced to delay crossing until conditions improved. The Lewis and Clark Expedition experienced these difficulties while in North Dakota.

Bismarck was a center of steamboat activity from the 1870s to the late 1880s. The completion of the transcontinental railway in 1883 brought an inevitable end to a business that could only operate about seven months out of the year. The most famous steamboat excursion in this area took place in 1876 from the Battle of the Little Bighorn in Montana to Bismarck in a record time of 54 hours. River captain Grant Marsh made the 700-mile trip on the steamboat *Far West* carrying wounded soldiers and news of the battle. The *Far West* was fairly typical of the steamers that traveled the Missouri River. She drew only 20 inches of water when empty but needed 54 inches of clearance when carrying a full load of 400 tons. In winter, steamboats were either sent south to warmer climates or pulled out of the river to prevent shifting ice from damaging their hulls and paddle wheels. During their winter at Fort Mandan, Lewis and Clark experienced firsthand the damage that ice can do to the hull of a boat frozen in the river. By the 1930s, only one steamboat operated between Bismarck, North Dakota, and Yankton, South Dakota. The steamboat docks and warehouses were along the east bank of the river, adjacent to the present-day Bismarck water treatment plant and just south of the Northern Pacific Railway bridge.

Tracks of the Northern Pacific Railway Company reached Bismarck in 1873. Construction was halted there for about six years due to financial problems and difficulty crossing the Missouri River. Construction of the Bismarck railroad bridge began in 1880. This was the first bridge across the upper Missouri River and the widely fluctuating flows complicated construction and design. The $1 million cost was also a huge capital investment for the Northern Pacific Railway Company. Prior to bridge completion in 1882, ferries transported railroad supplies across the river during the openwater season. During winter, tracks were laid directly on the ice, and trains ran across the frozen river. During bridge construction, a dike was built to confine the river against the east bank in this area, the first of many attempts to manage the upper Missouri.

The Northern Pacific bridge, the only railroad bridge that crosses the Missouri River in North Dakota, is unique for many reasons, including

Snags (Sunken Trees) on the Missouri *by Karl Bodmer depicts sandbars and snags along the Missouri River route of the steamboat* Yellow Stone. —Art courtesy of the Joslyn Art Museum, Omaha, Nebraska; gift of Enron Art Foundation

Mih-Tutta-Hang-Kusch, Mandan Village *by Karl Bodmer. Mandans are crossing the frozen Missouri River at Fort Clark. The Mandan village and Fort Clark were built on a Missouri River terrace.* —Art courtesy of the Joslyn Art Museum, Omaha, Nebraska; gift of Enron Art Foundation

its engineer's pioneering use of steel and caissons to construct piers. The middle piers of the bridge were sunk approximately 50 feet before they intercepted strata that could bear the weight of the bridge. The massive granite support columns were constructed with metal edges to cut through ice to minimize ice jams. The bridge engineer designed these massive columns after witnessing an ice jam that formed south of Bismarck. The ice jam contained huge ice blocks that had floated downriver and restricted the flow of a vast amount of water. He also noted the power the ice blocks exerted as they snapped full-grown cottonwood trees. These innovative steel spans had to be replaced in 1904.

For decades, ferries conducted a brisk business transporting horses and wagons across the Missouri River near towns such as Fort Yates, Bismarck, Washburn, Stanton, and Williston. The advent of the automobile soon made the time spent waiting for, loading, and unloading the ferry a major inconvenience, and citizens demanded that bridges be built. Prior to bridge construction, wagons and automobiles could cross the river in only three ways: by ferry (weather permitting), by driving on the frozen river during the winter, or by driving across the railroad bridge. All, particularly the latter two, involved a certain amount of risk.

The first highway bridge across the Missouri River in North Dakota was the Liberty Memorial Bridge at Bismarck, completed in 1922. Within six years, two additional bridges were completed: the Verendrye Bridge at Sanish (near New Town) and one at Williston. Four Bears Bridge was constructed at Elbowoods in 1934. The Four Bears Bridge and the Verendrye Bridge at Sanish were dismantled in 1953 during the construction of Garrison Dam. The original Four Bears Bridge was incorporated into a new, much longer bridge, completed in 1955 just south of the abandoned town of Sanish. Since the 1960s, four additional highway bridges have been built across the Missouri River: two at Bismarck, one at Washburn, and one near Buford. In Bismarck, Interstate 94 crosses the Missouri River via the Grant Marsh Bridge, completed in 1965 and named after the famous steamboat pilot who captained boats on the upper Missouri. Today, eight bridges—seven highway and one railroad—span the Missouri River in North Dakota.

Dams on the Upper Missouri

In the mid-1900s, crews constructed a series of seven dams on the upper Missouri River in Montana and the Dakotas to tame the widely variable flow conditions that were once so characteristic of the upper Missouri River. Construction of the Fort Peck Dam in eastern Montana began in the 1930s and construction on the Oahe Dam in South Dakota and the Garrison Dam in North Dakota began in the 1940s. They were constructed for flood control, power generation, irrigation, recreation, and—to the disdain of many in the upper Missouri River area—to insure adequate flow for barge traffic on the lower Missouri River. Fort Peck is the largest earthen-dam structure in the United States, Oahe is the second largest, and Garrison is the fifth largest. Lake Sakakawea, the reservoir behind Garrison Dam, is the third largest reservoir in the United States.

For thousands of years prior to dam control, floods generally occurred in spring or early summer. Now, the highest flows typically occur in the fall, when the reservoirs are lowered to make room for next spring's runoff. The U.S. Army Corps of Engineers tightly controls river discharge, keeping peak flows within 23,000 to 68,900 cubic feet per second (cfs), averaging about 37,200 cfs. Prior to these controls, peak flow rates in the Missouri River at Bismarck ranged from 31,800 to 500,000 cfs, averaging 123,000 cfs. Before dam construction, the historic high and low river levels were more than 29 feet apart at the Bismarck gauging station. Since dam construction, the highs and lows have been dampened to less than 13 feet.

The Army Corps of Engineers' current management practice, which gives precedence to barge traffic over tourism and environmental concerns, is highly controversial with upper Missouri River states. Barge traffic reportedly peaked at 3.3 million tons on the Missouri River in 1977. Today, the river carries less than half of that amount (1.3 million tons in 2000), generating less than $7 million annually compared to the hundreds of millions of dollars generated annually by boating, fishing, and other forms of river recreation. In 1997, fishing and recreation at Lake Sakakawea alone generated an estimated $175 million, significantly more than that of barge traffic. In recent years, widely fluctuating Lake Sakakawea water levels, exacerbated by the Corps of Engineers' mandate to provide water for downstream barge traffic, has negatively impacted boat ramps and other infrastructure of the reservoir. Negative impacts to Lake Sakakawea, the number one tourist destination in North Dakota, translate directly into reduced revenues for the state.

Garrison Dam contains five electric generators that have a combined rating of over 500 megawatts, about the size of the largest coal-fired power plant unit in North Dakota (most power plants have two units). This is equal to about 13 percent of the electrical generation capacity of the seven coal-fired power plants currently operating in the state (4,071 megawatts).

Railway bridge and steamboats along the Missouri River in Bismarck during the spring flood of 1884. —Photograph courtesy of the State Historical Society of North Dakota (SHSND B0125-1)

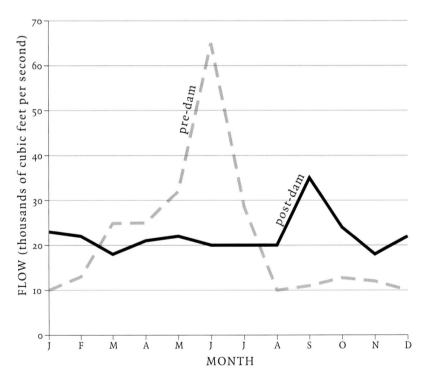

The yearly peak flow of the Missouri River at Bismarck occurred in spring prior to construction of Garrison Dam and was much greater than the post-dam peak flow that now typically occurs in the fall.

The River as a Water Source

The moniker "The Muddy Missouri" was well earned prior to the advent of the dams; the river literally carried tons of suspended silt and clay. Based on journal entries, the Lewis and Clark Expedition primarily obtained drinking water directly from the Missouri River. The expedition members most likely filled barrels with river water and did not consume it until at least some of the clay and silt had settled to the bottom. The expedition members tested springs in the Missouri River valley and likely supplemented their supply with spring water whenever possible. However, several journal entries note the poor quality of this water. In this area, springs emanating from bedrock such as sandstone and lignite are often high in sodium and sulfate, which is bitter tasting and may act as a laxative to those unaccustomed to drinking it. Springs emerging from sand and gravel deposits in terraces along the river valley often contain better-quality water although they occasionally contain high iron concentrations.

> many of the springs which flow from the base of the river hills are so strongly impregnated with this substance that the water is extreemly unpleasant to the taste and has a purgative effect.
>
> —LEWIS, April 11, 1805

> all the Streams which head a fiew miles in the hills discharge water which is black & unfit for use (and can Safely Say that I have not Seen one drop of water fit for use above fort Mandan except Knife and little Missouris Rivers and the Missouri, the other Streams being So much impregnated with mineral as to be verry disagreeble in its present State.)
>
> —CLARK, April 15, 1805

Bison herds crossing the river increased its turbidity and added fecal matter, and the rotting carcasses of drowned animals, noted in many of the expedition's journal entries, would not have improved the taste. Waterborne illnesses, primarily dysentery, were a constant problem for the group.

Towns along the Missouri River, such as Bismarck, Mandan, Washburn, and Williston, have traditionally used the river for their drinking water supply. Starting in the mid-1880s, the Bismarck Water Company pumped water from the river into large wooden reservoirs situated on a hilltop from which it was gravity fed into Bismarck. The majority of the clay and silt settled out in the reservoirs, but not all, judging from the recorded complaints of homeowners. Thick layers of mud had to be routinely dredged out of the reservoirs with shovels.

Beginning around 1908, cities and towns along the river began using different forms of water disinfection, which correlated with a rapid decline in typhoid and other waterborne illnesses.

Now, Fort Peck Reservoir and Lake Sakakawea act as giant sediment traps, removing millions of tons of silt and clay from the water. The Missouri River at Bismarck carries only a fraction of the sediment that it used to transport, and the once familiar brown hue has changed to clear. The clarity has made recreation more enjoyable and has decreased costs to municipal water treatment plants along the river, but it may have a negative impact on native species of fish that thrive in muddy water. The dams have also lowered the summer water temperature. The large, deep reservoirs provide a constant supply of cold, clear, river water downstream from the dams. In August 1937, river temperature at Bismarck reached 75 degrees Fahrenheit. In August 2000, the river temperature was more than 10 degrees cooler.

The long, wheeled arms of center-pivot irrigation systems are a common sight throughout the Missouri River valley in North Dakota. Irrigation takes place where soil conditions are conducive to irrigation and where the large capital outlay required for such a system can be justified. Heavy or clay-rich soils are typically not conducive to irrigation because, rather than infiltrating into the root system, water is often trapped at the surface and is lost through evaporation, leaving dissolved ions behind. These ions can create a hard pan layer that makes water infiltration more difficult, further increasing salinity and decreasing crop yield.

After years of debate, many people are realizing that we cannot continue to manage the upper Missouri River system as we have in the past without further impacting the remaining native animal and plant inhabitants and diminishing the fertility of the soils. Managing the river in a manner more consistent with natural flows may be a viable means to reduce our negative impacts on the river's ecosystem. It is impossible, and in many cases undesirable, to restore the Missouri River to the natural conditions that Lewis and Clark encountered, but we need to seek a balance between flood protection, natural flows, and development at the water's edge.

Two containers of water from the Missouri River. The water in the container on the right was collected on June 21, 1937, and the one on the left on November 14, 2001. The sample from 1937 contains the highest turbidity (a measure of cloudiness due to fine sediment in the water) ever recorded at Bismarck (recording began in 1931). The 1937 sample is courtesy of Charlie Jaszkowiak, City of Bismarck Water Treatment Plant.

A section of the McClusky Canal, which is part of the Garrison Diversion Project, a program tied to the Pick-Sloan Program that was originally intended to irrigate more than 1 million acres in central and eastern North Dakota. Environmental concerns have stalled the project since the 1980s. Landslides are common along the unstable banks of the canal.

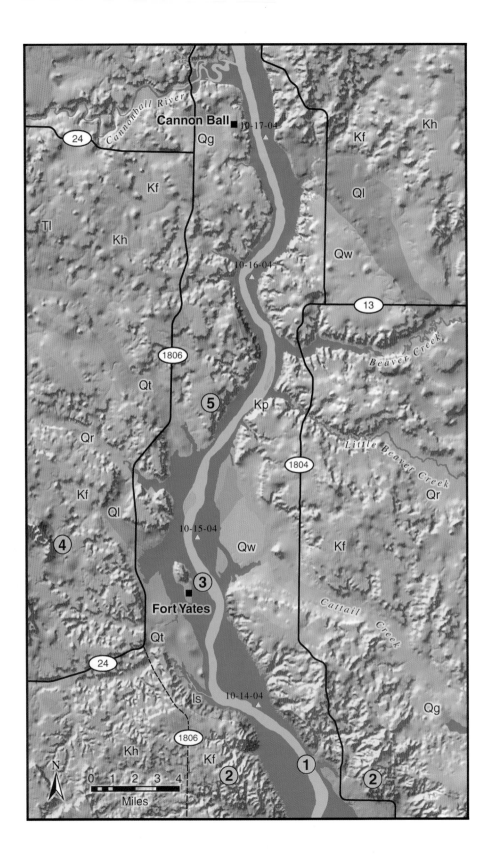

GEOLOGIC GUIDES

South Dakota to Bismarck-Mandan

October 14–21, 1804
August 19, 1806

Between South Dakota and Bismarck-Mandan, Highway 1804 and Highway 1806 are never more than 4 miles east or west of the old Missouri River channel now inundated by the Oahe Reservoir. In some places the rolling topography precludes anything beyond glimpses of the river, but Highway 1806 between Fort Rice and Mandan boasts one of the longest stretches of continuous Missouri River viewing in North Dakota. Likewise, a 15-mile stretch of Highway 1804 south of Glencoe is, in most places, less than a mile from the river valley. Many gravel roads lead to the reservoir; some roads cross private property, but public access areas are scattered throughout this stretch.

Large center-pivot irrigation systems supply water to fields along both highways. Many of these systems withdraw water from the Oahe Reservoir, but some tap groundwater from shallow aquifers in sand and

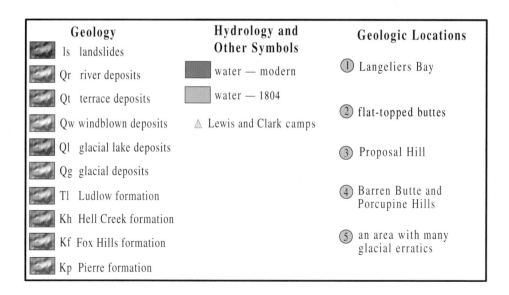

Geology	Hydrology and Other Symbols	Geologic Locations
ls landslides	water — modern	① Langeliers Bay
Qr river deposits	water — 1804	
Qt terrace deposits		② flat-topped buttes
Qw windblown deposits	△ Lewis and Clark camps	
Ql glacial lake deposits		③ Proposal Hill
Qg glacial deposits		
Tl Ludlow formation		④ Barren Butte and Porcupine Hills
Kh Hell Creek formation		
Kf Fox Hills formation		⑤ an area with many glacial erratics
Kp Pierre formation		

gravel that were deposited by melting glaciers. The arc of the center-pivot systems creates large, round fields that, when seen from the air, contrast visually with traditional rectangular fields.

PIERRE FORMATION

When the Lewis and Clark Expedition entered what is now North Dakota on October 14, 1804, they passed through an area where some of the oldest bedrock formations in the state are exposed along the Missouri River shoreline and in the bluffs adjacent to the river. The oldest of these, the Pierre formation, consists primarily of massive gray shale with occasional lenses of siltstone. It was deposited about 75 million years ago in a shallow, inland sea that teemed with life. The Pierre formation has yielded the fossil remains of invertebrate marine animals such as snails, clams, cephalopods, and crabs; vertebrate marine animals including plesiosaurs and mosasaurs, which were giant reptiles; and many kinds of fish including several species of sharks. The most spectacular fossil found in North Dakota in the Pierre formation is the skeleton of a 23-foot-long mosasaur that is on display at the North Dakota Heritage Center in Bismarck. The Pierre formation generally erodes into rounded, well-vegetated slopes that are visible along both sides of the river between the South Dakota border and Fort Yates. Although the Lewis and Clark Expedition camped near Fort Yates on October 15, 1804, none of the journalists reported fossils in this area.

At low-water levels the gray Pierre shale is exposed along the east bank of the Oahe Reservoir at Langeliers Bay, a public-access area on the east side of the reservoir near the South Dakota border. Above the shale, the bank consists of alluvium overlain by loess. Water covers these shales during high to moderate pool levels.

FLAT-TOPPED BUTTES OF THE FOX HILLS FORMATION

The Fox Hills formation overlies the Pierre shale. It comprises many of the bluffs near the Missouri River and is exposed in roadcuts on both sides of the river from the South Dakota border to Huff. This formation consists mostly of sandstone and mudstone deposited in lagoons, estuaries, and shoreline environments at the edge of the inland sea during Late Cretaceous time, about 68 million years ago. By this time, the sea had receded to the east, and a large delta, similar in size to the present-day Mississippi Delta, occupied western North Dakota. The shallow marine sediments of the Fox Hills formation were deposited along the eastern margin of this delta.

This painting by David Miller, based on fossils found in North Dakota, is a habitat reconstruction of the Western Interior Seaway during deposition of the Pierre shale. The mosasaur, Plioplatecarpus, *large seabird,* Hesperornis, *large shark,* Carcharias, *small sharks,* Squalus, *and snails, clams, and ammonites are illustrated. A 23-foot-long mosasaur skeleton, collected from the Pierre shale in North Dakota, is exhibited next to this mural at the North Dakota Heritage Center in Bismarck.* —Art courtesy of the North Dakota Geological Survey

Lenses of cemented sandstone form thin ledges within the poorly cemented sandstone of the Fox Hills formation. View is to the west from south of the intersection of Highway 13 and Highway 1804.

(2)   The topography along this reach is gently rolling interspersed with an occasional flat-topped butte. The degree of cementation in sandstones within the Fox Hills formation determines the topography. Soft or poorly cemented sandstone and mudstone form the rolling topography, and the occasional layer of well-cemented sandstone protects the underlying rock from erosion and forms the flat-topped buttes. These are the hills that Clark noted resembled a "house with a hiped roof." A prominent one, Fireheart Butte, is on the west side of the river near the sandbar where the court martial and punishment of John Newman took place on October 14, 1804. Generally vegetation is able to establish itself in the poorly cemented sandstone. Areas of poorly vegetated, gray sand and occasional concretionary ledges stained reddish brown by iron are characteristic of the Fox Hills formation. Wind often creates pits or blowouts in the area, exposing the formation.

> Saw many Curious hills, high and much the resemblance of a house [NB: *like ours*] with a hiped roof, at 12 oClock it Cleared away and the evening was pleasant.
>
> —CLARK, October 15, 1804

Fossils of marine invertebrate animals such as clams, snails, cephalopods, crabs, lobsters, and vertebrate animals including sharks, rays, other fish, turtles, and mosasaurs are common in the Fox Hills formation, but the expedition journalists did not report any finds. Some of the most spectacular fossils found in the Fox Hills formation along the Missouri River are ammonites. These cephalopods often retain the pearly luster of their original shells of aragonite, a carbonate mineral. Ammonites have also been found in archeological sites near the Missouri River. One specimen recovered from the Taylor Bluff Village at the Knife River Indian Village National Historic Site had a hole drilled in it. Archeologists think it may have been drilled to be worn as a pendant.

Ammonites occasionally break naturally along suture lines between chambers in the shell and the fragments resemble animals. Some Native peoples kept them as effigies. The Blackfoot refer to such ammonite fragments as *iniskim*, or "buffalo stones," because they resemble sleeping bison. They may have been used in hunting rituals. Archeologists have recovered these ammonite fragments from the Fireheart Creek Site near Fireheart Butte and at the Anton Rygh excavations just south of the North Dakota-South Dakota border. Buffalo stones have also been noted in medicine bundles.

Fireheart Butte is the prominent flat-topped butte at the right side of the photograph. View is to the west from the east side of Lake Oahe.

Flat-topped buttes of the Fox Hills formation east of the Missouri River valley and Fort Yates. View is to the east from Highway 1804.

Fossil cephalopod, an ammonite called Jeletzkytes nebrascensis, *collected from the Fox Hills formation. Specimen is 6 inches in diameter and is on exhibit at the North Dakota Heritage Center in Bismarck.*
—North Dakota State Fossil Collection (ND 7.2)

Fragment of a drilled ammonite fossil from the Taylor Bluff archeological site in the Knife River Indian Villages National Historic Site. Archeologists believe this fossil may have been drilled to be worn as a pendant. Specimen is 1 inch in height. —Courtesy of the Knife River Indian Villages National Historic Site (KNRI 262)

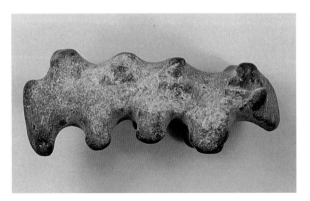

Segment of an ammonite fossil probably from the Pierre shale, called a "buffalo stone," collected at the Anton Rygh archeological site just south of the North Dakota-South Dakota border. Specimen is 2.5 inches in length.
—Courtesy of the South Dakota State Historical Society, State Archaeological Research Center (Acc. #88–38, Cat. #409)

Fort Yates

Fort Yates is located on an island, part of which is a large terrace of the Missouri River. Proposal Hill, the upland portion of this island, consists of rocks of the Fox Hills formation that resisted erosion when large volumes of glacial meltwater carved the Missouri River valley. West of Fort Yates, Barren Butte and Porcupine Hills rise above the surrounding Fox Hills formation and are comprised of the Hell Creek, Ludlow, and Cannonball formations. Several large landslides are present along these buttes. Clark referred to this area as the "barren hills," a name that at least partially stuck. Gass and Ordway referred to them as the "naked hills" in their journals.

Glacial Erratics

Glaciers sculpted the subtle rolling hills that Lewis and Clark noted and modern travelers experience. Glacial deposits between South Dakota and Bismarck are generally only a few feet thick on the uplands adjacent to the Missouri River but glacial erratics (boulders transported by the glaciers) are plentiful, some as large as 8 feet in diameter. They are exposed at the surface where the surrounding material has eroded away. Many of the larger boulders are polished and have trenches worn around them indicating that for thousands of years bison used them as rubbing stones. Erratics were used for the Standing Rock and the Sitting Bull burial monuments in Fort Yates. On October 17, 1804, Clark was observing erratics on the west side of the river south of the mouth of the Cannonball River when he noted "Great numbers of verry large Stone on the Sides of the hills."

Fossils of Ice Age Animals

Fossils of animals that lived about 12,000 years ago at the end of the Ice Age have been found along the shore of the Missouri River. Of particular interest is the 1999 discovery of a claw of the giant ground sloth called *Megalonyx*, meaning "giant claw," near Fort Yates. Thomas Jefferson was first to describe this 8-foot-tall prehistoric animal in a report to the American Philosophical Society in 1797 based on fossils found in a cave in West Virginia. Jefferson directed Lewis to look for fossil remains of Ice Age mammals, and possibly even living Ice Age animals. It is ironic that this ground sloth claw was found along the Missouri River near the expedition's October 15, 1804, campsite almost two hundred years later.

Aerial view to the west with Barren Butte and Porcupine Hills in the background. Proposal Hill and Fort Yates are on the island along the left side of the photograph. Flat terraces of the Missouri River edge both sides of the river.

Glacial erratics in pastureland north of Fort Yates. View is to the east.

GLACIAL MELTWATER STREAMS

Highways 1804 and 1806 cross large valleys, several containing very small streams, that empty into the Missouri River valley. These tributaries are too small to have eroded their valleys; instead, the valleys were incised by huge amounts of water generated by the melting of glacial ice. Cattail, Beaver, and Little Beaver Creeks are meltwater channels on the east side of the Missouri River. Terrace deposits of a meltwater river, consisting of 10 to 20 feet of sand and gravel, are visible along both sides of Beaver Bay on the east side of the Missouri River.

Highway 1806 crosses large valleys now occupied by the Cannonball River and Porcupine Creek. The extreme width of the Cannonball River valley suggests that it is older than many of the valleys in this area. About 30 miles upstream, a large meltwater channel system crosses the Cannonball River valley. This system, known as the Killdeer-Shields channel, extends from the Killdeer Mountains, about 150 miles to the northwest, to the Fort Yates area.

This 12,000-year-old, 7-inch-long claw of the giant Ice Age ground sloth Megalonyx jeffersoni *is on exhibit in the North Dakota Heritage Center in Bismarck.* —North Dakota State Fossil Collection (ND 00–10.1)

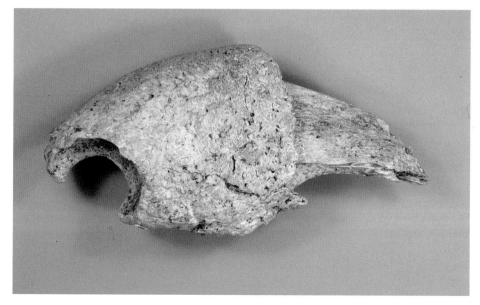

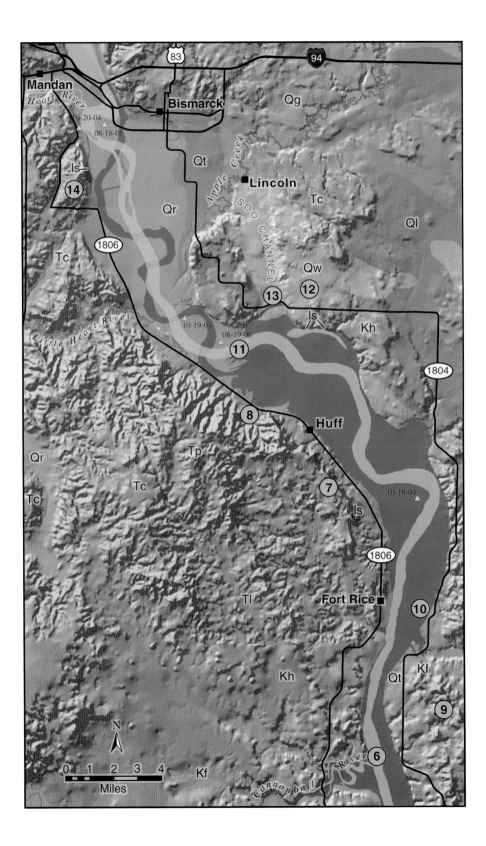

CANNONBALL RIVER

On October 18, 1804, Clark observed perfectly round stones near the mouth of the Cannonball River that to him resembled cannonballs. These large spherical concretions weathered out of Fox Hills sandstone. Concretions are bodies of rock that are more cemented than the surrounding rock. They generally form when minerals, typically calcium carbonate, crystallize from groundwater flowing through the sandstone. Organic-rich debris in the rock tends to trigger the crystallization. Concretions vary in size and shape but are generally flattened or elongated in one direction. Spherical concretions, such as these, are not common but occasionally occur in the marine rocks of the Fox Hills and Cannonball formations in North Dakota. Travelers along Highway 1804 and 1806 will note that these cannonball concretions are popular lawn ornaments in south-central North Dakota.

> above the mouth of the river Great numbers of Stone perfectly round with fine Grit are in the Bluff and on the Shore, the river takes its name from those Stones which resemble Cannon Balls.
>
> —CLARK, October 18, 1804

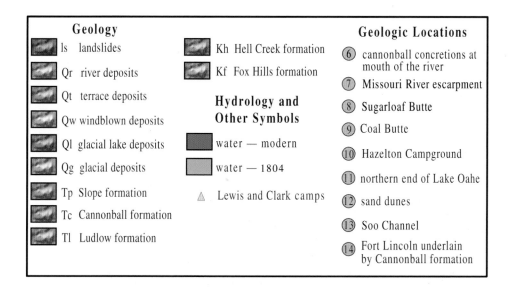

Geology

ls	landslides
Qr	river deposits
Qt	terrace deposits
Qw	windblown deposits
Ql	glacial lake deposits
Qg	glacial deposits
Tp	Slope formation
Tc	Cannonball formation
Tl	Ludlow formation
Kh	Hell Creek formation
Kf	Fox Hills formation

Hydrology and Other Symbols

water — modern

water — 1804

⚠ Lewis and Clark camps

Geologic Locations

- ⑥ cannonball concretions at mouth of the river
- ⑦ Missouri River escarpment
- ⑧ Sugarloaf Butte
- ⑨ Coal Butte
- ⑩ Hazelton Campground
- ⑪ northern end of Lake Oahe
- ⑫ sand dunes
- ⑬ Soo Channel
- ⑭ Fort Lincoln underlain by Cannonball formation

Aerial view to the northwest of the confluence of the Missouri and Cannonball Rivers. The Cannonball River migrates across a wide floodplain created by glacial meltwater. Note the sunlit cliff exposures of Fox Hills sandstone just north of the mouth of the Cannonball River. —Photograph taken by and courtesy of Jeffrey Olson

Fox Hills sandstone along the Missouri River north of the mouth of the Cannonball River. Spherical rocks on the beach are concretions that weathered out of the sandstone. View is to the north.

Fox Hills sandstone just north of the mouth of the Cannonball River. These sandstone concretions are approximately 2 feet in diameter.

French fur traders named many of the Missouri River tributaries prior to the Lewis and Clark Expedition. They named the Cannonball River *Le Boulet*—French for "the ball"—because of the numerous spherical concretions at its mouth. Lewis and Clark sent one of the concretions to Thomas Jefferson from Fort Mandan in the April 1805 shipment. The specimen has been lost.

> passed the mouth of Cannon Ball River on S. S. about 100 yds. wide passed Sand Stone Bluff on the Same Side abo. the River where we found round Stone in the form of cannon balls. Some of them verry large we took one of them on Board to answer for an anker.
>
> —ORDWAY, October 18, 1804

MISSOURI RIVER ESCARPMENT AND BUTTES OF HELL CREEK FORMATION

Throughout its course in North Dakota, the Missouri River is situated at the base of a valley as much as 600 feet below the surrounding countryside. In some areas, the top of the valley is prominently marked by steep cliff faces called escarpments. In the Huff-Glencoe area, escarpments are readily visible from the highways on both sides of the river, especially the western escarpment. Clark dutifully mapped the approximate position of the river valley and escarpments of the Missouri River in North Dakota. West of the escarpment was the "beautiful high plain" marked on the late-1700s map by Evans that Clark carried. In his journal entry of October 20, 1804, Clark noted that he "walked out to view those remarkable places pointed out by Evans."

Small buttes form outliers east of the western escarpment, and landslides along the edge of this escarpment have created an area of badland terrain. A prominent, rounded outlier called Sugarloaf Butte is undoubtedly one of the hills referred to by Clark as "remarkable round hills." The Fox Hills formation is exposed at river level in many places in this area, but the primary rock formation exposed in the buttes and escarpment is the Hell Creek formation of Cretaceous age. The Hell Creek formation, which overlies the Fox Hills formation, consists of mudstones, siltstones, and sandstones deposited primarily by rivers in the delta that formed in western North Dakota at the end of Cretaceous time, about 65 million years ago.

> I saw Som remarkable round hills forming a Cone at top one about 90 foot one 60 & Several others Smaller, the Indian Chief Say that the Callemet bird live in the holes of those hills, the holes form by the water washing thro Some parts in its passage Down from the top— near one

of those noles, on a point of a hill 90 feet above the lower plane I observed the remains of an old village, [NB: *high, strong, watchtower &c.*] which
had been fortified, the Indian Chief with us tels me, a party of Mandins
lived there, Here first saw ruins of Mandan nation we proceeded on &
Camped on the L. S. opposit the upper of those conocal hills.

—CLARK, October 19, 1804

The Hell Creek formation contains a number of layers of swelling
claystone that are susceptible to landslides. Large landslides are visible
on both sides of the Missouri River along this stretch. Lewis and Clark
did not mention these landslides in their journals although they did
mention landslides in other parts of North Dakota. As is true of most
landslides, they are best viewed from the air. Vegetation, slopewash (a
thin layer of eroded sediments that has washed down from rocks above),
or the lack of prominent bedding often make large landslide complexes
difficult to identify on the ground.

North Dakota's and perhaps this nation's shortest underground coal
mine—at least in terms of height—is located at Coal Butte, a prominent butte 3 miles west of Highway 1804 in northwestern Emmons
County. The mine operated from the early 1900s to the 1950s. The coal,
one of the few Cretaceous coals known in North Dakota, is in the Hell
Creek formation. The coal bed is only 1.5 feet thick and was mined to
provide fuel to local farms and ranches. The underground workings
extended several hundred feet into the butte and were only about 3 feet
high. Room heights for typical underground mines were 8 to 10 feet.
Miners had to crawl through this mine on their hands and knees; they
laid on their sides to excavate the coal with picks.

The dinosaur fossil-bearing, dull-colored rocks of the Hell Creek
formation are well exposed in the vicinity of Sugarloaf and Eagle Nose
Buttes on either side of Highway 1806 in the Huff area. Between the
Hazelton Campground and Glencoe, Highway 1804 is on or near the contact between the Fox Hills and Hell Creek formations. The Hell Creek
formation is well exposed in the buttes east of Highway 1804 and in a
small, prominent butte on the west edge of the highway.

Sodium Sulfate

The "Globesalts" that Clark referred to in his October 19, 1804, journal
entry is Glauber's salt, a naturally occurring compound of sodium sulfate named for the German chemist J. R. Glauber, who first created it in
his laboratory in 1658. Sodium and sulfate ions often occur abundantly
in surface waters and groundwaters in North Dakota. These waters carry
large quantities of these salts when warm but, when water temperatures

Aerial view of the western edge of the Missouri River escarpment near Huff. View is to the northwest. A landslide complex is visible in the foreground and Highway 1806 is visible in the upper right.

Lewis and Clark Expedition, October 19, 1804, *by Vern Erickson. The Lewis and Clark Expedition is passing Sugarloaf Butte and the Eagle Nose Village Site. View is to the west.* —Art Courtesy of Vern Erickson

Layers of Hell Creek sandstone and claystone exposed in Sugarloaf Butte north of Huff just west of Highway 1806. View is to the northwest.

A gray channel sandstone in the Cretaceous Hell Creek formation forms the base of this small butte just west of Highway 1804 south of Glencoe. View is to the northwest.

decline in the fall, the salts precipitate out of solution, typically as thin white crusts on the margins of streams or at the mouths of springs. Lewis and Clark noted these salts in many of their journal entries.

> water is brackish and near the Hills (the Salts are) and the Sides of the Hills & edges of the Streems, the mineral salts appear
>
> —CLARK, October 19, 1804

DINOSAUR BONES IN THE HELL CREEK FORMATION

Fossils from at least twelve different species of dinosaurs, including *Triceratops* and *Tyrannosaurus rex*, turtles, crocodiles, lizards, mammals, freshwater snails and clams, and many kinds of plants have been recovered from the Hell Creek formation in North Dakota. Many of these fossils are exhibited at the North Dakota Heritage Center in Bismarck. Much of what we know about the life, environment, and climate at the end of Cretaceous time in North Dakota comes from the many dinosaur and other fossil sites along this stretch of the Missouri River. The Stumpf Site, 7 miles south of Huff, is registered as a North Dakota Natural Area because of the scientifically important fossils found there.

It is somewhat surprising that dinosaur fossils were not noted, particularly by Lewis, because they must have been abundant and conspicuous two hundred years ago in the badland terrain adjacent to the river. Because of concern for Teton Sioux warriors, Lewis may not have ventured far from shore and likely moved quickly through this area. The expedition was so concerned about safety that they traveled through this area on their return trip in 1806 without stopping. Even if Lewis had observed dinosaur bones he would not have known what they were because the first dinosaur fossils were not identified until the 1820s in England. If he had seen any large fossil bones, he would likely have attributed them to be the remains of mammoths or mastodons.

Dinosaurs such as *Triceratops*, which inhabited North Dakota at the end of Cretaceous time, were some of the last dinosaurs (excluding birds, which most paleontologists consider descendants of dinosaurs) to live on Earth. A major extinction event at the end of Cretaceous time wiped out the last of these dinosaurs and many other animals and plants. This major biological catastrophe, called the Cretaceous-Tertiary boundary extinction event, occurred about 65 million years ago and may have been caused by an asteroid collision with Earth.

The Cretaceous-Tertiary boundary in the Huff area is generally the contact between the Hell Creek formation and the overlying Ludlow formation. Where these formations meet, near the top of the escarpment and buttes, the color changes from gray to brown. This area is one of the few places in the United States where the boundary is exposed, and geologists have studied it to determine the cause of the extinction event.

Missouri River Terraces

River terraces are well preserved in the Huff and Glencoe areas. The Hazelton Campground is situated on a 30-foot-high fill terrace of the Missouri River. Terrace exposures consist primarily of silt and clay with occasional sand and gravel lenses that were deposited when the river flowed at a higher elevation. The upper 5 feet of these terraces commonly consist of windblown deposits and weakly to well-formed ancient soils, which are 1- to 2-foot-thick, organic-rich layers of brown to black silt.

In many places, Highway 1806 parallels the edge of a flat, upper terrace between Fort Rice and Mandan. Coarse, occasionally iron-cemented gravels are exposed along the edge of terraces in this area. Over the years, several companies have mined sand and gravel from the Missouri River terrace deposits south of Fort Lincoln.

Northern End of Oahe Reservoir

At Glencoe and Huff, near the northern terminus of Lake Oahe, the river valley is approximately 4 miles wide. The rising water table and lake levels after construction of Oahe Dam drowned the once-thriving riparian cottonwood forest. Dead cottonwood trees quickly lose their thick dark bark, exposing the underlying light-colored wood. At sunset, these tree stumps often shine a ghostly, eerie white against a dark background. Drought years in the 1980s enabled vehicles access to this area, and people clearcut the stand of dead trees for firewood.

Windblown Deposits

Windblown deposits are prevalent along Highway 1804 between the 90-degree turn west of Moffit and southeast of Bismarck. Westerly winds transporting silt and sand from terraces and sandbars in the Missouri River valley formed these partially to well-vegetated sand dunes during the last 10,000 years. Windblown deposits blanket the area and individual dunes within the dune fields are generally less than 10 feet high. Although much of this area has been stabilized by vegetation, high winds still stir the sand where it is exposed at the surface.

This 65-million-year-old, 7-foot-long Triceratops *skull, on exhibit at the North Dakota Heritage Center in Bismarck, was excavated from the Hell Creek formation on land administered by the United States Forest Service in North Dakota in 1995.* —North Dakota State Fossil Collection (ND95–117.1)

Fluvial deposits exposed along the edge of a Missouri River terrace at the Hazelton Campground. Old, buried soil horizons, represented by thin, light to dark gray layers of organic material, are visible in many of these river cuts. View is to the north.

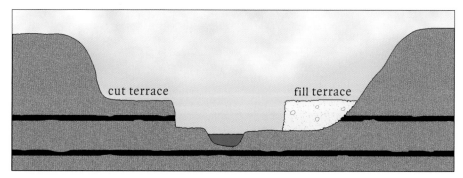

Cut terraces are carved into existing bedrock. Fill terraces are sediments deposited by the river. Bedrock strata is brown, sand and gravel are yellow, and the black layers are seams of lignite.

Cottonwood stumps near the northern terminus of Lake Oahe. Prior to dam construction, a thriving cottonwood forest grew on this floodplain. The Missouri River escarpment west of Huff is evident in the background. View is to the west.

Partially stabilized sand dunes along Highway 1804 south of Lincoln. An ancient soil layer is visible in the dune cut. The Missouri River escarpment is visible in the background. View is to the southwest.

Soo Channel

Highway 1804 crosses the southern terminus of a 1- to 2-mile-wide valley 4 miles southeast of Bismarck. This valley is the Soo Channel, a 5-mile-long, 180-foot-deep diversion channel of the ancestral Missouri River, which flowed through here tens of thousands of years ago.

Bismarck and Mandan

Bismarck was founded on the uplands overlooking one of the widest parts of the Missouri River valley. For a 5-mile stretch, the valley is almost 6 miles wide. Hay Creek and Apple Creek enter along the east side, and the Heart River joins the Missouri from the west. Mandan is situated on the floodplain of the Heart River and on the adjacent rolling hills. These drainages carried significant amounts of water and sediment, as did the ancestral Missouri River during the melting of the glaciers. The large amounts of sand and gravel deposited as river terraces are now important resources; sand and gravel pits dot the area.

A number of devastating floods occurred in south Mandan during spring thaws, the latest occurring in 1943. Since Heart Butte Dam was constructed 70 miles upstream in 1949 on the Heart River and Garrison Dam 75 miles upstream on the Missouri River in 1954, the flood threat has been greatly reduced but not eliminated. After Garrison Dam was constructed, Bismarck began expanding to the south onto the floodplain of the Missouri River. Urban sprawl onto the lower terraces of the Missouri River has made it difficult, and in some cases impossible, to excavate sand and gravel.

During the last Ice Age, glaciers sculpted the poorly indurated mudstone and poorly cemented sandstone of the Cannonball formation of Paleocene age into the rolling topography of the Bismarck area. Occasionally, well-cemented lenses of sandstone form flat-topped hills or buttes in this area. Glacial till overlying the Cannonball formation is generally less than 15 feet thick.

Glacial erratics are common along many of the hillsides near Fort Lincoln State Park. In 1872, an infantry post was established to provide protection for railroad workers and settlers. Originally called Fort McKeen, it was renamed Fort Lincoln when cavalry was added later that same year. George Armstrong Custer and the Seventh Cavalry departed for the Battle of the Little Bighorn from Fort Lincoln. Fort Lincoln and North Dakota's Veteran's Cemetery, just south of the fort, are situated on hillslopes underlain by the Cannonball formation.

You can find exposures of the Cannonball formation along the Heart River west of its confluence with the Missouri River and in a major slump on the University of Mary campus west of Highway 1804.

Aerial view of the southwest portion of Bismarck. View is to the north. Buildings below the dashed line are situated on the Missouri River floodplain. Prior to 1954, this area was susceptible to spring floods.

Fort Lincoln in foreground was constructed at the base of hills consisting of the Cannonball formation. The Missouri River escarpment is visible in the distance to the southeast. Next to the river, Highway 1806 parallels an abandoned Northern Pacific Railway embankment that operated from the late 1800s until the 1960s. The old line ran from Mandan to the town of Cannon Ball before turning west. The embankment, up to 20 feet high, remains along many stretches. —Photograph by Will Kincaid courtesy of the Tourism Division of the North Dakota State Department of Commerce

Lewis and Clark Expedition, October 20, 1804, *by Vern Erickson.*
The Lewis and Clark Expedition is at the abandoned On-A-Slant vil-
lage. The hill that expedition members are standing on consists of
the Cannonball formation. The Missouri River escarpment is visible in
the distance. View is to the southeast. —Art courtesy of Vern Erickson

Interbedded mudstone and sandstone of the Cannon-
ball formation exposed along the Heart River near
Mandan. View is to the north. Pick is 3 feet long.

On October 20, 1804, Clark mentioned the occurrence of an inferior
quality coal in the bluff "above the old Village of the Mandans." He labeled this site on his map "coal hill." The On-A-Slant Village, one of a
number of earthlodge village sites protected and managed by the State
of North Dakota, is at the base of the hill adjacent to Fort Lincoln.
Clark's report of coal in the hill above the village is puzzling because
the hills in this area consist of the Cannonball formation, which does
not contain coal. Drilling has detected thin lignites in the subsurface
below the roadway, but these coals probably extend *beneath* the village

(14) site, not above it. The Cannonball formation contains organic-rich storm deposits that Clark may have mistaken for coal. On the other hand, Clark may have meant upriver when he used the term "above." Upriver from the village site, the basal layer of the glacial deposits contains reworked granules of oxidized lignite. The organic sediment in both situations would have very low heating values, which might explain Clark's comment about the coal's inferior quality.

> Camped on the L. S. above a Bluff containing Coal of an inferior quallity, this bank is immediately above the old Village of the Mandans.
>
> —CLARK, October 20, 1804

MEDICINE ROCK

Clark wrote about a painted stone sacred to Native peoples on the Heart River. Some scholars believe that this stone is Medicine Rock, a North Dakota State Historic Site located along the Cannonball River, not the Heart River as Clark thought, about 50 miles southwest of Bismarck. Native peoples probably headed southwest along the Heart River valley to reach this site, which is southeast of Elgin. The Mandan and Hidatsa regarded Medicine Rock as an oracle and still consider it a sacred place. Incised pictures (petroglyphs) and painted figures (pictographs) cover a soft, fluvial sandstone outcrop of the Paleocene-age Slope formation.

> a Small river on the L. S. Called by Indians Chiss-cho-tar this river is about 38 yards wide Containing a good Deel of water Some Distance up this River is Situated a Stone which the Indians have great fath in & Say they See painted on the Stone, ["]all the Calemites & good fortune to hapin the nation & parties who visit it."
>
> —CLARK, October 21, 1804

> a Delightfull Day put out our Clothes to Sun— Visited by the big white & Big Man they informed me that Several men of their nation was gorn to Consult their Medison Stone about 3 day march to the South West to know What was to be the result of the insuing year—. They have great confidence in this Stone and Say that it informs them of every thing which is to happen, & visit it every Spring & Sometimes in the Summer—. "They haveing arrived at the Stone give it Smoke and proceed to the wood at Some distance to Sleep the next morning return to the Stone, and find marks white & raised on the Stone representing the peece or war which they are to meet with, and other changes, which they are to meet" ["]This Stone has a lavel Surface of about 20 feet in Surcumfrance, thick [NB: thick] and pores," and no doubt has Some mineral qualtites effected by the Sun.
>
> —CLARK, February 21, 1805

Six-inch-thick layer of reworked lignite at the contact between the Cannonball formation and overlying glacial deposits (head of 3-foot-long pick is at the contact). Photograph taken on a hillside adjacent to Highway 1806, 1 mile south of the Heart River.

Medicine Rock State Historic Site, Grant County, North Dakota. At this site, considered sacred by Native peoples, petroglyphs and pictographs cover an outcrop of Paleocene-age Slope formation sandstone.
—Photograph courtesy of the State Historical Society of North Dakota

Close-up of petroglyphs carved into Slope formation sandstone at Medicine Rock State Historic Site.
—Photograph courtesy of the State Historical Society of North Dakota

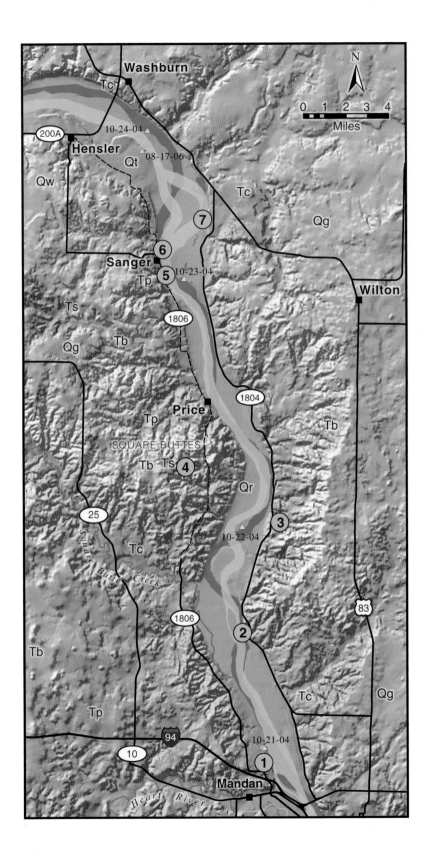

Bismarck-Mandan to Washburn

October 21–24, 1804
August 18, 1806

Highways 1804 and 1806 closely parallel the Missouri River from Bismarck-Mandan to Washburn, offering many views. Dam construction has not directly altered this 36-mile-long stretch, which is the longest natural reach of the Missouri River in North Dakota. This area remains as close to the original river conditions that the Lewis and Clark Expedition experienced as anywhere in the state. Although upstream dams control water levels and the entire river system has undergone significant changes in the past two hundred years, the numerous sandbars visible during low-water conditions and the remaining riparian cottonwood forests would have been familiar to Lewis and Clark. Much of the highway routes are on or near old terraces of the Missouri River, especially the north half of Highway 1806.

Two major industrial plants, Tesoro's Mandan oil refinery and Montana-Dakota Utilities Company's lignite-fired R. M. Heskett power plant, are situated on a Missouri River terrace east of Highway 1806 north of Mandan. This is a cut terrace, rather than a fill terrace, and ①

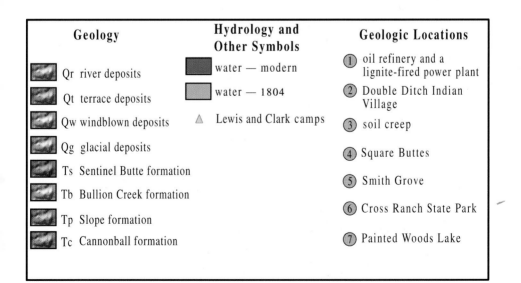

Geology	Hydrology and Other Symbols	Geologic Locations
Qr river deposits	water — modern	① oil refinery and a lignite-fired power plant
Qt terrace deposits	water — 1804	② Double Ditch Indian Village
Qw windblown deposits	△ Lewis and Clark camps	③ soil creep
Qg glacial deposits		④ Square Buttes
Ts Sentinel Butte formation		⑤ Smith Grove
Tb Bullion Creek formation		⑥ Cross Ranch State Park
Tp Slope formation		⑦ Painted Woods Lake
Tc Cannonball formation		

consists primarily of Cannonball formation mudstone. The mudstone is overlain by a thin layer of gravel and is capped by up to 5 feet of wind-blown silt, or loess. Few outcrops of marine mudstone and sandstone of Paleocene age occur from Bismarck-Mandan to Washburn, but you can find isolated exposures of Cannonball sandstones and mudstones along River Road in Bismarck, along Highway 1804, and at the base of Square Buttes.

Both the refinery and power plant were located adjacent to the Missouri River to utilize river water for cooling. Standard Oil of Indiana constructed the refinery in 1954 at a cost of $30 million. They spent an additional $12 million on crude and product pipelines, reportedly making it the single largest commercial facility in North Dakota up to that time. Over the years, the refinery capacity has increased from 15,000 to 60,000 barrels per day. The Heskett station was constructed in 1954 with a unit 1 capacity of 25,000 kilowatts. Unit 2, with a capacity of 75,000 kilowatts, was added in 1963 and retrofitted to a fluidized-bed combustor in 1987. Virtually all of the 30 million tons of lignite mined in North Dakota annually is consumed in the seven coal-fired power plants in the state.

Double Ditch Indian Village State Historic Site

Double Ditch Indian Village State Historic Site is one of the best areas on the Missouri River to note rapid channel changes and sandbar movements that are typical of rivers flowing across low-relief landscapes. The river erodes sand from terrace deposits on the outside of meanders where the current is strongest and on upstream points of sandbars. Sand is deposited on the inside of meanders where the current is weakest and on the downstream end of sandbars. At Double Ditch, a Mandan village site occupied between 1500 and 1781, Clark noted that the river was a "bad place," referring to difficulties the expedition had navigating through sandbars on October 22, 1804. Other expedition journalists and later explorers to the region also recorded difficulties with sandbars and snags on the upper Missouri River. Double Ditch is situated on an upper terrace of the Missouri River. Approximately 20 feet of alluvium is exposed in a terrace cut beneath the village site. North of the village site, approximately 10 feet of alluvium and loess overlie Cannonball formation mudstone.

> Camped on the L Side, passed an Island Situated on the L. Side at the head of which & Mandans village S. S. [NB: *2 miles above*] we passd a bad place.
>
> —CLARK, October 22, 1804

River terrace cut into Cannonball formation mudstone and till upon which the Tesoro refinery and Heskett power plant are situated. The top of the pick is located at the mudstone-till contact. The jointed till is overlain by windblown sediments.

Sandbars at Double Ditch Indian Village State Historic Site. Square Buttes are in the distance. View is to the northwest.

SOIL CREEP

Soil slides, or soil creep, are common phenomena along the hillslopes in western North Dakota and are readily visible in this area where Tertiary-age rocks are poorly consolidated. Soil creep is the slow, imperceptible downslope movement of fine-grained rocks, such as mudstone and shale, caused by gravity. Even though soil creep generally involves only the top 2 to 6 feet of soil and subsoil bedrock, it can seriously damage trees and human-made structures such as roads and buildings. Trees on a hillslope undergoing slow soil creep will often grow with the lower trunk bent in the downslope direction as the tree attempts to right itself. Soil creep is a more significant erosional process than landslides are in most areas of western North Dakota. You can see numerous benches or terraces caused by soil creep along hillsides adjacent to Highway 1804 north of Bismarck.

③

Soil creep formed the numerous benches or terraces on this hillside adjacent to Highway 1804 north of Bismarck.

Aerial view of Square Buttes. View is to the southeast. Note sandbar development in the Missouri River.

SQUARE BUTTES

The best exposures of Paleocene-age rocks between Bismarck and Washburn are along Highway 1806 where it passes through Square Buttes, a half dozen or so sandstone-capped buttes that rise 200 to 300 feet above the surrounding countryside. Visible for more than 20 miles up and down the river, Square Buttes are a significant landmark. It is surprising that these buttes were not mentioned in any of the expedition journals or depicted on Clark's map of this area. During the winter at Fort Mandan, hunting parties had to come at least this far south to escape the hunting pressures of the Knife River villages.

Square Buttes consist of, from oldest to youngest, the Slope, Bullion Creek, and Sentinel Butte formations. These formations are Paleocene in age and consist of nonmarine sandstones, mudstones, and coal deposited in river, lake, and swamp environments. Thick channel

Thick channel sandstones of the Sentinel Butte formation cap the Square Buttes. View is to the southwest.

Lewis and Clark Expedition, October 23, 1804, *by Vern Erickson. The* Lewis and Clark Expedition *is traveling upstream past the Square Buttes. This painting is on display at the North Dakota Lewis and Clark Interpretive Center in Washburn.*
—Art courtesy of Vern Erickson

sandstones, deposited in rivers flowing east-southeast that emptied into the Cannonball Sea, form the caprock of these buttes, which protect the underlying mudstones from erosion.

The lowest rock unit exposed in drainages surrounding the buttes are dark gray mudstones of the Cannonball formation. The mud was deposited in a shallow, warm-water inland sea that covered much of North Dakota about 60 million years ago, the last sea to inundate the state. Beautifully preserved fossils of animals that inhabited this sea—shells of snails, clams, crabs, lobsters and corals, and teeth of sharks, stingrays, and other fish—have been recovered from the Cannonball formation.

North Dakota's state fossil, *Teredo* petrified wood, also occurs in this formation. The wood is named for the *Teredo* genus (actually *Nototeredo*) of wormlike clams, called shipworms, that bored holes in the driftwood of the Cannonball Sea and lined these tube-shaped borings with calcium carbonate to create living chambers.

The Don Steckel Boat Landing, south of Washburn just west of Highway 1804, offers a good view of Square Buttes from across the Missouri River. This is also a good place to observe sandbar development in the river when water levels are low, and you can see 10 to 15 feet of recent, grayish brown, silty alluvium and windblown silt that contains ancient soils in cutbank exposures at the landing.

Old Growth Cottonwood Forests

Cottonwood forests covered extensive areas on the floodplains of the Missouri River and its tributaries prior to construction of the dams. The cottonwood is a large, shallow-rooted tree with waxy, heart-shaped leaves that make a unique rustling sound in the wind, similar to the related quaking aspen. For thousands of years, the white, puffy, cottony seeds, from which the name *cottonwood* is derived, germinated in the thin layers of mud left behind when the Missouri River overflowed its banks in the spring and early summer. Lake Oahe and Lake Sakakawea, reservoirs created by Oahe and Garrison Dams on the Missouri River, not only drowned these vast stands of trees, but also made it difficult for cottonwood seeds to germinate due to the absence of flood-deposited mud. Few, if any, trees now grow along Lakes Oahe and Sakakawea, where stands of cottonwood trees once extended for miles and miles. There are also very few places remaining where the setting is suitable for rejuvenation of cottonwood trees.

Smith Grove, a few miles south of Cross Ranch State Park and just east of Highway 1806, is one of the few remaining old-growth cottonwood forests in North Dakota. Some of the cottonwood trees in this

Geologists believe this interbedded sandstone and mudstone was deposited on a tidal flat of the Cannonball Sea about 60 million years ago. The roadcut, adjacent to Highway 1806 on the north side of the Square Buttes, was created when a contractor mined the area for material to construct a clay liner for an impoundment. View is to the north. Pick is 3 feet long.

Railroad cut in glacial till near Price along Highway 1806. In this area the railroad follows along the top of, or just above, the upper terrace of the Missouri River. View is to the east.

Aerial view to the east with Smith Grove, an old growth cottonwood forest, in the foreground. Highway 1806 parallels the forest at the bottom of the photograph.

Old growth cottonwood trees in Smith Grove. Some trees in this forest are about 275 years old and would have been mature trees when the Lewis and Clark Expedition traveled through this area.

stand have diameters of up to 7 feet and are estimated to be 275 years old. These are the oldest known cottonwood trees in the Missouri River valley in central North Dakota and the only ones known to have been living when Lewis and Clark camped near here on October 23, 1804. Even in this relatively undisturbed stretch of the Missouri River, fire, disease, drought, and clearcutting have removed most of the cottonwood trees that lined the river in 1804. Even Lewis and Clark found it somewhat difficult to find trees suitable for construction of Fort Mandan in the fall of 1804 and for building large canoes in the spring of 1805.

CROSS RANCH STATE PARK

One of the best places to experience this relatively pristine part of the Missouri River is at Cross Ranch State Park just off Highway 1806 south of Hensler. The park extends from rolling uplands along the western edge of the valley to the river's edge, a 7-mile stretch of undeveloped riverfront property. You can see three well-developed river terraces in the park. The lower two terraces are easily recognized by their very flat surface, with the lowest terrace only 8 feet lower than the middle terrace. Edges of the lowest terrace are well exposed along the river, where a 10-foot-thick section of alluvium is primarily ripple-bedded fine sand overlain by several feet of finer-grained flood deposits and loess. The upper, older terrace is about 50 feet higher than the middle one, and it is not as well defined because its topographic expression is more rolling, at least in part, due to longer exposure to erosion. From Price to the Cross Ranch, Highway 1806 is generally situated on the eastern edge of the upper terrace.

At Cross Ranch, Highway 1806 passes out of the river valley and onto the glaciated, rolling topography characteristic of this prairie region. Topographic relief generally decreases with increasing distance from the river. A veneer of glacial drift, containing numerous glacial erratics, covers the Paleocene bedrock near Cross Ranch, so there are few outcrops of the Cannonball formation and overlying Slope formation.

PAINTED WOODS LAKE

The dynamic nature of the Missouri River is exemplified at Painted Woods Lake, an oxbow lake located where Highway 1804 joins U.S. 83, south of Washburn. An oxbow lake is a former river meander channel that the river abandoned when it cut a path across a neck of the meander, bypassing it. Painted Woods Lake was already an inactive meander channel of the Missouri River when the expedition passed through the area on October 24, 1804. Clark's sketch map of the area indicates that

Edge of the lower river terrace at Cross Ranch State Park. View is to the north.

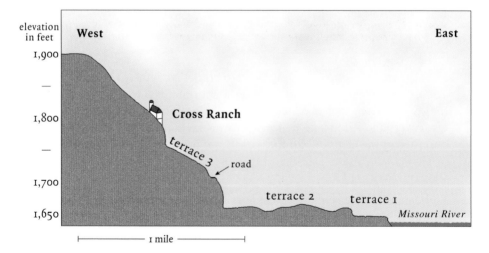

Profile of terrace deposits at Cross Ranch State Park. The lower terraces (terraces 1 and 2) are very flat, often with less than 20 feet of relief over an area up to 1½ miles wide. The upper terrace (terrace 3) is up to a half mile wide in this area and is generally not as flat.

necks of the meander were filled with sand from point-bar deposits that caused water to pond in the old channel. Clark's journal entry states that the river cutoff took place seven years before the expedition arrived, undoubtedly information he obtained from John Evans's map created seven years earlier.

> passed a Island on the S. S. made by the river Cutting through a point, by which the river is Shortened Several miles.
>
> —Clark, October 24, 1804

Aerial view to the northeast of Painted Woods Lake, the oxbow lake in the far background (arrow). Note sandbar development in the Missouri River.

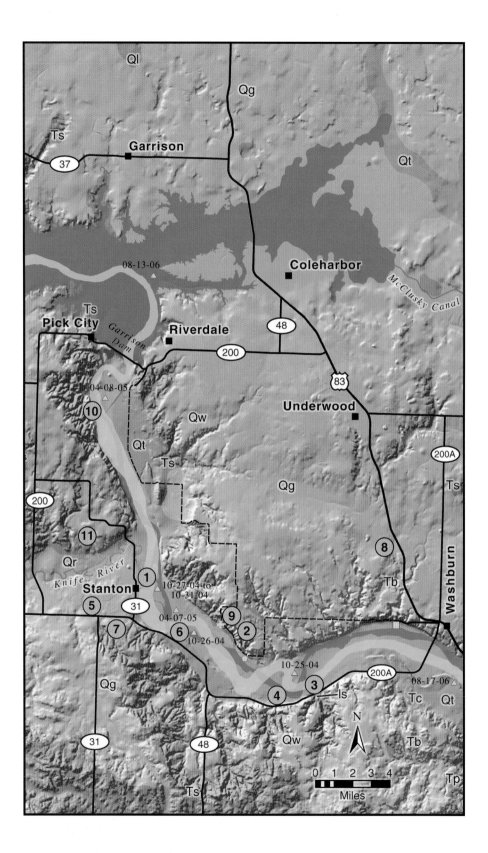

Washburn to Riverdale

October 25, 1804 to April 8, 1805
August 14–17, 1806

On October 27, 1804, the Lewis and Clark Expedition arrived at the Knife River Indian villages, a thriving community of Mandan and Hidatsa and the leading trade center on the upper Missouri River. The collective population of the villages near the confluence of the Missouri and Knife Rivers has been estimated at between three and five thousand people, exceeding the populations of both St. Louis and Washington City (present-day Washington D.C.) at that time. The Hidatsa inhabited three villages—Big Hidatsa (Manatara), Sakakawea (Metaharta or Awatixa), and Amahami (Mahawha)—when the expedition visited the area. (The names in parentheses are the names Native residents gave these villages.) A smallpox epidemic probably forced the Indians to abandon these villages in 1837, ending several hundred years of continuous Hidatsa occupation. Two large Mandan villages, Black Cat (Ruhptare or Rooptahee) and Big White (Matootonha), were a few miles south of the Hidatsa villages. The National Park Service administers the 1,700-acre Knife River Indian Villages National Historic Site, which

(1)

Geology		Hydrology and Other Symbols	Geologic Locations	
ls	landslides	water — modern	①	Knife River Indian villages
Qr	river deposits		②	river-channel sandstone
Qt	terrace deposits	water — 1804	③	landslide along 200A
Qw	windblown deposits		④	concretion along 200A
Ql	glacial lake deposits	△ Lewis and Clark camps	⑤	sand dunes
Qg	glacial deposits	⬠ approximate location of Fort Mandan	⑥	coal-fired electric plants
Ts	Sentinel Butte formation	▢ Fort Mandan Reconstruction	⑦	Glenharold coal mine
Tb	Bullion Creek formation		⑧	Coal Creek Station
Tp	Slope formation	✚ Fort Mandan Historic Monument	⑨	clinker in ridge northeast of Fort Mandan
Tc	Cannonball formation		⑩	lignite-bearing rocks of the Sentinel Butte formation
			⑪	bison trails

contains remnants of three Hidatsa villages. Information gained from the more than fifty archeological sites in the national historic site indicate that humans have inhabited this area for almost eight thousand years.

The Lewis and Clark party arriving at the first Mandan village *by Ralph W. Smith. Outcrops of the Bullion Creek formation are evident across the Missouri River. View is to the east.* —Art courtesy of the State Historical Society of North Dakota (SHSND 11549)

Mih-Tutta-Hangkusch, a Mandan village *by Karl Bodmer. The village is situated on a terrace of the Missouri River. The women are crossing the river in buffalo hide-covered bullboats.* —Art courtesy of the Joslyn Art Museum, Omaha, Nebraska; gift of Enron Art Foundation

The Knife River Indian villages, visited by fur trappers and explorers for many years before the expedition, were a hub of commerce and the northern terminus for which Lewis and Clark had reliable information about the Missouri River. From here to the Columbia River, the expedition traveled through country widely believed to have never been seen by white men.

Aerial view of the Knife River Indian Villages National Historic Site and the confluence of the Missouri and Knife Rivers. View is to the south. Stanton is west of the confluence. Arrow points to Sakakawea Village Site. Note sandbar development in the Missouri River.

Aerial view of the Sakakawea Village Site along the Knife River. View is to the southeast. Circular depressions mark locations of former earthlodges. —Photograph courtesy of the University of North Dakota and Knife River Indian Villages National Historic Site

The expedition's arrival at the Knife River Indian villages began a five-month-long stay, their longest in any one place. The men hurriedly began building living quarters for a winter encampment that they called Fort Mandan. In North Dakota, winter weather often starts at the end of October.

> we Spoke to the Indians in council— tho' the wind was so hard it was extreemly disagreeable. the sand was blown on us in clouds.
>
> —LEWIS, October 29, 1804
> (From Lewis's Weather Diary)

> The river being very low and the season so far advanced that it frequently shuts up with ice in this climate we determined to spend the Winter in this neighbourhood, accordingly Capt. Clark with a party of men reconnoitred the countery for some miles above our encampment: he returned in the evening without having succeed in finding an eligible situation for our purpose.
>
> —LEWIS, October 31, 1804

Lewis and Clark chose to build the fort on the floodplain because of the availability of wood for construction and the close proximity to the Mandan and Hidatsa villages. Closeness to the villages made trade for food easier and allowed Clark to query the Native peoples for geographical information about the uncharted areas to the west, including information about rivers like the Yellowstone, or *Roche Jaune*, misspelled by Clark on January 7, 1805, as *Rejone*.

> Big White Chef of the Lower Mandan Village, Dined with us, and gave me a Scetch of the Countrey as far as the high mountains, & on the South Side of the River Rejone, he Says that the river rejone recves 6 Small rivers on the S. Side, & that the Countrey is verry hilley and the greater part Covered with timber.
>
> —CLARK, January 7, 1805

Gass provided the only sketch of Fort Mandan and noted that some of the cottonwood trees they used to construct the fort were 18 inches in diameter. Alan Woolworth (1988) estimated that it took over 2.4 miles of linear board to construct the fort; about 660 logs that were at least 1 foot in diameter and 14 to 21 feet long. The men felled hundreds of trees in a race to establish permanent shelter before winter set in. They used stones, probably glacial erratics, for the fireplaces, and clay from Missouri River alluvium for chinking.

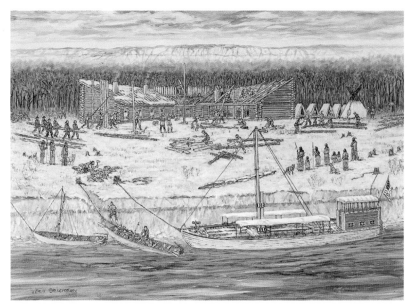

Lewis and Clark Expedition, Constructing Fort Mandan *by Vern Erickson.*
Expedition members are building Fort Mandan. Men are unloading rocks
from a perogue for chimney construction. —Art courtesy of Vern Erickson

Capt. Lewis & 6 men went in the pearogue up the River through the
Ice to the first village of the Mandens after Stone for the backs of our
Chimneys.

—ORDWAY, November 13, 1804

men imployed untill late in dobing their huts.

—CLARK, November 16, 1804

The exact location of the original fort site is not known. Lewis and
Clark attempted to determine the longitude and latitude of Fort Mandan,
and they reported an average latitude of 47°21'32.8"N. Lewis calculated
longitude by using observations from a lunar eclipse that resulted in
two readings, 99°22'45.3"W and 99°26'45"W. Scholars have proven
that Lewis's longitude measurements were off by about 100 miles, probably because of faulty methodology (Bergantino, 2001). Two leading au-
thorities used historical maps and detailed reconstructions of the compass readings and recorded distances in the Lewis and Clark journals to
determine the latitude and longitude of the fort: Bob Bergantino

(2001) calculated 46°16'52"N latitude and 101°16'44"W longitude and Martin Plamondon II (2000) calculated 47°16'47"N latitude and 101°16'19"W longitude. These sites occur about 2,000 feet apart on private land about 12 miles west-southwest of Washburn. Ken Karsmizki (personal communication, 2002) believes that the site was several miles south of Bergantino's and Plamondon's locations. He is attempting to find the fort's remains using standard archeological techniques and remote sensing. He hopes to find metal from the expedition's blacksmith operation, 200-year-old soil horizons, sediment baked by fire, wood used to construct the fort, and stones from the chimneys.

Fire had destroyed much of Fort Mandan by the time the expedition passed through this area on their return trip in August 1806. Thirty years later, Prince Maximilian of Weid commented on Fort Mandan and wrote in his journal that "at present, there is not the smallest trace of that post. The river has since changed its bed in such manner, that the site of that building, which was then at some distance from the shore, is now in the middle of the stream" (Thwaites, 1905).

Since Fort Mandan was constructed, the Missouri River has meandered across its floodplain in this area for almost two centuries. After Clark's initial survey, ninety years passed before the Missouri River in this area was mapped again, this time by the Missouri River Commission. The earliest aerial photographs of North Dakota were taken in 1938 and provided the river's position on topographic maps published in 1948. Topographic maps available in 2002 used aerial photographs taken in 1980. A comparison of the Missouri River's position at these four times in history demonstrates how quickly and extensively the river has changed its course within its floodplain and suggests that the Fort Mandan ruins were probably destroyed by the meanderings of the Missouri River. The exact location of Fort Mandan may never be found.

> we then Saluted them with a gun and Set out and proceeded on to Fort Mandan where I landed and went to view the old works the houses except one in the rear bastion was burnt by accident. Some pickets were Standing in front next to the river.
>
> —CLARK, August 17, 1806

Fort Mandan Overlook State Historic Site. This site, established by the State Historical Society of North Dakota, overlooks the general area where Lewis and Clark established Fort Mandan. The site is on a 30-foot-high, poorly defined, upper terrace of the Missouri River 14 miles west of Washburn and 1 or more miles northwest of the actual location of the fort site.

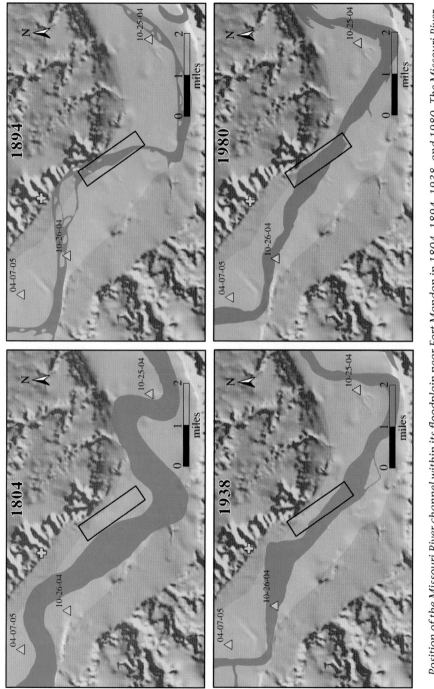

Position of the Missouri River channel within its floodplain near Fort Mandan in 1804, 1894, 1938, and 1980. The Missouri River is blue, the floodplain gray, and the uplands brown. The rectangle encloses the possible locations of Fort Mandan as proposed by Bergantino, Plamondon, and Karsmizki. The yellow cross is the location of Fort Mandan Overlook State Historic Site. The yellow triangles are Lewis and Clark Expedition campsites.

The cut terrace consists primarily of Bullion Creek formation fluvial sandstones. Archeological evidence indicates that the terrace was inhabited several hundred years before the expedition visited this area. The wooded floodplain west of the overlook probably appears much as it did when the expedition passed through. Two monuments at the site are made from glacial erratics, which North Dakotans often call "fieldstones." A plaque mounted on a fieldstone identifies the location as a state historic site. A pyramidal monument, made of numerous smaller glacial erratics, was erected by the Order of the Masons. Lewis was a Mason at the time of the expedition and Clark became one shortly after.

Fort Mandan Reconstruction. The McLean County Historical Society completed a reconstruction of Fort Mandan in 1972 about 2 miles west of Washburn. The triangular fortification is about 10 miles east of the original fort site and was based on Gass's sketch of Fort Mandan, his journal entry, and other information in the Lewis and Clark journals. The newly constructed visitor center is made of coal-combustion by-products. The North Dakota Lewis and Clark Bicentennial Foundation manages the reconstructed fort and visitor center.

North Dakota Lewis and Clark Interpretive Center. This Interpretive Center is 2 miles east of the reconstructed Fort Mandan and just north of Washburn. Displays in the Bergquist Gallery include Mandan and Hidatsa artifacts, objects from the fur trade, a clasp from one of the Lewis and Clark journals, and a full-scale replica of a canoe carved from the trunk of a large cottonwood tree, similar to the canoes the expedition made at Fort Mandan in the spring of 1805. The Interpretive Center's Sheldon Gallery exhibits a collection of Karl Bodmer's artwork. Bodmer, a Swiss artist, accompanied Prince Maximilian of Weid on a journey to the upper Missouri River country in 1833 and documented the people living in the area and its landscape in paintings. The Center also features artwork by contemporary Lewis and Clark theme artists such as Vern Erickson, Gary P. Miller, Michael Haynes, and Charles Fritz.

A Long Winter at Fort Mandan

During the long, harsh winter of 1804–1805, the expedition members experienced several days of blizzard conditions and extremely cold temperatures, at times more than 40° F below zero. Most of the hardy crew were from the mild climes of Kentucky and Virginia and had never encountered the bitter cold of a northern-plains winter. Lewis and Clark dutifully noted the daily temperatures and other meteorological observations in their journals and recorded forty-eight days of subzero temperatures, seven with lows more than 30 degrees below zero. When the thermometer read -12°F on December 8, Ordway noted in his journal entry, "the weather is 12 degrees colder this morning than I ever new it to be in the States." The coldest recorded temperature was either -43°F or -45°F, depending upon the journal source. Their recorded low was colder than the record cold for fourteen of the seventeen states that were in the Union at the time of the Lewis and Clark Expedition. The expedition conducted few experiments, but on December 10, 1804, as reported by Gass, they determined that it took only fifteen minutes for a glass of "proof spirits" to freeze when the temperature was -10°F. The Fort Mandan area generally has forty-five to fifty days of below-zero temperatures over the course of a normal North Dakota winter.

North Dakota is located at the geographical center of the North American continent—far from the temperature-stabilizing effects of the oceans. North Dakota is tied for sixth place among the states for the coldest temperature ever recorded (-60°F; Alaska holds the record at -80°F). What is often most surprising to visitors is our ranking of fifth (tied with Kansas) among the hottest recorded temperatures in the United States (121°F; California holds the record at 134°F). The range in temperature (181°F) between our hottest and coldest records is exceeded only by Utah and Montana. North Dakota is probably unique in that both the record high and record low were set in the same year, 1936.

The expedition journalists observed a number of natural phenomena associated with North Dakota winters. A heavy white frost, called *hoarfrost*, forms on the branches of trees and shrubs during times of relatively mild temperatures in the winter. Hoarfrost is composed of interlocking crystals of ice that form by sublimation on small-diameter objects such as tree branches and wires that are exposed to the air. In this situation, sublimation is the transformation of water vapor in the air into ice on cooled objects. The process is similar to the formation of dew except hoarfrost only forms on objects that have temperatures below freezing.

> a cold frosty night. the Trees were covered with frost which was verry course white & thick even on the Bows of the trees all this day. Such a frost I never Saw in the States.
>
> —ORDWAY, November 16, 1804

> the frost of yesterday remained on the trees untill 2 P. M. when it descended like a shower of snow.
>
> —LEWIS, November 17, 1804
> (Weather Journal)

They also observed sun dogs, also called *parhelion*, which are two bright, often colored spots, that occur on each side of the sun or moon, often on a halo. They are produced by the prismatic refraction of light on ice crystals floating in the air. These ice crystals form in temperatures between 15–25 ° F although sun dogs may be visible when the temperatures are much colder due to temperature inversions.

> below o which is 53° below the freesing point and getting colder, the Sun Shows and reflects two imigies, the ice floating in the atmespear being So thick that the appearance is like a fog Despurceing.
>
> —CLARK, December 11, 1804

> singular appearance of three distinct *Halo* or luminus rings about the moon appeared this evening at half after 9 P. M. and continued one hour. the moon formed the center of the middle ring, the other two which lay N & S. of the moon & had each of them a limb passing through the Moons Center and projecting N & S a simidiameter beyond the middle ring to which last they were equal in dimentions, each ring appearing to subtend an angle of 15 degrees of a great circle.
>
> —LEWIS and CLARK, January 12, 1805
> (Weather Journal)

Expedition members frequently gazed at the stars during the cold, clear winter nights and they experienced an eclipse of the moon on January 14, 1805. They were also treated to spectacular displays of northern lights on November 5, 1804. Northern lights, or *aurora borealis*, are bands or streams of light that dance across the night sky at high latitudes. Electrical discharge in the atmosphere causes this phenomenon. When upper atmospheric atoms and molecules collide with current-carrying electrons, they emit streamers of various-colored light. Intense solar flares generate the charged electrons. High latitude areas such as North Dakota are good places to see northern lights, particularly in fall and winter.

> Observed an Eclips of the Moon. I had no other glass to assist me in this observation but a small refracting telescope belonging to my sextant, which however was of considerable service, as it enabled me to define the edge of the moon's immage with much more precision that I could have done with the natural eye. The commencement of the eclips was obscured by clouds, which continued to interrupt me throughout the whole observation; to this cause is also attributable the inacuracy of the observation of the *commencement of total darkness.* I do not put much confidence in the observation of the middle of the Eclips, as it is the wo[r]st point of the eclips to distinguish with accuracy. The two last

Sun dogs, two bright spots on either side of the sun, are produced by the prismatic refraction of light on ice crystals floating in the air.

Northern Lights *by Michael Haynes. Members of the Lewis and Clark Expedition observing aurora borealis during construction of Fort Mandan. They saw the northern lights on several occasions during the winter of 1804–1805. Painting on exhibit at the North Dakota Lewis and Clark Interpretive Center, Washburn.* —Art courtesy of Michael Haynes

observations (i. e.) the *end of total darkness*, and the *end of the eclips*, were more satisfactory; they are as accurate as the circumstances under which I laboured would permit me to make them.

—LEWIS, January 14, 1805

last night late we wer awoke by the Sergeant of the Guard to See a nothern light, which was light, [NB: *light but*] not red, and appeared to Darken and Some times nearly obscered [NB: *about twenty degrees above horizon—various shapes*], and <open> [NB: *divided*], many times appeared in light Streeks, and at other times a great Space light & containing floating Collomns which appeared <to> opposite each other & retreat leaveing the lighter Space at no time of the Same appearance.

—CLARK, November 6, 1804

saw the arrora. borialis at 10 P. M. it was very briliant in perpendiculer collums frequently changing position.

—LEWIS, November 7, 1804
(Weather Journal)

The Frozen Missouri River

The processes that govern the formation and breakup of ice in rivers and lakes are different. In general, flowing water weakens ice, and river ice is more dangerous than lake ice. Individual ice crystals often form at the surface of rivers where they mix to form slush and are transported downstream until they coalesce to form ice floes. Under subfreezing temperatures, ice floes expand upstream as floating crystals attach to the edge of the ice floes. Rivers seldom freeze solid although they can contain up to 4 feet of ice. Ice breakup often involves a mixture of degrading forces: solar radiation and warm water under the ice melt it and the pressure exerted by increased river discharge causes cracking and fragmentation.

> The ice on the parts of the River which was verry rough, as I went down, was Smothe on my return, this is owing to the rise and fall of the water, which takes place every day or two, and Caused by partial thaws, and obstructions in the passage of the water thro the Ice, which frequently attaches itself to the bottom.— the water when riseing forses its way thro the cracks & air holes above the old ice, & in one night becoms a Smothe Surface of ice 4 to 6 Inchs thick,— the river falls & the ice Sink in places with the water and attaches itself to the bottom, and when it again rises to its former hite, frequently leavs a valley of Several feet to Supply with water to bring it on a leavel Surface.

—CLARK, no date

For some unexplained reason, Lewis and Clark allowed the expedition boats to become frozen in the river. Perhaps they were unaware that in a cold North Dakota winter the Missouri River can freeze in a matter of days. In late January the captains became concerned, and they decided to free the trapped boats before the force of expanding ice crushed them. First, the men unsuccessfully tried chopping the ice away from the boats with axes. Next, they tried heating water in the bottom of the boats by adding hot rocks. This failed because the rocks kept exploding or breaking apart when heated. Lewis said these rocks were of a "calcarious genus," so it is likely that they were sandstone concretions cemented with calcium carbonate from either the Sentinel Butte or Bullion Creek formations exposed in the steep cliff faces east and northeast of the fort. Perhaps they took the rocks from a massive channel sandstone that crops out east of the fort.

Ordway noted that they tried heating rocks collected from different localities but ended up with the same result. The rocks broke because gases were released or moisture expanded when the rocks were heated. It is surprising that the men did not use igneous or metamorphic glacial erratics for this purpose since they probably would not have fragmented during heating. They may have picked the concretions out of a pile of discarded rocks they created while constructing the fort's chimneys. Lewis was capable of identifying granitic rocks as noted in his journal entries. The exploding rock incident must have made quite an impression on members of the expedition because Lewis, Clark, Gass, Ordway, and Whitehouse all mentioned it in their journals. A month later, they were able to free the boats by chopping the ice away.

> all hands during this time were employed at work on the boat & Pettyaugers to get them free from the Ice, and hawled Stones on a Sled which they made warm in a fire, in order to thaw the Ice from about the said Crafts, when the Stones were put into the fire, they would not stand the heat of the fire but all of them broke, so that their labour was lost.
>
> —WHITEHOUSE, January 23, 1805

> Sergt Gass Sent up the River to an other bluff in order to look for another kind of Stone that would not Split with heat he brought one home & het it found it was the Same kind of the other as soon as it was hot it bursted asunder So we Gave up that plan.
>
> —ORDWAY, January 30, 1805

the situation of our boat and perogues is now allarming, they are firmly inclosed in the Ice and almost covered with snow. The ice which incloses them lyes in several stratas of unequal thicknesses which are seperated by streams of water. this peculiarly unfortunate because so soon as we cut through the first strata of ice the water rushes up and rises as high as the upper surface of the ice and thus creates such a debth of water as <had> renders it impracticable to cut away the lower strata which appears firmly attatched to, and confining the bottom of the vessels. the instruments we have hitherto used has been the ax only, with which, we have made several attempts that proved unsuccessfull from the cause above mentioned. we then determined to attempt freeing them from the ice by means of boiling water which we purposed heating in the vessels by means of hot stones, but this expedient proved also fruit-less, as every species of stone which we could procure in the neighbourhood partook so much of the calcarious genus that they burst into small particles on being exposed to the heat of the fire. we now determined as the dernier resort to prepare a parsel of Iron spikes and attatch them to the end of small poles of convenient length and endeavour by means of them to free the vessels from the ice. we have already prepared a large rope of Elk-skin and a windless by means of which we have no doubt of being able to draw the boat on the bank provided we can free from the ice.

—LEWIS, February 3, 1805

All hands employed in Cutting the Perogus Loose from the ice, which was nearly even with their top; we found great difficuelty in effecting this work owing to the Different devisions of Ice & water after Cutting as much as we Could with axes, we had all the Iron we Could get & Some axes put on long poles and picked throught the ice, under the first water, which was not more the 6 or 8 inches deep— we disengaged one Perogue, and nearly disingaged the 2nd in Course of this day which has been warm & pleasant.

—CLARK, February 23, 1805

ice running the [river] Blocked up in view for the Space of 4 hours and gave way leaveing great quantity of ice on the Shallow Sand bars.

—CLARK, March 28, 1805

The obstickle broke away above & the ice came dow in great quantites the river rose 13 inches the last 24 hours.

—CLARK, March 30, 1805

Mapping the Missouri–Winter Afternoon at Fort Mandan *by Charles Fritz. A resident of the Mandan-Hidatsa villages is drawing a map in the snow on the frozen Missouri River for expedition members. Note that the expedition boats are frozen in the river, which became a major concern to Lewis and Clark.* —Art courtesy of Charles Fritz

Blocks of ice float down the Missouri River near the Fort Mandan reconstruction.

MANDAN AND HIDATSA LORE AND GAMES

In his December 15, 1804, journal entry, Ordway recorded a game played by the Mandan using stones and sticks. The game was probably *tchung-kee*, in which contestants rolled a donut-shaped stone on the ground and tossed a decorated stick ahead of it. The objective was to have the stone ring fall on the stick. Moulton (1995) incorrectly suggested that this was the Mandan hoop-and-pole game, in which a large, rawhide-covered hoop, not a donut-shaped stone, was used. Ordway reported, probably wrongly, that the *tchung-kee* stone was made of clay. Stones for *tschung-kee* were generally made from igneous or metamorphic glacial erratics.

One of the recreational activities of the expedition members during their stay at Fort Mandan was backgammon. It is therefore surprising that none of the journalists recorded the Native residents' games in which they used gaming pieces, such as the Mandan women's *Sha-we* dice game. These gaming pieces were often incised with geometric designs and consisted of stones found in the area, including clinker.

BULLION CREEK AND SENTINEL BUTTE FORMATIONS

The Fort Mandan area is the farthest upstream point where marine rocks of the Cannonball formation are exposed at river level. About 6 miles northwest of Washburn, 60-million-year-old rocks of the Fort Union group, primarily the Bullion Creek and Sentinel Butte formations, occur along the Missouri River and Lake Sakakawea all the way to the North Dakota–Montana border. These formations consist of sandstones, siltstones, mudstones, and lignite deposited in a dynamic system of rivers flowing across a low-relief landscape. Sand was deposited in river channels, and the finer-grained sediments were deposited when the rivers overflowed their banks during flooding events. Lakes, ponds, and swampy areas punctuated the landscape. Some of the swampy areas were vast and existed for a long enough time that vegetation built up and formed thick peat deposits. After millions of years of burial these thick and extensive peat deposits turned into lignite.

You can see excellent exposures of the Bullion Creek formation east of Highway 1804 near the Fort Mandan site. A 50-foot-thick river channel sandstone or series of stacked channel sandstones crop out in the steep cliffs along the east edge of the Missouri River floodplain. The sandstone is very fine grained, contains some ripup clasts (clay pebbles eroded at the base of a river or stream channel), exhibits large-scale crossbeds, and is generally poorly cemented, though it contains well-cemented concretionary zones. It was deposited in a large river that flowed to the east-southeast across this area. Blocks of this sandstone

This 1¾-inch-wide game piece, made of clinker, was recovered from the Big Hidasta Village at the Knife River Indian Villages National Historic Site. —Courtesy of the Knife River Indian Villages National Historic Site (KNRI 1867)

Donut-shaped tchung-kee *game stones from Big Hidatsa Village on exhibit at the Knife River Indian Villages National Historic Site. The large stone is 4¼ inches in diameter and made of basalt, a dark igneous rock.* —Photograph courtesy of the University of North Dakota and the Knife River Indian Villages National Historic Site (KNRI 1867)

Tchung-kee, a Mandan Game Played with a Ring and Pole *by George Catlin. The donut-shaped game stones are carved out of rock, mostly igneous glacial erratics.* —Art courtesy of the Smithsonian American Art Museum; gift of Mrs. Joseph Harrison, Jr.

have tumbled to the base of the cliff. It seems reasonable to assume that members of the expedition might have carved their names into this soft channel sandstone during their long stay at Fort Mandan—as Clark did during a very brief visit to Pompeys Pillar in Montana. Although graffiti covers this sandstone today, none can be attributed to members of the expedition. Glacial till veneers upland surfaces in this area, and

Thick channel sandstone in the Bullion Creek formation exposed along the eastern edge of the Missouri River valley near the Fort Mandan site.

Active landslide along Highway 200A. The toe or base of the slide is at road level. Landslide material is present both above and below road level.

glacial erratics are strewn across the landscape in many places. The orientation of northeast-southwest-trending linear, low-relief ridges of glacial till and gravel suggest that glaciers advanced from the northeast.

LANDSLIDES ALONG HIGHWAY 200A

You can see landslides, which are fairly common in the Sentinel Butte formation, at some roadcuts and along the bluffs of the Missouri River. The scarp, or vertical face, of a moderate-sized landslide is present on the south side of Highway 200A west of Washburn. Landslides, which have been damaging the roadside in this area for many years, are occurring along the north side of the butte that Clark referred to as a "high hill" on October 25, 1804. The highway is situated between the toe (bottom) of one set of landslides and the head (top) of another set of landslides, and the railroad tracks are located closer to the toe of this latter group of slides. Disturbed strata are exposed along the walls of the railroad cut, indicating that landslides occurred in this area before the railroad was constructed. Excavation by the railroad at the base of the slide and highway activity in and around the head of the slide have likely added to slope instability. The close proximity of the highway and railroad makes stabilization of this area more difficult.

CONCRETION TURNOFF

Along Highway 200A west of Washburn is a large concretion that workers exhumed in the early 1970s while constructing the earthen dams that created the small fishing lake south of the highway. This red, semispherical concretion is about 8 feet in diameter and is from the Sentinel Butte formation. The shape of this concretion is unusual because concretions in nonmarine rocks like the Sentinel Butte formation are usually elongate. Concretions in marine rocks are more often spherical, like those of the Cannonball formation. The red is from iron oxide, a common chemical component of the Sentinel Butte formation. A thin crack developed in this concretion when it was excavated. Expansion and contraction from heating and cooling during extreme weather fluctuations and the pressure exerted by ice that formed in the crack split the concretion into several pieces.

FLUVIAL TERRACE DEPOSITS

Fort Mandan and the Mandan and Hidatsa villages were built on terraces of the Knife and Missouri Rivers. The Knife River valley is wider and has gentler slopes than the Missouri River valley, indicating that the Knife River valley predates the Missouri River valley in this area. In

Round concretion from the Sentinel Butte formation covered with graffiti along Highway 200A. View is to the north.

The edge of a middle terrace of the Missouri River that was an active cutbank north of the Knife River Indian villages in 1804, at which time the Missouri River covered the flat area on the left side of the photograph. Vegetation now covers many of the cutbanks that were active in 1804, 1805, and 1806.

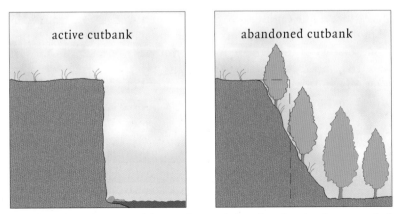

Active cutbanks have steep slopes; slopes of abandoned cutbanks are eroded into gentler grades.

fact, the Missouri River between the Knife River and Washburn occupies part of the ancestral valley of the Knife River, which flowed east and then north to Hudson Bay more than 1 million years ago. Geologists have mapped eight river terraces in this area. Stanton is situated on a terrace that marks the position of the Missouri River floodplain about 13,000 years ago. One terracelike landform is actually a strandline, or beach, of Glacial Lake McKenzie, which formed when ice dammed the Missouri River channel in Late Wisconsinan time, about 14,000 years ago. This lake spilled over into lowlands as far south as Bismarck.

Sand Dunes

A 6-square-mile area of sand dunes west of Stanton formed during dry periods over the past five hundred years. Crests of the dunes are 15 to 30 feet high and are now stabilized by prairie grasses. Terrace deposits of the Knife and Missouri Rivers, the source of the sand, were made vulnerable to wind erosion when drought conditions reduced vegetation cover. Most dunes are a half mile long. Longitudinal dunes oriented northwest to southeast indicate a prevailing wind out of the northwest during dune formation, similar to prevailing wind directions in North Dakota today.

Aerial view of northwest-southeast-oriented sand dunes west of Stanton. View is to the northwest. Stanton is along the right edge of the photograph.

Ancient Soils

Ancient soil layers are often well preserved within river terrace deposits and are best exposed along active river cutbanks. These ancient soils consist of dark gray to black organic-rich layers that are 1 to 3 feet thick and stand out in contrast to the adjacent tan-colored silts and clays of the terraces. Gass and Ordway reported seeing coal in bluffs along the Missouri River in their October 27, 1804, journal entries as did Clark on October 30. We have not observed any coal in outcrops in this area, so we believe Clark, Gass, and Ordway probably mistook ancient soils for coal. Ancient soils are especially well exposed in cutbanks along the Knife River just north of Sakakawea Village in the Knife River Indian Villages National Historic Site. The soils exposed there are less than 4,500 years old.

> passed a Bluff on the S. S. with a black Stripe through the center of it resembling Stone coal, a bottom opposite on N. S. on which is the 2d village of the Mandens.
>
> —ORDWAY, October 27, 1804

Coal

Although Clark, Gass, and Ordway reported seeing coal earlier, the first time the expedition encountered coal-bearing rocks adjacent to the river was just north of Fort Mandan. The Paleocene-age Sentinel Butte formation is the primary source of lignite in North Dakota. About 60 million years ago, vegetation accumulated in the bottom of swamps. Millions of years of burial, heat, and pressure turned the mats of plant debris into lignite. The coal beds often contain stumps, logs, and branches of carbonized trees. In some areas, particularly west of Washburn, Sentinel Butte lignites attain thicknesses of 20 feet or more. Approximately 10 feet of peat is required to produce 1 foot of coal, which means that the ancient swamps were vast and existed for long periods of time.

Expedition members were familiar with coal found in the northeastern part of the United States, which is a much higher grade coal than that found in the Sentinel Butte formation, so they referred to this coal as being of inferior quality. The men relied on wood for heat at Fort Mandan and their evening campsites. Whitehouse's journal entry for March 3, 1805, where he mentioned the "burning of Coal for the Armourer & Blacksmiths," is misleading because they made charcoal by burning wood, as recorded by Ordway and Gass. Apparently the Mandan and Hidatsa did not burn coal and maybe that is one of the reasons why the expedition did not.

Ancient soils (dark layers) in a river terrace along the Knife River across the river from Sakakawea Village Site in the Knife River Indian Villages National Historic Site. Note the mass wasting at the base of the cutbank. View is to the east.

Lewis and Clark Expedition Visits Black Cat Village August 14, 1806, *by Andy Knutson. Note the ancient soils (dark bands) in the Missouri River cutbank in foreground and pink clinker beds in the Bullion Creek formation outcrops at the base of the hills behind the village.* —Art courtesy of the State Historical Society of North Dakota (SHSND 2003.9)

⑥ A few miles northwest of Fort Mandan, on the west side of the Missouri River, are two coal-fired electric generating stations. The Stanton Station was built in 1966 and contains one lignite-fired unit rated at 202,000 kilowatts. The Leland Olds Station contains two units: the first was built in 1966 and is rated at 210,000 kilowatts and the second was built in 1975 and is rated at 440,000 kilowatts. Both plants burn North Dakota lignite and were built next to the Missouri River to take advantage of abundant cold water as a coolant.

⑦ On the south side of Highway 200A across from the power plants is the old Glenharold surface coal mine that operated from 1964 to 1990. Most of the uplands south of Highway 200A between Stanton and the Highway 31 exit were mined and reclaimed. The lignite was about 12 feet thick and about 100 feet below the surface in this area. The land was returned to its pre-mined contour and, except for the absence of outcrops, looks much like it did prior to mining.

⑧ Coal Creek Station, north of Washburn on U.S. 83, is the largest lignite-fired electric generating station in North Dakota. The plant contains two units that are rated at 550,000 kilowatts apiece. Unit 1 became operational in 1979 and Unit 2 in 1981. Coal from the adjacent Falkirk Mine is burned in this plant. The Hagel coal bed, one of the primary lignite beds mined in the Sentinel Butte formation, is 5 to 15 feet thick and is mined at depths less than 150 feet.

The first time that the expedition encountered clinker, brittle sedimentary rock baked by burning coal veins, was near Fort Mandan. Throughout the remainder of their journey in North Dakota they noted the occurrence of pink layers in the bluffs along the Missouri River and floating "pumice stone" in the water. A 20- to 30-foot-thick layer of clin-

⑨ ker is present in the upper part of the ridge northeast of the Fort Mandan Historic Monument. Clark passed by this area on March 21, 1805, and it is evident from his journal entry that he understood these rocks had been heated, although he likely did not realize that burning coal veins were the source of the heat. The Mandan and Hidatsa often set fire to the prairie, and these fires probably ignited the lignite veins. Clark collected several specimens of the frothy and nonfrothy varieties of clinker from this site and experimented by heating them in a furnace. The explorers sent one clinker specimen from this site to Thomas Jefferson in the April 7, 1805, shipment from Fort Mandan. It is listed as Specimen Number 67 in the November 16, 1805, American Philosophical Society donation book and is now in the collection of the Academy of Natural Sciences in Philadelphia.

> on my return to day to the Fort I came on the points of the high hills, Saw
> an emence quantity of Pumice Stone on the Sides & foot of the hills and

emence beds of Pumice Stone near the Tops of the [hills] with evident marks of the Hill haveing once been on fire, I collected Some the differnt i e Stone Pumice Stone & a hard earth and put them into a furnace the hard earth melted and glazed the others two and the hard Clay became a pumice Stone Glazed.

—CLARK, March 21, 1805

The Plains are on fire in view of the fort on both Sides of the River, it is Said to be common for the Indians to burn the Plains near their villages every Spring for the benifit of ther horse, and to induce the Buffalow to come near to them.

—CLARK, March 30, 1805

In early April, as the expedition reached a point about 6 miles below the present-day location of Garrison Dam, they entered an area containing extensive, well-exposed outcrops of the lignite-bearing rocks of the Sentinel Butte formation. The 100- to 200-foot-high cliffs adjacent to the west edge of the Missouri River provided them with the first good look at these coal-bearing strata, which continued from here to the North Dakota–Montana border. These were the most lithologically

Sentinel Butte formation exposures 2 miles south of Garrison Dam where expedition journalists first mentioned thick coal.

diverse rocks that they had encountered in North Dakota and possibly in all of their journey upriver from St. Louis.

Gass noted "a strong smell of sulphur" on April 8, 1805, which was caused by sulphur oxides released from burning lignite. This was the first of many actively burning coal veins that the expedition would encounter during the remainder of their trip through North Dakota. It was later that Lewis and Clark made the connection between burning coal veins and the formation of clinker.

> From the upper part of an island just below Morparperyoopatoo's camp to a point of wood land on the Stad. Side *passing* a high bluff on the Lad. containing many horizontal narrow Stratas of Carbonated wood, some of which are Sixty feet above the Surface of the water.
>
> —CLARK, April 8, 1805

THE NORTH DAKOTA EVERGLADES

Numerous fossils recovered from the Bullion Creek and Sentinel Butte formations indicate that North Dakota was dramatically different during Paleocene time than today. The most common fossils found in these formations are petrified wood and leaf fossils of dawn redwood, bald cypress, magnolia, ginkgo, palm, and many other kinds of exotic plants that grow in subtropical to tropical climates. These rain forests occupied vast areas of North Dakota: many fossil tree-stumps, some 10 feet or more in diameter, are still in an upright growth position. The dominant predators that inhabited these forested, swampy areas were crocodiles, some up to 12 feet long, and crocodile-like, fish-eating champsosaurs. Numerous kinds of fish, turtles, clams and snails, and insects lived in the ponds, lakes, and swamps. Snake, bird, and mammal fossils have also been found.

Clark was the first expedition member to report the occurrence of fossils in North Dakota when he noted carbonized wood on April 8, 1805, as the expedition left Fort Mandan. He encountered these fossils when the expedition passed the high bluffs along the shore between Fort Mandan and Riverdale. Members of the Lewis and Clark Expedition (we are not sure who) were also the first people to collect fossils for scientific purposes in North Dakota. Lewis and Clark sent a specimen of petrified wood, recorded as Specimen Number 66 in the November 16, 1805, American Philosophical Society donation book, to Thomas Jefferson along with other biological, ethnological, and geological specimens from Fort Mandan. A label on the specimen, believed to have been written by Lewis, stated that the fossil was "Found in the Bluffs near Fort mandan." This specimen has since been lost.

This 60-million-year-old, seven-foot-long skeleton of a crocodile-like champsosaur from the Sentinel Butte formation, found on land administered by the United States Forest Service in North Dakota, is on exhibit at the North Dakota Heritage Center in Bismarck. —North Dakota State Fossil Collection (ND 94–225.1)

Painting by Julie Martinez of a pond habitat during Paleocene time in North Dakota. Crocodiles, crocodile-like champsosaurs, and several kinds of turtles, fish, insects, and mollusks lived in these ponds and lakes about 60 million years ago. Exotic plants such as bald-cypress, dawn redwood, magnolia (large white flower), ginkgo, and palm grew along the margins of the ponds and lakes. Mammals and birds lived in the forests. Painting is based on fossils found in North Dakota. —Art courtesy of the Science Museum of Minnesota

The Mandan and Hidatsa collected fossils from the Sentinel Butte formation to wear as ornaments. Archeologists have found fossils of the freshwater snail *Campeloma*, perforated near the aperture and worn as jewelry, in earthlodge village sites in North Dakota.

Bison Trails

In the 1970s, geologist Lee Clayton examined linear features on aerial photographs and realized that a number of intersecting trenches across North Dakota's landscape were bison trails. These trails are typically 15 to 30 feet wide and are 3 feet deep where they cross areas of

Perforated Campeloma *snail fossil from the Sentinel Butte or Bullion Creek formation recovered from the Elbee archeological site in the Knife River Indian Village National Historic Site. This fossil shell, which is 1 inch tall, would have been worn as jewelry.* —Courtesy of the Knife River Indian Villages National Historic Site (KNRI 1225)

The Expedition II "The Hunt" by Gary P. Miller. Members of the Lewis and Clark Expedition are on a buffalo hunt north of Fort Mandan. View is the east. Fort Mandan was situated across the river. —Art courtesy of Gary P. Miller.

moderate relief. Vast herds of bison migrated across landforms at the same place for thousands of years, forming trails. The trails are often oriented northwest-southeast in areas where the surface topography did not hinder herd movement. The bison may have created this trail orientation, which parallels the prevailing wind direction in North Dakota, following the smell of water or edible plants. Though visible on aerial photographs, most of these subtle trails are difficult to identify on the ground. Gullying and human activities have obliterated many of them. While in North Dakota, the expedition journalists often commented on the abundance of wildlife, particularly bison.

Aerial photograph of a 1-square-mile area near Stanton shows parallel linear depressions that geologist Jon Reiten has identified as bison trails. These trails may be oriented north-south because the Knife River valley is just a few miles due north.

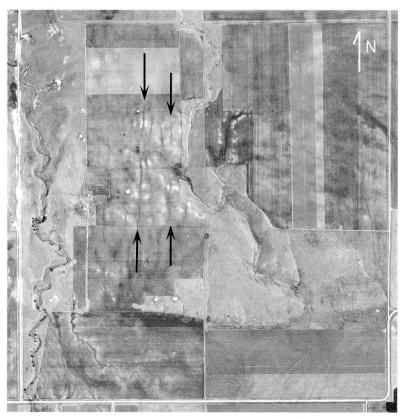

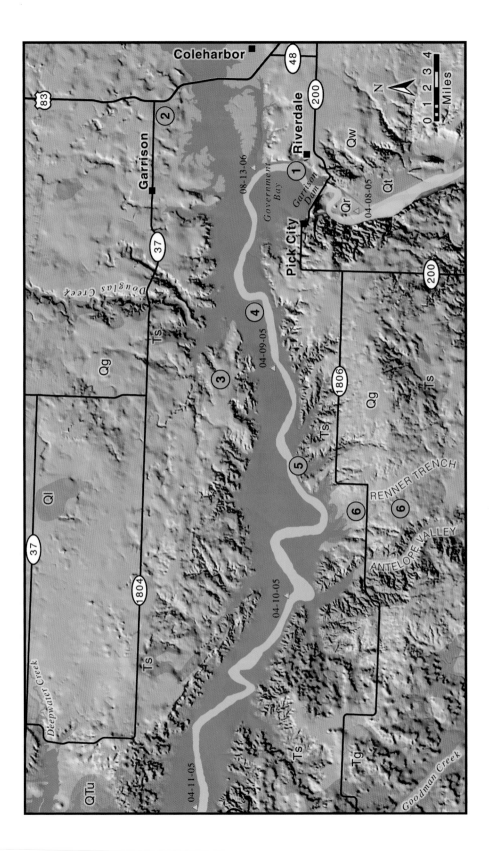

Riverdale to New Town

April 9–15, 1805
August 12–13, 1806

Highways 1804 and 1806 do not parallel the Missouri River valley as closely along this stretch as they do from the South Dakota border to Riverdale. Throughout much of this segment, you cannot see the lake from the highways. However, you can access public use areas along the lake by side roads, and there are notable geologic features along Highways 200, 22, and 23.

Garrison Dam at Riverdale is one of seven mainstem dams in the upper Missouri River basin in Montana and the Dakotas. Completed in 1954, the dam was authorized under the Pick-Sloan project. The fifth-largest earthen dam in the world, it is more than 2 miles long (11,300 feet) and has a maximum height of 210 feet. The reservoir created by the dam, Lake Sakakawea, extends almost to the Montana border, a distance of about 180 miles, and has a maximum width of about 6 miles. The total storage capacity of the reservoir is 23.8 million acre-feet. The shoreline of the lake extends for roughly 1,300 miles, making it one of the largest human-made lakes in the United States.

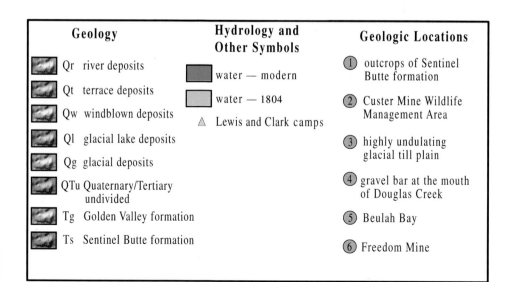

Geology	Hydrology and Other Symbols	Geologic Locations
Qr river deposits	water — modern	① outcrops of Sentinel Butte formation
Qt terrace deposits	water — 1804	② Custer Mine Wildlife Management Area
Qw windblown deposits	△ Lewis and Clark camps	
Ql glacial lake deposits		③ highly undulating glacial till plain
Qg glacial deposits		
QTu Quaternary/Tertiary undivided		④ gravel bar at the mouth of Douglas Creek
Tg Golden Valley formation		⑤ Beulah Bay
Ts Sentinel Butte formation		⑥ Freedom Mine

Lake Sakakawea is named after the young Hidatsa woman who accompanied Lewis and Clark on their journey from Fort Mandan to the West Coast and back. Tribal leaders of the Three Affiliated Tribes (Mandan, Hidatsa, and Arikara) were instrumental in getting the reservoir named in honor of Sakakawea. The spelling of Sakakawea's name has been a controversy for many years. Charbonneau said her name meant "Bird Woman" in Hidatsa and according to the linguist Washington Matthews it should be spelled Tsakaka-wias (Russell, 1986). For ease in pronunciation it became Sakakawea (Sakaka=bird and weawoman). This became the official spelling in North Dakota and is accepted as such by the State Historical Society of North Dakota. Although the United States Geographic Board acknowledged that her name is a Hidatsa word meaning Bird Woman, people started spelling it Sacagawea. This became the official spelling of her name by federal agencies. Elsewhere, particularly in Wyoming, her name is spelled *Sacajawea*, which is a Shoshone word that has been translated as "Boat Launcher" or "Carrying Burden." Lewis and Clark spelled her name many ways and often just referred to her as "the Indian woman." Even today there is debate within the Three Affiliated Tribes as to how her name should be spelled.

During low-water phases of Lake Sakakawea, the foot of the steep banks and shoreline are wonderful places to hike and explore. You can find chunks of coal, fossilized tree trunks and stumps, leaf fossil impressions, spherical and elongated concretions, clinker, and glacial rocks of many igneous and metamorphic types such as granite, basalt, diorite, and schist. The U.S. Army Corps of Engineers, which manages the shoreline of Lake Sakakawea, prohibits the collection of artifacts, rocks, or fossils without a permit.

"THE BLUFFS OF THE RIVER"

On April 9, 1805, the expedition traveled from a few miles below to about 13 miles above the position of Garrison Dam. Impressive outcrops of the Sentinel Butte formation were, and still are, exposed along the shore. These exposures prompted Lewis to include a lengthy and detailed description of the stratigraphy of these rocks in his journal. This is the first geological description that Lewis recorded since entering North Dakota. Prior to this time, Clark was the principle recorder of geological information, and his comments were generally not as detailed as Lewis's descriptions. Lewis's lack of daily journal entries up to this point is a mystery, and his detailed description on this day adds to our disappointment over their absence.

The Riverdale area prior to construction of Garrison Dam. View is to the north. The wooded floodplain is now under as much as 150 feet of water in this area. Rocks of the Sentinel Butte formation are exposed in the foreground. —Photo courtesy of the State Historical Society of North Dakota (SHSND 0760–24)

Aerial view of the Riverdale area with Garrison Dam in the center. View is to the southeast. Note the beginning of badlands terrain just a few miles south of the dam.

the Bluffs of the river which we passed today were upwards of a hundred feet high, formed of a mixture of yellow clay and sand— many horizontal stratas of carbonated wood, having every appearance of pitcoal at a distance; were seen in the face of these bluffs. these stratas are of unequal thicknesses from 1 to 5 feet, and appear at different elivations above the water some of them as much as eighty feet. the hills of the river are very broken and many of them have the apearance of having been on fire at some former period. considerable quantities of pumice stone and lava appear in many parts of these hills where they are broken and washed down by the rain and melting snow.

—LEWIS, April 9, 1805

all the hills have more or Less indefferent Coal in Stratias at different hites from the waters edge to 80 feet. those Stratias from 1 inch to 5 feet thick.

—CLARK, April 9, 1805

The April 9 journal entries illustrate the different terms that the expedition members used to refer to lignite: pit coal, stone coal, and carbonated wood. In the early 1800s, the term *stone coal* referred to harder and more mature qualities of coal such as anthracite and possibly bituminous coal mined in the eastern part of the United States. These were the kinds of coal that Lewis and Clark were familiar with, and it is probably the reason the journalists typically referred to the lignite, the softest grade of coal, as "inferior" quality. *Pit coal* was also a frequently used eastern term for coal that could be mined from a pit or through excavation. Thomas Jefferson used the term *pit coal* in his June 20, 1803, instruction letter to Lewis: "the mineral productions of every kind; but more particularly metals, limestone, pit coal, & saltpetre; salines" (Jackson, 1962).

Lignite occurs at several stratigraphic positions in the Sentinel Butte formation in beds typically 3 to 5 feet thick. The Sentinel Butte formation, consisting of alternating beds of mudstone, claystone, siltstone, sandstone, and lignite, attains a thickness of more than 600 feet. It is the dominant bedrock formation exposed in the Missouri River bluffs between Garrison Dam and the Montana border. When the expedition traveled through this area, more that 200 feet of Sentinel Butte strata were exposed in the steep, 250-foot-high cliffs, capped with glacial till, along the east end of the river valley near Riverdale. Lake Sakakawea inundated the bottom one-half to two-thirds (about 140 feet) of the cliff faces observed by the expedition. The cliff faces along the west side of the river south of Garrison Dam provide a good indication of how the east end of the river valley appeared prior to dam construction.

Sentinel Butte formation overlain by glacial sediments along a cliff face at Government Bay north of Riverdale on Lake Sakakawea. Black layers are lignite beds. A bald eagle is perched on the ice eating a fish in the lower left.

Boulder pavement, an accumulation of glacial boulders and gravel from which finer material has been removed by water or wind, separates two layers of glacial till along the banks of Lake Sakakawea. The lower till is believed to be more than 600,000 years old and the upper till about 70,000 years old.

Fertile Plains

One of the missions of the Lewis and Clark Expedition was to assess the agricultural potential of areas explored. John Logan Allen, an eminent Lewis and Clark scholar, noted that the prevailing concept of the West in the early 1800s was that it was a garden with extremely fertile soil. He quoted the *National Intelligencer* (Washington D.C.), October 24, 1803, which noted, "No country enlightened by the sun has a better soil to expose to its rays; or a soil capable of higher cultivation, or richer or greater variety of produce" (Allen, 1998). Along this stretch of the Missouri River, the agrarian inhabitants had utilized the agricultural attributes of the valley for generations. The expedition traversed this area in the springtime when rejuvenation of life after winter dormancy was, and still is, starkly evident in North Dakota. The leading industry in the state today is agriculture, even though Lake Sakakawea inundated many of the fertile floodplains the expedition observed. The glacial plains, however, are also fertile.

A canola field in bloom in McLean County in an area noted by Lewis as being a "level fertile plain." In 2001, North Dakota led the nation in production of spring wheat, durum, oats, barley, flaxseed, dry edible beans, dry edible peas, sunflowers, and canola.

2¼ miles higher we passed the entrance of Miry Creek, which discharges itself on the Stard. side. this creek is but small, takes it's rise in some small lakes near the Mouse river and passes in it's course to the Missouri, through beatifull, level, and fertile plains, intirely destitute of timber.

—LEWIS, April 9, 1805

The country on both sides of the missouri from the tops of the river hills, is one continued level fertile plain as far as the eye can reach, in which there is not even a solitary tree or shrub to be seen except such as from their moist situations or the steep declivities of hills are sheltered from the ravages of the fire.

—LEWIS, April 10, 1805

CUSTER MINE WILDLIFE MANAGEMENT AREA

The Custer Mine Wildlife Management Area encompasses about 700 acres that were mined by underground methods from 1926 to 1938 and by surface mining from 1947 to 1964. At Custer Mine the 7-foot-thick coal seam is about 45 feet below the land surface. The surface mining occurred before reclamation laws were established in the mid-1970s, so soil was not segregated and saved and the mine spoils were not reclaimed. Beginning in the early 1950s, an area sportsmen's club, along with youth groups and other volunteers, began hand-planting trees on the old spoils to create wildlife habitat. In 1984, the mining company deeded the land to the North Dakota Game and fish Department, and the abandoned mine became a wildlife management area. In the 1990s The North Dakota Public Service Commission used abandoned-mine land funds to reduce the potential danger of the area by resloping the steep, 60-foot-high walls that remained after mining ended.

HIGHLY UNDULATING GLACIAL TILL PLAIN

The landscape east of the town of Garrison and north of Highway 1804 is a highly undulating glacial till plain. West of Garrison, the topography flattens out though it is still a till plain. Several factors, including possible differences in the variable rate of glacial melt or the type and amount of sediment that slid off melting glaciers, produced the topographic differences. Sediments derived from quickly melting glaciers tend to produce a more highly undulating topography than slowly melting glaciers where sediments spread out more evenly. The primary reason for the difference in topography is that the area to the west is older and therefore more worn and subdued. The large boulders on the

Aerial view of the Custer Mine Wildlife Management Area. View is to the north. Note the linear ridges of mine spoils and the rows of hand-planted trees. Highly undulating glacial topography is visible in the background.

Vegetated mine spoils at the Custer Mine Wildlife Management Area.

hillsides that Clark mentioned in his April 11, 1805, journal entry are glacial erratics that were transported to the area by glaciers, deposited with the rest of the till when the glaciers melted, and exposed at the surface as the finer particles of till eroded away.

3

> The plains are high and rich Some of them are Sandy Containing Small pebble, and on Some of the hill Sides large Stones are to be Seen.
>
> —CLARK, April 11, 1805

Highly undulating glacial topography of the till plain east of Garrison.

Gently undulating glacial topography in the Douglas Creek area.

GRAVEL BARS IN THE MISSOURI RIVER

For the past 10,000 years, the Missouri River has primarily transported and deposited sand, silt, and clay as it flowed through North Dakota. However, this has not always been the case. At the end of the last Ice Age, melting glaciers contributed vast amounts of water to the river, and it was able to transport and deposit coarse sand and gravel. Terrace deposits in the modern valley preserve lenses of some of this sand and gravel. Where the river undercuts a terrace or bank containing a lens of gravel, it removes the finer-grained material and leaves the layer of gravel. This apparently happened near the mouth of Douglas Creek where Ordway noted gravel bars. Six days later, Lewis reported similar gravel in an area northwest of New Town.

> Saw Gravelly bars which was the first we Saw on this River. they were round and large. Saw Some on Shore also.
>
> —ORDWAY, April 9, 1805

> we passed a rock this evening standing in the middle of the river, and the bed of the river was formed principally of gravel.
>
> —LEWIS, April 15, 1805

BEULAH BAY

Beulah Bay has excellent exposures of the Sentinel Butte formation which contains many petrified logs and stumps. Based on leaf fossils associated with them, the 60-million-year-old fossilized trees are probably dawn redwood (*Metasequoia*) and bald cypress (*Taxodium*). Some of the petrified trees are extremely well preserved and still show bark and knotholes. During one of the Lake Sakakawea low-water phases, a beautifully preserved, 80-foot-long fossil tree was collected from the Beulah Bay area and is now on exhibit along the arboretum trail on the state capitol grounds in Bismarck. Some trunks maintain their original shape, but many have been flattened by the weight of overlying sediments deposited on them before they were mineralized. The whitish trunks and stumps are often embedded in black lignite and are easy to see because of this color contrast. Often, silica has only replaced the outer edges of fossil wood in the Sentinel Butte formation, and the wood is carbonized (black) in the center.

The 20- to 50-foot-high vertical banks adjacent to the lake in Beulah Bay are excellent places to examine the typical claystone, mudstone, siltstone, and lignite of the Sentinel Butte formation and the overlying, highly jointed, glacial till capped by windblown sediments (loess). Be

A sandbar capped with a thin layer of gravel north of Stanton. Lewis and Ordway described similar sites in the stretch of river now submerged beneath Lake Sakakawea.

Leaf fossil from the Sentinel Butte formation found along the shore in Beulah Bay.

Fossil tree trunks weathered out of the Sentinel Butte formation along the shore of Lake Sakakawea in the Beulah Bay area. This trunk is 3 feet in diameter and 20 feet long.

This 4-foot-tall fossil stump from the Sentinel Butte formation is in its original growing position along the shore of Lake Sakakawea.

careful when hiking along these cutbanks because rocks of the Sentinel Butte formation have a tendency to slump in large blocks.

> Set out at an early hour. our peroge and the Canoes passed over to the Lard side in order to avoid a bank which was rappidly falling in on the Stard.
>
> —LEWIS, April 12, 1805

The expedition encountered and recorded veins of burning lignite near what is now the Beulah Bay Public Use Area. We searched the area but were unable to locate any clinker deposit that might have resulted from this burn.

> at the distance of 12 miles from our encampment of last night we arrived at the lower point of a bluff on the Lard side; about 1 1/2 miles down this bluff from this point, the bluff is now on fire and throws out considerable quantities of smoke which has a strong sulphurious smell. the appearance of the coal in the blufs continues as yesterday.
>
> —LEWIS, April 10, 1805

Smoke rises from a burning lignite bed that was ignited by a prairie fire. This photograph was taken a few months after the prairie fire had swept through this area. Note pink, baked rock called "clinker."

Cutbank of till overlying the Sentinel Butte formation along the southern shore of Lake Sakakawea. Two layers of lignite, one at lake level, are evident. Petrified wood and glacial boulders cover the beach.

Rounded and elongate concretions from the Sentinel Butte formation along the edge of Lake Sakakawea. The Sentinel Butte formation is overlain by till at the midpoint of the bluff in the background.

Coal-Based Energy Plants near Antelope Valley

Highway 1806 passes through the Coteau Properties Company's Freedom Mine, the largest lignite mine in North Dakota. This mine produces more than half of North Dakota's annual 30 million tons of lignite. The lignite is consumed in the adjacent Antelope Valley Station power plant. It is also converted to synthetic natural gas at Dakota Gasification Company's neighboring Great Plains Synfuel Plant. The synfuels plant, conceived and built as a result of the 1970s energy crisis, began operation in 1984. The plant consumes, on an annual basis, about 6 million tons of lignite to produce approximately 54 billion standard cubic feet of natural gas. In addition to natural gas, the plant produces a host of products including anhydrous ammonia, phenols, solvents, carbon dioxide, and other chemicals.

Antelope Valley and Renner Trench are two large, southeast-trending glacial meltwater channels that likely formed during the Early Wisconsinan (about 40,000 years ago). They are about 3 miles apart and contain as much as 400 feet of fill material. Although similar in depth, the surface expression of these two channels is quite different. Antelope Valley is about 1 mile wide with 150- to 200-foot-high valley walls. The Renner Trench is two to three times wider and has low, gentle slopes. Because the Renner Trench has such a subtle topographic expression, it is difficult to see from the ground. The readvance of a retreating ice sheet or the advance of another glacier overrode the trench and filled it with glacial sediments. Antelope Valley was not overridden in this area and retained a valley profile. These two meltwater trenches exemplify the difficulties associated with attempting to place glacial events in the context of time in the absence of dateable material. These trenches could have been formed anytime between 60,000 and 14,000 years ago—40,000 years ago is an educated guess assuming that both formed as the 60,000-year-old glacial advance retreated through this area. We do know that both these systems carried water into the Knife River valley. Glacial meltwater in these trenches eroded through the 15-foot-thick Beulah-Zap lignite bed, removing about 635 million tons of mineable coal, an amount equal to more than twenty years of current mine production in North Dakota.

The gasification and power plants use water from an intake system in Renner Bay. The intake system was constructed about 3,000 feet offshore in 80 feet of water. An 8-foot-diameter pipe, 200 feet below the bottom of Lake Sakakawea, carries water from the intake system to shore. This system is also used to supply water to the Southwest Water Pipeline, which transports water to many communities and rural water systems in southwestern North Dakota. The Southwest Water Pipeline

*View to the west across Antelope Valley, a channel
eroded by glacial meltwater about 40,000 years ago.*

*Two lignite beds exposed in a cutbank near Indian Hills Resort on Lake
Sakakawea near where expedition members tried burning lignite on April
11, 1805. Petrified wood (white) is visible at bottom center of photograph.*

delivers a reliable supply of good-quality water to people living in this area. Prior to establishment of this system, many people obtained their drinking water from groundwater that contained relatively high concentrations of total dissolved solids, sodium, and sulphate.

On April 11, 1805, expedition members experimented with burning lignite. This was the second of only three attempts to burn what they thought was coal. They had previously tried burning lignite near Mandan.

> the plains begin to have a green appearance, the hills on either side are from 5 to 7 miles asunder and in maney places have been burnt, appearing at a distance of a redish brown choler, containing Pumic Stone & lava, Some of which rolin down to the base of those hills— In maney of those hills forming bluffs to the river we procieve Several Stratums of bituminious Substance which resembles Coal; thoug Some of the pieces appear to be excellent Coal it resists the fire for Some[time], and consumes without emiting much flaim.
>
> —CLARK, April 11, 1805

Confluence of the Missouri and Little Missouri Rivers

The expedition reached the confluence of the Missouri and Little Missouri Rivers on April 12, 1805. They camped early, having only traveled about 6 miles that day, so that Lewis would have time to make celestial observations that he used to determine the longitude and latitude of this confluence. Lewis and Clark determined that the Little Missouri was 134 yards wide at its mouth and 30 inches deep. Lewis concluded that since the Little Missouri River resembled the Missouri River in color and the type of sediment it transported, the geology it passed through must also be similar to that encountered by the larger river—an astute and accurate observation. Both he and Clark correctly noted that the headwaters of the Little Missouri River are near the Black Hills in South Dakota, information that they probably received from the Mandan and Hidatsa at Fort Mandan. Lewis also noted the rugged badlands topography in this area. The Little Missouri River valley is underlain by up to 200 feet of sand, gravel, and glacial till.

> The little Missouri disembogues on the S. side of the Missouri 1693 miles from the confluence of the latter with the Mississippi. it is 134 yards wide at it's mouth, and sets in with a bould current but it's greatest debth is not more than 2 1/2 feet. it's navigation is extreemly difficult, owing to it's rapidity, shoals and sand bars. . . . this river passes through the Northern extremity of the black hills where is very narrow and rapid and it's banks high and perpendicular. it takes it's rise in a broken country West

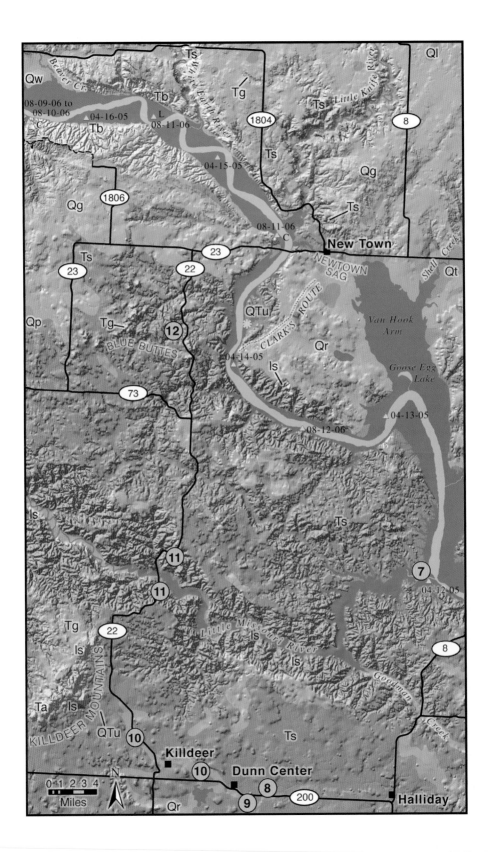

of the Black hills with the waters of the yellow stone river, and a considerable distance S. W. of the point at which it passes the black hills. the country through which it passes is generally broken and the highlands possess but little timber. . . . the country is extreamly broken about the mouth of this river, and as far up <and> on both sides, as we could observe it from the tops of some elivated hills, which stand betwen these two rivers, about 3 miles from their junction. the soil appears fertile and deep, it consists generally of a dark rich loam intermixed with a small proportion of fine sand. . . . the colour of the water, the bed of the river, and it's appearance <of this river> in every respect, resembles the Missouri; I am therefore induced to believe that the texture of the soil of the country in which it takes it's rise, and that through which it passes, is similar to the country through which the Missouri passes after leaving the woody country, or such as we are now in.

—LEWIS, April 12, 1805

Another fine day. We set out early as usual. About 8 we came to the mouth of the Little Missouri, a handsome small river that comes in on the South side where we halted and took breakfast. The river is very properly called the Little Missouri, for it exactly resembles the Missouri in colour, current and taste.

—GASS, April 12, 1805

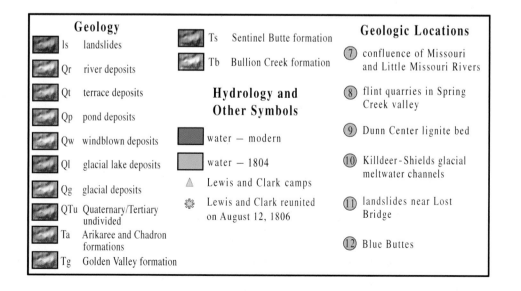

Geology

ls	landslides	
Qr	river deposits	
Qt	terrace deposits	
Qp	pond deposits	
Qw	windblown deposits	
Ql	glacial lake deposits	
Qg	glacial deposits	
QTu	Quaternary/Tertiary undivided	
Ta	Arikaree and Chadron formations	
Tg	Golden Valley formation	
Ts	Sentinel Butte formation	
Tb	Bullion Creek formation	

Hydrology and Other Symbols

water — modern

water — 1804

△ Lewis and Clark camps

❋ Lewis and Clark reunited on August 12, 1806

Geologic Locations

⑦ confluence of Missouri and Little Missouri Rivers

⑧ flint quarries in Spring Creek valley

⑨ Dunn Center lignite bed

⑩ Killdeer-Shields glacial meltwater channels

⑪ landslides near Lost Bridge

⑫ Blue Buttes

Aerial view of the confluence of the Missouri and Little Missouri Rivers (arrow). View is to the west. Lake Sakakawea in this area is nine times the width that the Missouri River was in the spring of 1805.

Aerial view of the Little Missouri River badlands. View is to the west. The Hans Creek/Goodman Creek channel in the foreground is a half-mile-wide, northwest-southeast-trending valley that extends for 30 miles before it empties into the Knife River valley. The Little Missouri River created this channel when it was diverted into this area by glaciers. Sometime later, advancing ice blocked the flow of water through this channel and the Little Missouri River turned north at this location to occupy its present channel. This channel may by contemporaneous with the Renner Trench and Antelope Valley.

Floating Clinker

Expedition members observed the frothy variety of clinker, which they called "pumice stone", floating on the water at the mouth of the Little Missouri River. Lewis and Clark also reported clinker floating in the Missouri River in the Charlson area. Occasionally people witness this phenomenon today. The establishment of farms and ranches has reduced the spread of prairie fires that ignite lignite beds. With fewer burning coal veins, less clinker is formed. The frothy clinker is also soft and susceptible to weathering. Moreover, Garrison and Fort Peck Dams have reduced spring flooding so less clinker is eroded from the bedrock and introduced into the Missouri River.

> the mineral appearances of salts, coal and sulpher, together with birnt hills & pumicestone still continue— while we remained at the entrance of the little Missouri, we saw several pieces of pumice stone floating down that stream, a considerable quanty of which had lodged <and collected> against a point of drift wood a little above it's entrance.
>
> —LEWIS, April 14, 1805

Knife River Flint

A 2- to 3-foot-thick layer of dark brown to black flint, called Knife River flint, formed in western North Dakota sometime between 20 and 50 million years ago. Geologists don't know its exact age or formation source because they have never been found it in place. This flint, which is silicified peat, contains fragments of fossil plants, indicating that it was deposited in ponds and swamps. Cobbles and boulders of this flint have been found in preglacial river deposits, glacial meltwater deposits, glacial till, modern fluvial deposits, and lag deposits (coarse grained material left behind after the finer-grained material eroded away). Because it has not been found in situ, geologists don't known whether it came from Fort Union, Golden Valley, White River, or Arikaree strata.

Native peoples mined pockets of this flint for thousands of years from several quarries in the Knife River valley in Dunn and Mercer Counties. Small pits and depressions are evident north of Highway 200 in the valley of Spring Creek where Paleo-Indians of late Pleistocene time collected the flint. They considered it a high quality material for making tools because of its conchoidal fracturing. They traded it extensively throughout North America, and artifacts made from Knife River flint have been recovered from as far away as New York, New Mexico, and northern Canada. It is likely that Clark was observing Knife River flint at the mouth of the Little Missouri River when he reported seeing a "black flint" in his April 12 journal entry.

> I walked out on the lower Side of this river and found the countrey hilley the Soil composed of black mole & a Small perportion of Sand containing great quantity of Small peable Some limestone, black flint, & Sand Stone.
>
> —CLARK, April 12, 1805

Frothy varieties of clinker collected near Lewis and Clark State Park. The specimen on the right will float on water and is similar to the floating rocks that Lewis and Clark encountered and called "pumice stone."

Hand specimen of Knife River flint (left), a knife blade made of Knife River flint (State Historical Society of North Dakota 95.118.1) collected in Dunn County, and a spear point (right) made of Knife River flint (State Historical Society of North Dakota 10028) collected in north-central North Dakota. Knife blade is 4½ inches in height. Note the white crust or patina on the unworked specimen.

Lag deposits of Knife River flint were collected from the adjacent field and dumped along this fence line. Though Knife River flint has never been found in outcrop, large blocks like this indicate to geologists that it comes from 2- to 3-foot-thick layers.

Aerial photograph of Knife River flint quarries, dug by Paleo-Indians in glacial meltwater terrace deposits along Spring Creek in Dunn County. —Photograph courtesy of the University of North Dakota and the Knife River Indian Villages National Historic Site

DUNN CENTER COAL FIELD

The Dunn Center bed, a 15- to 20-foot-thick lignite bed in the Sentinel Butte formation, crops out in ravines south of Highway 200 in the Dunn Center area. The highway bisects a 50-square-mile deposit that contains approximately 900 million tons of mineable lignite. In response to the energy crisis of the mid-1970s, over 1,500 test holes were drilled in this area to determine if this lignite deposit could sustain a coal gasification plant. Plans for the plant were abandoned when natural gas prices fell below projected price levels in the late 1970s.

KILLDEER-SHIELDS CHANNELS

The Killdeer Mountains are at the head of a large, intricate system of buried glacial meltwater channels that extend southeastward for more than 140 miles to the Missouri River near Fort Yates in south-central North Dakota. The channels are 1/4 to 1 mile wide at the surface and contain up to 200 feet of fill, mostly glacial deposits. Some channels are enclosed by moderately high walls while others have very little surface relief. Highway 200 crosses several of these channels between Dunn Center and Killdeer in an area where the topographic relief of the channels is subtle. Highway 22 is within, or in some places adjacent to, one of these channels from the town of Killdeer to the Killdeer Mountains. The channels followed the edge of the ice lobe capturing meltwater from the ice as well as north-flowing streams that were blocked by the ice and forced to turn southeast.

KILLDEER MOUNTAINS

The Killdeer Mountains, two prominent mesas, rise approximately 700 feet above the surrounding countryside. They are capped by several hundred feet of volcanic ash-rich siltstones, sandstones, and freshwater carbonates of the Arikaree formation, the most extensive deposits of this 25-million-year-old strata in North Dakota. The Miocene-age Arikaree formation is the youngest bedrock formation in the state. Mudstones and sandstones of the Eocene/Oligocene-age White River group underlie Arikaree strata. The White River group extends from the Dakotas to Nebraska, Colorado, and Wyoming. The Paleocene/Eocene-age Golden Valley formation, which underlies the White River beds, is exposed at the base of the Killdeer Mountains.

Fossils from rocks exposed in the Killdeer Mountains and other buttes in southwestern North Dakota document the dramatic change from a humid, subtropical climate with swampy forests during Paleocene time to a cooler, drier, and more seasonal climate with open savannas during

In Pre-Wisconsinan or Early Wisconsinan time, more than 60,000 years ago, meltwater flowed along the southern margin of the continental glacier, forming the Killdeer–Shields channels.

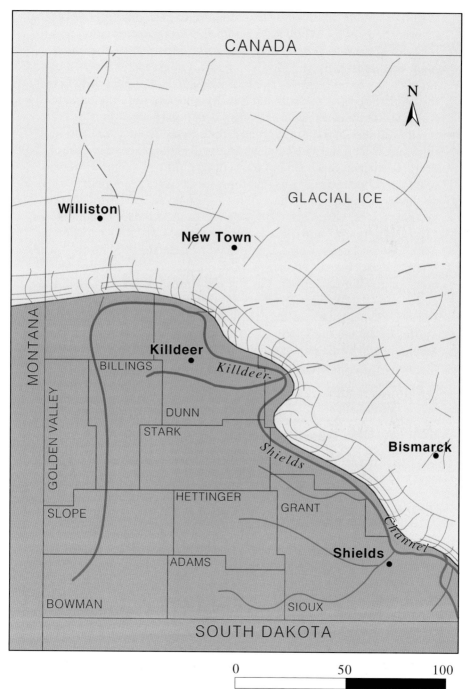

CANADA

N

GLACIAL ICE

Williston

New Town

MONTANA

Killdeer

BILLINGS

Killdeer

DUNN

STARK

Shields

Bismarck

GOLDEN VALLEY

HETTINGER

GRANT

SLOPE

Channel

Shields

ADAMS

BOWMAN

SIOUX

SOUTH DAKOTA

0   50   100

miles

Oligocene and Miocene time. The fossil remains of more than eighty kinds of animals, particularly mammals, have been discovered in sedimentary beds of the White River group and Arikaree formation. Hornless rhinoceroses, ancestral camels, diminutive three-toed horses, giant pigs, sheeplike oreodonts, ancestral dogs, saber-toothed cats, squirrel-like rodents, mice, giant tortoises, fish, and many other creatures inhabited the savanna habitat. By Miocene time the climate of North Dakota was semiarid to arid and cool temperate.

The Killdeer Mountains received their name from a translation of the Sioux word *Tah-kah-o-kuty*, which means "the place where they kill deer." Lewis and Clark did not travel up the Little Missouri River to explore the Killdeer Mountains, but these mesas were prominent features on the horizon for several days of their journey. In their April 15, 1805, journal entries, Lewis and Clark referred to the Killdeer Mountains as "Turtle Mountain," and Clark labeled the mesas with this name on his map. This has been a source of confusion because the present-day Turtle Mountains are located about 150 miles northeast of the Killdeer Mountains, on the border between Canada and North Dakota. It is likely that Lewis and Clark referred to these mesas as Turtle Mountain because David Thompson had plotted the Killdeer Mountains but labeled them Turtle Hill on his 1798 map, referring to them in his journal as Turtle Mountain and Turtle Mountain of the West. Thompson may have gotten the name from the Mandan and Hidatsa; if so, the English translation of the Sioux name eventually won out over the translation of the Mandan and Hidatsa name. In his April 12 entry, Lewis pointed out that the location of the Killdeer Mountains had been "laid down too far S. W." from where they had earlier thought.

> passed high range of hills on the South Side of the River.
>
> —ORDWAY, April 12, 1805

> proceeded on to the mouth of the Little Missouri river and formed a Camp in a butifull elivated plain on the lower Side for the purpose of taking Some observations to fix Latitude & Longitude of this river this river falls in on the L. Side and is 134 yards wide and 2 feet 6 Inches deep at the mouth, it takes its rise in the N W extremity of the black mountains, and through a broken countrey in its whole course washing the N W base of the Turtle Mountain which is Situated about 6 Leagues S W of its mouth.
>
> —CLARK, April 12, 1805

> this river in it's course passed near the N. W. side of turtle mountain, which is said to be no more than 4 or 5 leagues distant from it's entrance

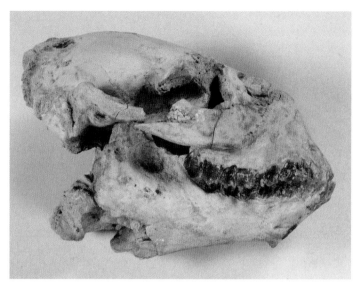

Skull of a 25-million-year-old, sheep-like oreodont from the Arikaree formation that was collected from the summit of the Killdeer Mountains. Skull is 4½ inches long.
—North Dakota State Fossil Collection (ND 93–93.1)

Volcanic ash-rich sandstone and carbonate rocks of the Arikaree formation cap Indian Knob, an outlier along the southern edge of South Killdeer Mountain.

in a straight direction, a little to the S. of West.— this mountain and the knife river have therefore been laid down too far S. W.

—LEWIS, April 12, 1805

LANDSLIDES NEAR LOST BRIDGE

Numerous landslides have occurred adjacent to Highway 22 where the road descends into the valley of the Little Missouri River. The base of the Little Missouri River valley is more than 500 feet lower than the surrounding countryside. This valley was cut relatively quickly when glaciers diverted the Little Missouri River into this area about 600,000 years ago. The high, steep slopes of the Sentinel Butte formation are susceptible to landslides, which have seriously impacted the highway on both sides of the valley. Highway engineers made large slope cuts to stabilize the north valley wall and rerouted the highway away from landslides on the south wall.

Lost Bridge, built in the early 1930s, received its name because lack of funds during the Depression and during World War II prevented the construction of a road to the bridge until the 1950s. The original bridge was dismantled in 1994, and a plaque and a piece of the old bridge now mark the bridge site.

NEW TOWN SAG

When the expedition was near Independence Point, Clark traced the source of a southeast-flowing stream to a small lake that he named Goose Egg Lake. The lake and stream were situated within a 5-mile-wide valley. Clark, in his April 13, 1805, journal entry, demonstrated keen insight when he reasoned that he was traversing an abandoned valley of the ancestral Missouri River. About 60,000 years ago, the ancestral Missouri River flowed through a southeast-trending channel, which is now called the New Town Sag. The now-flooded lowland is known also as the Van Hook Arm of Lake Sakakawea. Highway 23 passes through the northern end of this sag, a flat-bottomed channel, along a 2-mile stretch near New Town. About 14,000 years ago when a glacial ice lobe pushed south, the Missouri River abandoned this 19-mile-long channel and quickly downcut a longer, 27-mile-long loop that is its present course. Goose Egg Lake was near the southern end of the abandoned river channel.

I assended it 1 1/2 mes and found it the discharge of a pond or Small Lake which has appearance of haveing been once the bead of the river.

—CLARK, April 13, 1805

A series of landslides in the Sentinel Butte formation along Highway 22 south of Lost Bridge. Note the thick coal at the base of the slide in the foreground.

Aerial view of a 14-mile-long-by-12-mile-wide peninsula within Lake Sakakawea. View is to the north. The New Town Sag, a former course of the ancestral Missouri River, is at the far upper right. Note the steep-walled coulees that enter the lake from the west at far left.

The modern river valley is only a mile or so wide in this area and is bounded by relatively steep valley walls, a result of the rapid downcutting. The walls consisting of the Sentinel Butte formation are somewhat unstable and prone to landslides. As the ancestral Missouri River cut this valley, deep coulees quickly eroded into the west valley wall. Highway 22 crosses these east-trending coulees in the Blue Buttes area. The steep sides of these coulees are also prone to landslides.

> the lard. shore on which I walked was very broken, and the hills in many places had the appearance of having sliped down in masses of several acres of land in surface.
>
> —LEWIS, April 14, 1805

> Dusk at our Camp on the S. S. opposit a high hill Several parts of which had Sliped down.
>
> —CLARK, April 14, 1805

BLUE BUTTES

Highway 22 crosses the eastern edge of a dozen or so buttes known collectively as the Blue Buttes. These buttes extend over an area of about 50 square miles and are capped by sandstone of the upper member of the Golden Valley formation. Bright white kaolinite clays, the lower member of the Golden Valley formation, crop out along the sides of some of these buttes. This clay is used for making brick in western North Dakota. Although these buttes are prominent features, neither Lewis nor Clark made specific reference to them in their journals, and they were not plotted on Clark's map. This is puzzling because Blue Butte, one of the easternmost buttes of the Blue Buttes complex, just east of Highway 22, would have been a highly visible landmark to Clark when he walked the uplands north and east of the Missouri River on April 14 and 15. Blue Butte would also have been visible from river level, but Ordway was the only member of the expedition who made note of these buttes.

> A high mountain back of the hills S. S.
>
> —ORDWAY, April 14, 1805

EXPLORING ON FOOT

Lewis and Clark took turns walking along the shore or in the uplands adjacent to the Missouri River. In his April 15, 1805, journal entry, Lewis

Aerial view of landslides (arrows) along the western edge of the Missouri River valley north of Bear Den Creek. View is to the west. This may be the landslide complex that Lewis and Clark referred to on April 14, 1805. Blue Butte and other buttes in the Blue Buttes complex are visible in the background.

The Bear Den member, the white, kaolinitic-rich (clay rich) lower member of the Golden Valley formation, is exposed in some of the Blue Buttes.

An unnamed butte to the right of Blue Butte exhibits the thick, capping sandstone of the Camels Butte member, the upper member of the Golden Valley formation. View is to the north along Highway 22.

described the exploration system that he and Clark had developed: "I walked on shore, and Capt. Clark continued with the party it being an invariable rule with us not to be both absent from our vessels at the same time." It seems that most of the time they walked along the Missouri River floodplain. On occasion, they ventured to the uplands overlooking the river valley and beyond.

On April 15, 1805, Lewis noted that Clark had "assended to the high country, about 9 miles distant from the Missouri." However, on the same day Clark wrote, "I walked on shore and assended to the high Countrey on the S.S. and off from the Missouri about three miles." Clark plotted his course on a map—the only time he did so in North Dakota—and his plotted course resolves the discrepancy between the two reported distances: while the length of his traverse may have been nine miles, he was never more than three miles east of the river. This was probably the farthest either Lewis or Clark journeyed out of the river valley while in North Dakota, except during the winter at Fort Mandan.

From a high point along his route, Clark observed that "the countrey is butifull open fertile plain the dreans take theer rise near the Clifts of the river and run from the river in a N E derection as far as I could See, this is the part of the River which Mouse river the waters of Lake Winnipec approaches within a fiew miles of <the> Missouri, and I believe those dreans lead into that river." The waterways ("dreans") that he was referring to are Shell Creek and East Shell Creek. Clark overestimated the extent of these creeks. Shell Creek extends to the northeast for about 25 miles and East Shell Creek for only about 15 miles, 40 or 50 miles short of the Mouse River. Standing upon this overlook today, it its difficult to discern the valleys of these creeks with the unaided eye. Clark probably used his telescope when he viewed them, although they would have been easier to see before trees were planted around farmsteads in this area.

PAUL BROSTE ROCK MUSEUM

One of the most unusual and interesting museums in North Dakota is the Paul Broste Rock Museum south of Highway 1804 in Parshall. Paul Broste was a farmer, philosopher, poet, painter, and rock hound. Over a span of twenty-five years, Broste amassed a huge collection of rocks, minerals, and fossils from around the world. Broste and his museum colleagues built a museum to house this collection in 1966. The outside walls of the museum are constructed of fieldstone, mostly granitic glacial erratics, handpicked by Broste from within a 20-mile radius of Parshall. The foyer floor of the museum is veneered with cut-and-polished local fieldstones of several lithologies, and the floor of the exhibit hall consists of 12-inch-square, 1-inch-thick, 8-pound tiles made of Mexican onyx. The exhibit consists of several thousand rock and mineral specimens, several of which are exquisite. The most unusual objects in the museum are the hundreds of lapidary spheres that Broste made by cutting and polishing rocks in special machines.

Lapidary spheres, some made from glacial erratics, exhibited in the Paul Broste Rock Museum.

The Paul Broste Rock Museum in Parshall is constructed of glacial erratics collected from the local area.

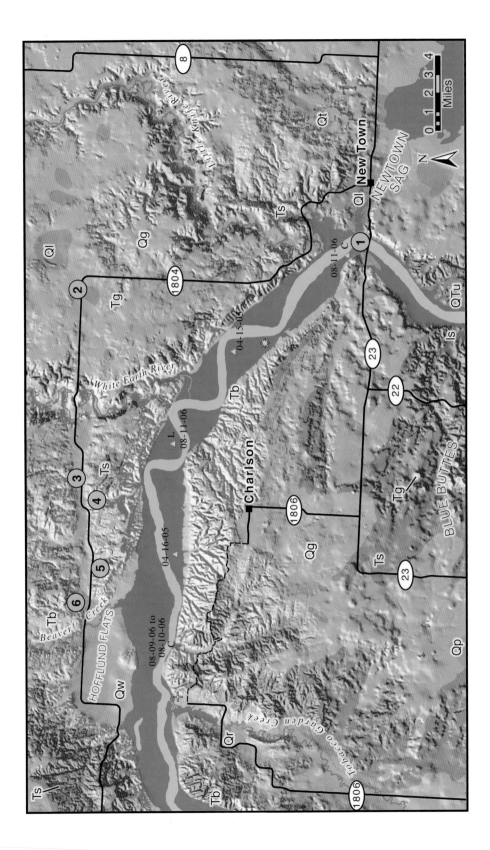

New Town to Williston

April 15–22, 1805
August 6–12, 1806

Highway 1804 closely parallels the Missouri River valley for the west half of this stretch. A short, unpaved stretch of Highway 1806 between Charlson and Tobacco Garden Bay is one of the most scenic routes along the river in North Dakota and offers spectacular views of the badlands topography adjacent to Lake Sakakawea.

On the return trip from the West Coast, the Lewis and Clark Expedition split into two parties at Travelers Rest in Montana so they could explore several areas of what is now eastern Montana. Lewis led one group and Clark the other. The two parties planned to rendezvous near the confluence of the Missouri and Yellowstone Rivers, but mosquitoes were so troublesome there that Clark decided he could not wait for Lewis. The two groups did not rejoin until farther downstream at a place now called Reunion Bay south of New Town on August 12, 1806. On the maps in this book from the Montana border to New Town, you'll notice that return campsites specify "Lewis" or "Clark."

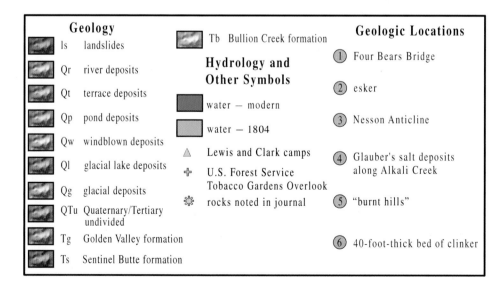

Geology

- ls landslides
- Qr river deposits
- Qt terrace deposits
- Qp pond deposits
- Qw windblown deposits
- Ql glacial lake deposits
- Qg glacial deposits
- QTu Quaternary/Tertiary undivided
- Tg Golden Valley formation
- Ts Sentinel Butte formation
- Tb Bullion Creek formation

Hydrology and Other Symbols

- water — modern
- water — 1804
- △ Lewis and Clark camps
- ✛ U.S. Forest Service Tobacco Gardens Overlook
- ✾ rocks noted in journal

Geologic Locations

- ① Four Bears Bridge
- ② esker
- ③ Nesson Anticline
- ④ Glauber's salt deposits along Alkali Creek
- ⑤ "burnt hills"
- ⑥ 40-foot-thick bed of clinker

Four Bears Bridge

① The Four Bears Bridge has the distinction of being not only the longest bridge across the Missouri River in North Dakota but, with a 20-foot-wide roadway, also the narrowest. The first bridge built across the river in this area, the Verendrye Bridge, stood about a mile north of this site from 1928 until 1953. Crews dismantled it when Garrison Dam was constructed, which created Lake Sakakawea. Four Bears Bridge—named after two prominent leaders, one of whom was Hidasta and the other Mandan—replaced the Verendrye Bridge and was completed in 1955. About one-third of Four Bears Bridge, the center spans, was salvaged from the original Four Bears Bridge that once carried Highway 8 across the Missouri River 30 miles southeast of this location prior to construction of Garrison Dam. Several other bridges were planned to span Lake Sakakawea as part of the Garrison Dam project, but none were ever built. A new bridge across the Missouri River valley at New Town will be completed in 2004, close to where the old and obsolete Four Bears Bridge is now.

Little Knife River

North of New Town, Highway 1804 passes through rugged badlands along the northern edge of the Missouri River valley. Strata of the Bullion Creek and overlying Sentinel Butte formations are well exposed. The Bullion Creek formation generally consists of light-colored rocks and the Sentinel Butte formation consists of darker, gray rocks. However, dark beds in the Bullion Creek formation and light beds in the Sentinel Butte formation complicate this distinction. A lignite bed, or a pinkish clinker where the lignite has burned, often marks the contact between these two formations. Bright strata of the Golden Valley formation are present along the rim of the Little Knife River valley.

As with many features, Lewis and Clark named the Little Knife River, but their name has not been used. On his map, Clark named it Goat Pen Creek because the Assiniboine had constructed a pen along the creek to catch antelope, which the expedition members often referred to as "goats."

> only about 8 feet deep in some places. we poled across in one place with a Small canoe. passd. goat pen creek.
>
> —ORDWAY, April 15, 1805

The town of Sanish and the Verendrye Bridge, circa the late 1940s. View is to the northwest. This bridge was named after the French fur-trader and explorer, Pierre de la Verendrye, who led the first party of white men into what is now North Dakota in 1738. Note the thick cottonwood riparian forest, common along the Missouri River before Lake Sakakawea drowned the floodplain. —Photograph courtesy of the State Historical Society of North Dakota (SHSND 0739-Vol 1-p28A)

Four Bears Bridge carries Highway 23 across Lake Sakakawea. The center span is from an old dismantled bridge that crossed the Missouri River prior to construction of Garrison Dam. Blue Buttes are in the distance. View is to the southwest from Crow Flies High Overlook.

The brightly colored lower member of the Golden Valley formation in the western road ditch of Highway 1804 about 15 miles north of New Town.

Highway 1804 cuts through an esker, a long, linear ridge of gravel deposited by a stream flowing beneath a glacier. View is to the northeast.

GLACIAL DEPOSITS

North of New Town, the thickness of glacial till ranges from very thin deposits overlying relatively flat topography to moderately thick deposits that create rolling topography. Erratics and glacial outwash gravels are exposed on hilltops along both sides of the Highway 1804. These gravels are quarried and used as road-surfacing material. Where Highway 1804 turns west it crosses an area of moderately thick glacial material where the hills are generally capped with gravel. About a mile west of this turn, the highway passes through a southwest-trending row of small hills that are part of an esker, a long, linear ridge consisting primarily of sand and gravel. The sand and gravel were deposited in a river that flowed in a crack or ice tunnel beneath the glacier about 14,000 years ago.

Glacial outwash sands and gravels and other deposits in North Dakota have yielded the fossil remains of animals that lived during the Ice Age. About 14,000 years ago, glaciers reached their maximum extent and covered about three-quarters of the state. Prior to that time, ice lobes repeatedly advanced over and retreated from this area, each time affecting the animal and plant communities. All types of plant and animal fossils, even the remains of insects and mites, have been recovered from the glacial deposits. They indicate that, at least during the last part of the Ice Age, forests dominated by spruce and aspen covered much of North Dakota. The most spectacular animals were the large mammals. In addition to the giant ground sloth (*Megalonyx jeffersoni*), fossils of mammoths, horses, deer, and bison with horn spans of 7 feet or more (*Bison latifrons*) have been recovered from sites adjacent to the Missouri River. Artifacts, such as finely crafted projectile points called *Clovis*, indicate that the first people to inhabit North Dakota were in the Missouri River valley by about 11,000 years ago. They were big game hunters harvesting many of the large mammals including mammoth and bison.

WHITE EARTH RIVER

The deep, winding, north-trending White Earth River valley is a prominent topographic feature for more than 30 miles before merging with Lake Sakakawea at White Earth Bay. The valley is too wide to have been cut by the existing river. Glacial meltwater may have contributed to its formation, but the valley does not have the typical U-shaped geometry associated with a meltwater trench. Water flowing south from a short-lived lake that formed in front of or within a glacier may have eroded it, or it may have been initially formed by the north-flowing ancestral Little Missouri River, which may have been diverted into this area for a while.

This skull of Bison latifrons, *which was found near New Town, is on exhibit in the North Dakota Heritage Center in Bismarck. Skull has a horn span of 7 feet. The Three Affiliated Tribes Museum in New Town displays a cast of this fossil.*
—North Dakota State Fossil Collection (ND 98–44.1)

This mural, which is in the Pembina State Museum, shows Paleo-Indians butchering a large bison at the end of the Ice Age while a mammoth looks on. A glacier, with meltwater forming streams and lakes, is in the background. —Art courtesy of the State Historical Society of North Dakota (SHSND 1996.26.1)

There is evidence that for a time, the ancestral Little Missouri River was diverted eastward into the lower portion of the White Earth River valley, at a point about 6 miles above its mouth.

The Bullion Creek and Sentinel Butte formations are well exposed along this valley. The contact between these two formations is about halfway up the buttes. Brightly colored siltstone and mudstone beds in the Bullion Creek formation differentiate it from the more somber colored rocks of the overlying Sentinel Butte formation. Clinker occurs near the tops of these buttes.

During the winter at Fort Mandan, Lewis and Clark wrote summary descriptions of rivers they had mapped on their trip upriver, and based on information from Native residents at the Knife River Indian villages they noted rivers that they expected to see when they continued their journey in the spring of 1805. In western North Dakota, they anticipated encountering the Little Missouri, White Earth, and Yellowstone Rivers, in that order. The name *White Earth* is believed to be derived from an Hidatsa word meaning "white clay sand." Yet when the expedition passed the waterway that we call the White Earth River, they did not identify it. Instead, they applied the name *White Earth River* to a river at Williston that is now known as the Little Muddy River.

The lower reaches of the White Earth River valley. View is to the north. The White Earth River meanders through a large valley which is typical of modern streams that occupy meltwater channels, but the White Earth River valley itself is somewhat sinuous. Note the sharp turn the valley makes to the northeast, which is not typical of meltwater channels.

What brought about the confusion in the names of these rivers? Lewis and Clark noted in their April 16, 1805, journal entries that they had passed three streams that entered the Missouri River on the north side. Moulton (1983, 1987) has suggested that one of these three streams is the White Earth River of today and that Lewis and Clark failed to recognize its significance. Cartographer Martin Plamondon (2001) suggested that they may have missed the river altogether. We believe that they correctly applied the name White Earth River to what is now called the Little Muddy River. The Mandan Chief Big White told them to look for a valley similar to that of the Cannonball River, which is broad and passes through open, level country. The White Earth River of today does not fit that description; near its mouth, it cuts a steep, narrow valley though rugged badlands. We discuss this name confusion in more depth under the subhead *Little Muddy River.*

Oil from the Nesson Anticline

The Nesson Anticline, a large north-trending, asymmetrical fold in the earth's crust, is the most prominent structural feature in the North Dakota portion of the Williston Basin. Highway 1804 crosses the axis of this anticline south of Tioga. This fold began forming during the Cambrian Period, about 500 million years ago, and continued folding periodically into the middle Tertiary. The anticline is visible at the surface by gently dipping beds of the Bullion Creek formation. The fold has trapped millions of barrels of oil into economically recoverable reserves in western North Dakota. Oil was discovered in this anticline in North Dakota near Tioga in 1951. To date, slightly more than 30 percent of North Dakota's oil production has come from the Nesson Anticline.

Highway 1804 passes through the Capa and Hofflund oil fields, and an unpaved segment of Highway 1806 passes through the Charlson oil field. The oil is produced from traps in limestones of the Mississippian-age Madison group. The wells produce from a depth of about 8,000 feet. Oil-field development is expensive in this area of badlands where topographic relief of 150 to 200 feet makes it difficult to build roads, oil pads, and pipelines.

The remnants of North Dakota's only "offshore" oil well are located in this area. In 1957, an oil company drilled an 8,300-foot-deep well in the Missouri River floodplain about a half mile north of the river. The company built a 10-foot-diameter concrete casing around the well 60 feet high to keep the well from being inundated by rising Lake Sakakawea water. The company also placed a mound of riprap around the casing to the top and constructed a pipeline to a treatment and storage

Alternating beds of sandstone, mudstone, and lignite in Bullion Creek and Sentinel Butte formations near Charlson. View is to the north. Arrow marks the contact between the two formations.

Aerial view to the north across Lake Sakakawea showing beds in the Bullion Creek and Sentinel Butte formations dipping slightly to the east along the eastern flank of the Nesson Anticline. This is one of the few places where the influence of the Nesson Anticline on surface rock exposures is visible. The concrete casing that protects the top of North Dakota's only "offshore" oil well is visible in the foreground.

facility north of the lake. The well sat idle for many years after it stopped producing until it was safely plugged in February 1989. At that time, during extremely cold weather, crews built a 30-inch-thick, 1-mile-long ice bridge on top of the frozen reservoir from the north shore to the well site. They had to construct the bridge because the existing 12-inch-thick ice was insufficient to support the weight of cement trucks, a crane, and a work-over rig. It cost more than $1 million to plug the well.

The Williston area has been an important center of oil activity for more than fifty years. The small Williston Basin Refinery, which processed a maximum of 5,000 barrels of oil per day, operated from 1954 to 1984 along the east edge of the Little Muddy River just south of Highway 1804. Projects to decontaminate the soil and groundwater at this site have been ongoing since the late 1980s at a reported cost of more than $1 million.

ALKALI CREEK AT LITTLE BEAVER BAY

Glauber's salt (sodium sulfate) deposits are abundant along the edges of Alkali Creek, particularly in the late summer and fall. Lewis and Clark noted the presence of salt in this area when they passed through in April 1805. Glauber's salt is so abundant in this part of the state that at least three attempts have been made to produce it commercially. One of these ventures occurred about 25 miles north of the Missouri River near Stanley, and a large stockpile of Glauber's salt from that operation is still present. The company pumped water from White Lake into a holding pond in the summer of 1961. Cooling temperatures in the fall caused the salt to precipitate out of the water that was in the holding pond. Crews then bulldozed the salt into the stockpile that still remains.

> the water of this creek as well as all those creeks and rivulets which we have passed since we left Fort Mandan was so strongly impregnated with salts and other miniral substances that I was incapable of drinking it.
>
> —LEWIS, April 15, 1805

> Some verry handsom high planes & extensive bottoms, the mineral appearances of Coal & Salt together with Some appearance of Burnt hils continue.
>
> —CLARK, April 16, 1805

CLINKER OF THE "BURNT HILLS"

By the time the expedition reached the Charlson area on April 16, 1805, the explorers had spent about five and a half months in an area characterized by extensive outcrops of clinker, which commonly occurs in the Bullion Creek and Sentinel Butte formations. It is exposed in the river bluffs throughout most of the area that the expedition traveled from April 16 to April 22, 1805. Lewis, Clark, and Gass's journal entries refer to this area as the "burnt hills" or "birnt hills" because of the extensive, brightly colored clinker.

Arrow marks the contact between the Bullion Creek formation (bottom) and Sentinel Butte formation (top) in the Alkali Creek valley. The thick coal occurs in the lower Sentinel Butte formation.

A 30-foot-high abandoned stockpile of Glauber's salt along the southern shore of White Lake near Stanley. The northeastern edge of the holding pond is visible along the left side of the photograph.

A crust of Glauber's salt encircles a small lake in northwestern North Dakota. These salts typically form along the shores of lakes and streams in fall when the water temperature drops and the water holds less salt in solution.

The expedition members had witnessed coal beds burning earlier in April, and it is clear from Lewis's journal entry of April 16 that he had concluded that clinker was formed by burning coal. Clark demonstrated an even clearer understanding about the process of clinker formation when he wrote, "the Pumies Stone which is found as low as the Illinois Country is formed by the bank or Stratums of Coal taking fire and burning the earth imedeately above it into either pumies Stone or Lavia, this Coal Country is principly above the Mandans." This entry is on an undated piece of letter paper that Moulton (1986, 1993) believes Clark wrote several months after traveling through this area of North Dakota, either while at Fort Clatsop or on the return journey.

> I believe it to be the stratas of Coal seen in those hills which causes the fire and birnt appearances frequently met with in this quarter. where those birnt appearances are to be seen in the face of the river bluffs, the coal is seldom seen, and when you meet with it in the neighbourhood of the stratas of birnt earth, the coal appears to be presisely at the same hight, and is nearly of the same thickness, togeter with the sand and a sulphurious substance which ususually accompanys it.
>
> —LEWIS, April 16, 1805

Aerial view to the north across Lake Sakakawea. Clinker beds in the Bullion Creek and Sentinel Butte formations are prominently exposed in the bluffs along the Missouri River west of Hofflund Flats. Clark ascended a hill on the north side of the valley in this area on April 18, 1805, and wrote, "Great appearance of Burnt hills Pumice Stone." Lewis and Clark referred to this area as "burnt hills" because of the pink clinker outcrops.

A delightfull morning, set out at an erly hour. the country though which we passed to day was much the same as that discribed of yesterday; there wase more appearance of birnt hills, furnishing large quanties of lava and pumice stone, of the latter some pieces were seen floating down the river.

—LEWIS, April 17, 1805

a fine morning wind from the S E. Genly to day handsom high extencive rich Plains on each Side, the mineral appearances continue with greater appearances of Coal, much greater appearance of the hills haveing been burnt, more Pumice Stone & Lava washed down to the bottoms and some Pumice Stone floating in the river.

—CLARK, April 17, 1805

I also saw where a hill had been on fire, and pumice stone around it.

—GASS, April 19, 1805

HOFFLUND FLATS

Shortly after crossing the White Earth River valley, Highway 1804 enters Hofflund Flats, a wide, flat-bottomed valley that is underlain by up to 150 feet of river deposits. The 18-square-mile fertile terrace is a prominent opening in the rugged badlands terrain. Neither Lewis nor Clark mentioned the Hofflund Flats in their journal entries, but Ordway, Gass, and Whitehouse did note this "beautiful plain" or "beautifull Priari" in their April 17, 1805, entries. Clark labeled the Hofflund Flats area as the "Great Bend" on his map.

Passed a beautiful plain and two large creeks on the North side, and another creek on the South.

—GASS, April 17, 1805

The highway traverses this east-west-trending valley for about 20 miles. At its eastern end, the valley is about 1 mile wide, but it is more than 3 miles wide where it intersects the Missouri River at Hofflund Bay. The north-flowing, ancestral Little Missouri and Missouri Rivers formed this valley when glaciers blocked the rivers between 1.5 and 0.6 million years ago. Unable to flow north, they followed the edge of the ice to the east, roughly parallel to Highway 1804 from Hofflund Flats to the White Earth River valley.

Just north of Highway 1804 on the edge of Hofflund Flats, a 40-foot-thick bed of clinker is mined for road-surfacing material. This deposit is thicker than most clinker deposits in North Dakota. Clinker thickness is a function of the thickness and quality of the lignite that burned, the mineralogy and grain size of the overlying deposits before they were baked, length of burning time, and temperature reached. People have long recognized that lightning, prairie fires, and spontaneous combustion could ignite lignite beds. More recently, geologists have theorized

Highway 1804 passes through Hofflund Flats, a wide, flat flood-plain of the ancestral Missouri River. View is to the west. Center-pivot irrigation systems created the circular patterns in the fields.

Aerial view of Lund's Landing at Whitetail Bay, just south of Highway 1804. View is to the south. Note the high and dry concrete boat landing at the head of the bay that is now several hundred feet from the lake. This is one of dozens of sites along Lake Sakakawea where boat landings have either had to be extended or abandoned due to historically low water levels in recent years. Lake level was at 1,825 feet when this photograph was taken.

that coal bed methane may be an important catalyst. Prairie fires may initially ignite the methane at the face of the outcrop, which in turn ignites the lignite. The presence of the gas may also increase the intensity of the burn. As is typical of most clinker, the color (black, yellow, green, blue, orange, purple, and red) and the hardness (friable to fused) are highly variable in this deposit.

Blocks of multi-colored clinker (foreground) in the Hofflund quarry. The wall of the quarry in the background contains the typical red-colored clinker.

The Hofflund clinker quarry in the Sentinel Butte formation just north of Highway 1804 on the northeastern edge of Hofflund Flats. View is to the northeast.

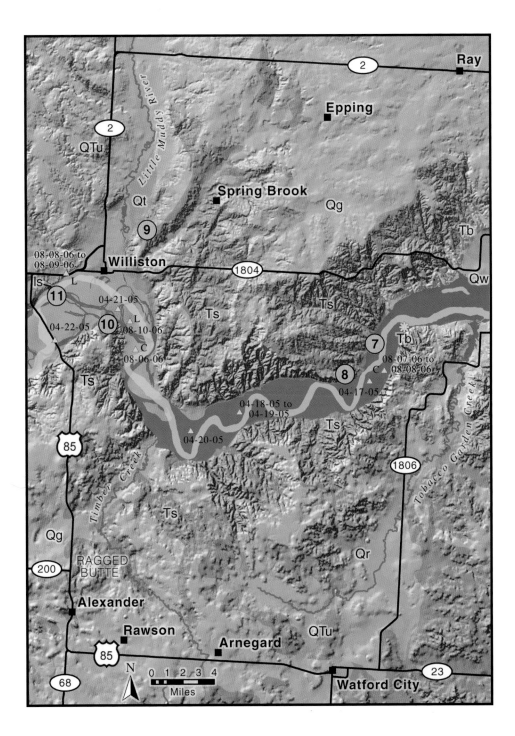

Ray

2

Epping

2

QTu

Little Muddy River

Qt

Spring Brook

Qg

Tb

9

08-08-06 to
08-09-06

Williston

1804

Qw

Is   L

11

04-21-05

Ts

Ts

Tb

7

L

10   08-10-06

08-07-06 to
08-08-06

04-22-05

C

C

08-06-06

8

Ts

04-17-05

Ts

04-18-05 to
04-19-05

1806

Tobacco Garden Creek

04-20-05

Ts

85

Timber Creek

Qg

Qr

200   RAGGED
BUTTE

Alexander

QTu

Rawson

Arnegard

85

N

0 1 2 3 4

68   Miles   Watford City   23

Tobacco Garden Creek

Two miles west of Watford City, U.S. 85 crosses a broad valley transected to the south by a large railroad embankment that was built in 1914. Known as the Madison Grade, it is one of the longest and highest earthen railroad embankments ever constructed in this country. Prior to its abandonment, the mile-long embankment enabled trains to cross the former valley of the ancestral Little Missouri River, which flowed to the northwest through this area until about 600,000 years ago when glaciers diverted it to the east about 25 miles south of here. This valley is underlain by 100 to 200 feet of sand and gravel, glacial till, and clay. North of Watford City, Highway 1806 parallels, and at times enters, this ancestral valley, and Tobacco Garden Creek flows north through it to Lake Sakakawea. There are few outcrops along Highway 1806 in this area, but Sentinel Butte strata are well exposed in the distant uplands.

Many people believe the name *Tobacco Garden* is derived from the abundant reeds that grew in the creek that had the same name as *tobacco* in the Sioux and Assiniboine languages. Clark called Tobacco Garden Creek "Pumic Stone Creek" on his map, though neither he nor Lewis mentioned pumice stone floating in the creek. In their journal entries of April 17, 1805, both of them noted large quantities of "pumice stone" floating down the Missouri River.

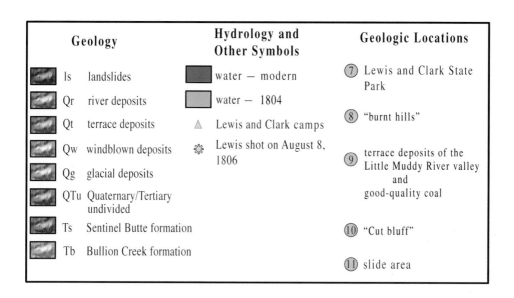

Geology	Hydrology and Other Symbols	Geologic Locations
ls landslides	water — modern	⑦ Lewis and Clark State Park
Qr river deposits	water — 1804	
Qt terrace deposits	△ Lewis and Clark camps	⑧ "burnt hills"
Qw windblown deposits	❄ Lewis shot on August 8, 1806	
Qg glacial deposits		⑨ terrace deposits of the Little Muddy River valley and good-quality coal
QTu Quaternary/Tertiary undivided		
Ts Sentinel Butte formation		⑩ "Cut bluff"
Tb Bullion Creek formation		
		⑪ slide area

West of Watford City, U.S. 85 crosses the valley that contained the ancestral Little Missouri River. Note the numerous small landslides along the north side of the Madison Grade railroad embankment. View is to the east.

View to the east across the mile-wide ancestral Little Missouri River valley now occupied by Tobacco Garden Creek.

Landslide in north-facing cutbank along Lake Sakakawea east of Tobacco Garden Creek. The 20-foot-high vertical cliffs consist of 600,000 year old till overlain by windblown deposits. Jointing in the till makes it susceptible to slope failure because large masses of till tend to break off the steep slopes along the joints. Wave action, during high lake levels, undercuts the base of the slopes creating the vertical cliff faces, eventually leading to slope failure. One of the expedition's boats nearly capsized because of slope failure along a cutbank.

LEWIS AND CLARK STATE PARK

A thick lignite seam in the upper Bullion Creek formation is exposed along the buttes in and adjacent to Lewis and Clark State Park and in the cutbanks along the south end of the reservoir. Thick beds of clinker occur in areas where the lignite has burned. Fossilized tree stumps are present just above road level. Many of these stumps have eroded, forming white blades of petrified wood that litter the ground at the fossil horizon.

Petrified wood, weathering out of the Bullion Creek and Sentinel Butte formations, is abundant along the Missouri River shore from New Town to Williston. Silica-rich groundwater flowing through the wood replaces organic matter and fills pores in the wood with minerals, causing petrification. Lewis expressed an understanding of the importance of water and time in the fossilization process in his April 16, 1805, journal entry. Lewis often put a practical spin on his observations, and on April 22 he wrote that petrified wood "makes excellent whetstones," as did Gass on April 19, 1805.

> I met with several stones today that had the appearance of wood first carbonated and then petrefyed by the water of the river, which I have discovered has that effect on many vegitable substances when exposed to it's influence for a length of time.
>
> —Lewis, April 16, 1805

> I saw a part of a log quite petrified, and of which good whetstones—or hones could be made.
>
> —Gass, April 19, 1805

LITTLE MUDDY RIVER

Williston is adjacent to the mouth of a large, mostly buried valley occupied by the Little Muddy River. The expedition reached the Little Muddy River area on April 21, 1805. On that day Lewis ascended a hill overlooking the Missouri River that he referred to as "Cut bluff." From this vantage point, Lewis was able to see up the Little Muddy River valley and noted:

> the course of this river as far as I could see from the top of Cut bluff, was due North. it passes through a beatifull level and fertile vally about five miles in width. I think I saw about 25 miles up this river, and did not discover one tree or bush of any description on it's borders.
>
> —Lewis, April 21, 1805

Petrified wood, which weathers to small, white, bladed pieces, litters the surface of the Bullion Creek formation at Lewis and Clark State Park.

Aerial view of the western edge of Lake Sakakawea near the mouth of Timber Creek. View is to the north. The lake level at the time of this photograph, in the fall of 2002, was 1,825 feet. During normal pool levels (1,850 feet) the terminus of the lake is 23 miles further west. Low lake levels create an extensive mud flat in this area.

Lewis, Clark, and Ordway referred to the Little Muddy River as the "White Earth River," a major tributary that the Mandan and Hidatsa described to them while at Fort Mandan. We now apply the name *White Earth River* to a river farther downstream, and many people assume Lewis and Clark simply missed it or failed to recognize it. However, we feel they named the correct river.

Lewis wrote in the winter of 1805 that the White Earth River "is said to be about the size of the Cannonball River; takes it's rise N. Westwardly from its mouth in level open plains with the waters of the S. Fork of the Saskashawin river, and passes through an open and level country generally without timber." The broad Cannonball River valley is about 6,500 feet wide at its mouth, intersects the Missouri River at right angles, and is surrounded by uplands that are 120 feet above the valley floor. The Cannonball River flows through a low-relief, rolling prairie and is a prominent landmark, similar to the Little Muddy River. The Little Muddy River valley is up to 3 miles wide. The uplands adjacent to the valley rise 100 to 200 feet above the surrounding countryside. Conversely the White Earth River of today bears little resemblance to the Cannonball River. Its steeper, narrower valley is only about 4,000 feet wide and much less conspicuous because it intersects the Missouri River valley at a 45-degree angle in an area of rugged badlands.

> passed the mouth of a large Creek on the N. S. Called White Earth River. it is about 15 yards wide at the mouth & Clear water & Gentle current.
>
> —ORDWAY, April 21, 1805

> the party halted and Cpt. Clark and myself walked to the white earth river which approaches Missouri very near at this place, being about 4 miles above it's entrance. we found that it contained more water than streams of it's size generally do at this season. the water is much clearer than that of the Missouri. the banks of the river are steep and not more than ten or twelve feet high; the bed seems to be composed of mud altogether. the salts which have been before mentioned as common on the Missouri, <and> appears in great quantities along the banks of this river, which are in many places so thickly covered with it that they appear perfectly white. perhaps it has been from this white appearance of it's banks that the river has derived it's name.
>
> —LEWIS, April 22, 1805

From their discussions with the Mandan and Hidatsa, Lewis and Clark estimated they would find the White Earth River 117 miles above the Little Missouri River. The actual distance from the Little Missouri

River to the Little Muddy River is about 90 miles. The present-day White Earth River is only about 50 miles. They also estimated that the distance between the White Earth River described to them by people at Fort Mandan and the Yellowstone River would be 3 miles. The Yellowstone is 20 miles above the Little Muddy River but nearly 70 miles above the present-day White Earth River.

The information Lewis and Clark received about the headwaters of the White Earth River does not fit either the present-day White Earth River or the Little Muddy River. The headwaters for both rivers are 25 to 30 miles north of the Missouri River, which places the rivers several hundred miles away from the South Fork of the Saskatchewan River.

Strong winds delayed the expedition on April 22, providing Lewis and Clark the opportunity to investigate the confluence area of the Missouri and Little Muddy Rivers. Lewis speculated that the river obtained its name from the "great quantities" of white salt that accumulated along its banks. Lewis was confident that this river was the White Earth River that people in the Knife River Indian villages had told him about. We think that, given the information Lewis and Clark had, they applied the name White Earth River correctly to what is today called the Little Muddy River. It was apparently the Fisk Expedition to gold fields in Montana in 1866 that incorrectly applied the name *White Earth* to the river that now bears that name (White, 1966).

The north-flowing ancestral Yellowstone River carved the large, mostly buried valley of the Little Muddy River, but glaciers diverted the Yellowstone River south and east in pre-Wisconsinan time (perhaps as long as 1 million years ago). These glaciers filled much of the 400-foot-deep Little Muddy River valley with sand, gravel, and glacial till. Lewis made some insightful geological comments about the valley of the Little Muddy River when he described terrace deposits nearly 200 feet above the water level. The flint pebbles and pieces of petrified wood noted by Lewis are common components of gravels deposited by these ancient streams.

> the broken hills of the Missouri about this place exhibit large irregular and broken masses of rocks and stones; some of which tho' 200 feet above the level of the water seem at some former period to have felt it's influence, for they appear smoth as if woarn by the agetation of the water. this collection consists of white & grey gannite, a brittle black rock, flint, limestone, freestone, some small specimens of an excellent pebble and occasionally broken stratas of a stone which appears to be petrefyed wood, it is of a black colour, and makes excellent whetstones.
>
> —LEWIS, April 22, 1805

Some of the high plains or the broken Revien of the river contains great
quantity of Pebble Stones of various Sizes

—CLARK, April 22, 1805

*Aerial view to the north showing, in the background, the Little Muddy
River on the east side of Williston. Lewis's "Cut bluff" is in the middle
(arrow). The Sentinel Butte formation is exposed in "Cut bluff" and
the badlands terrain adjacent to it.*

10

*Glacial erratics along a drainage divide between the Little Muddy
River and Stony Creek. Lewis called dark boulders of diorite, like
those at the left in the photograph, "brittle black rock." Diorite is an
igneous rock carried south to North Dakota by Pleistocene glaciers.*

Quality Coal

On April 22, 1805, for the first and only time in their journals, Lewis and Clark praised the quality of coal in North Dakota. The coal they sampled was likely from an extensive bed of lignite that was later mined (1909 to 1936) from several underground mines located on the ridge between the Little Muddy River and Stony Creek. Although Lewis and Clark were favorably impressed with this coal, mining records indicate that its heating value (6,600 btus per pound) was similar to the average value of other North Dakota lignites. What changed the explorers' impression of North Dakota lignite? This lignite may have been fresher than previous samples they had taken, which may have been weathered, or their previous samples could have been ancient soils they had mistaken for coal.

Underground mining of coal began in the area east of Williston in the late 1800s. In the early 1900s, a dozen or so mines operated between Williston and present-day Lewis and Clark State Park. The Cedar Coulee Mine, located just northeast of Lewis and Clark State Park, was the last underground mine to operate in North Dakota. This small mine ceased operation in 1967. As is typical of old underground mines throughout North Dakota, accurate maps of the extent of the mine workings do not exist. Sinkholes caused by the collapse of underground mines have damaged highways, county roads, and housing developments constructed in areas people thought were outside underground mine areas.

> Coal or carbonated wood pumice stone lava and other mineral apearances still continue. the coal appears to be of better quality; I exposed a specimen of it to the fire and found that it birnt tolerably well, it afforded but little flame or smoke, but produced a hot and lasting fire.
>
> —LEWIS, April 22, 1805

> The Stratum of Coal is much richer than below.
>
> —CLARK, April 22, 1805

Stony Creek Area

For almost thirty years, from 1960 to 1989, a salt plant operated on the floodplain of Stony Creek, north of Highway 1804 on the east side of Williston. The plant used a pair of 9,000-foot-deep wells to solution-mine about four million barrels of brine from 340-million-year-old salt deposits. Water was driven off by evaporators and the salt was filtered, screened, and packaged as table salt, livestock salt blocks,

A coal bed in the Sentinel Butte formation exposed along the east valley of the Little Muddy River. This may be the coal seam that Lewis sampled on April 22, 1805.

Aerial view of sinkholes formed by the collapse of underground coal mines. View is to the north. For the past fifteen years, the North Dakota Public Service Commission has been pumping grout into underground mines to reduce the chance of collapse.

Leonardite, which is weathered, earthy lignite, is mined from the Sentinel Butte formation at a quarry adjacent to the Little Muddy River at Williston.

Landslide in till along the Burlington Northern–Sante Fe railroad tracks near Williston. View is to the east. Engineers had railroad tracks, such as these, built at the edge of floodplains to get the tracks as far from the river's flood waters as possible while avoiding the expense of spanning the numerous ravines and coulees adjacent to the river valley. Unfortunately, steep-sided river valleys are prone to landslides that can damage tracks. The slide area in the foreground was eventually resloped and stabilized.

11

and water-softener pellets. Escalating energy costs and competition from a salt plant near Regina, Saskatchewan, forced the plant to close. During the early years of operation, the company dumped about 50,000 tons of waste salt on the ground behind its main building. The much more stringent environmental standards of today don't allow this type of waste disposal. Clean up of the salt pile cost the company hundreds of thousands of dollars.

Just west of Stony Creek, on the north side of Highway 1804, stands a large pile of black material that people commonly mistake for asphalt. This dark brown to black, earthy material is leonardite, lignite that has been weathered or oxidized because it is now, or has been in the past, at or near land surface. It is named for A. G. Leonard who was the state geologist of North Dakota from 1904 to 1932. For almost forty years, leonardite has been mined from the top of a ridge situated between Stony Creek and the Little Muddy River. The heating content of leonardite is too low for use as a fuel, but its high concentration of humate, or humic acid, makes it useful as a drilling fluid additive, a binding agent for molds in die-casting, an organic filter, and a soil-enhancement product. This mine and one other mine in the southwest corner of the state produce about 30,000 tons of leonardite annually.

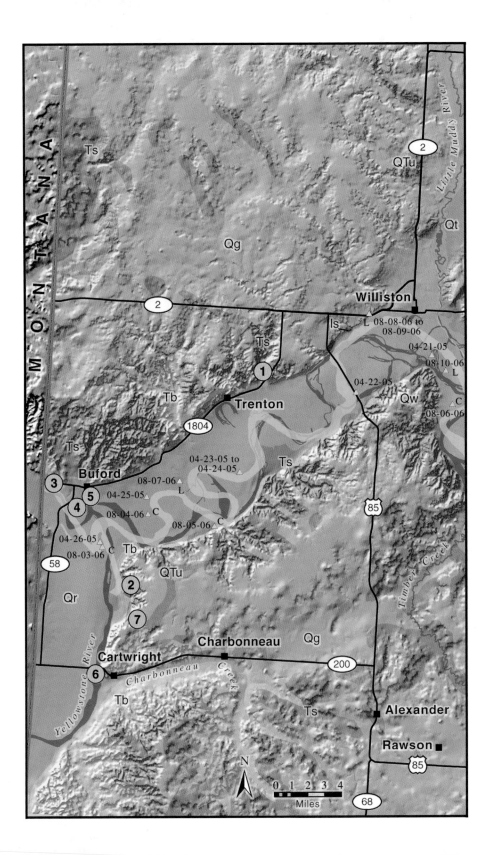

Williston to Fort Union

April 23–27, 1805
August 3–8, 1806

The edge or terminus of Lake Sakakawea ranges from near Trenton during lake levels of 1,850 feet—considered the normal pool level—to east of Timber Creek during low water (less than 1,830 feet), a distance of about 23 miles. In 1991, lake levels dropped to a historic low of 1,815 feet and in 1997 reached historic high levels of almost 1,855 feet. Lake levels have fluctuated more dramatically than they did during this six-year period. The lake level rose about 36 feet in a thirty-month period between March 1993 and September 1995. These widely fluctuating lake levels can create a multitude of problems. Low lake levels create an extensive mud flat in the area near the mouth of Timber Creek, which has proven to be difficult for boaters to navigate. High lake levels flood additional land and increase bank erosion.

From the Montana border to the terminus of the lake is one of only two stretches in North Dakota where the Missouri River still flows as a river. The other, much longer segment of the river flows from Huff to Riverdale. The floodplain of the Missouri River near Trenton contains

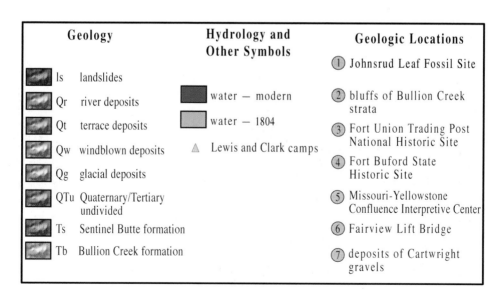

Geology	Hydrology and Other Symbols	Geologic Locations
ls landslides		① Johnsrud Leaf Fossil Site
Qr river deposits	▮ water — modern	② bluffs of Bullion Creek strata
Qt terrace deposits	▯ water — 1804	③ Fort Union Trading Post National Historic Site
Qw windblown deposits	△ Lewis and Clark camps	
Qg glacial deposits		④ Fort Buford State Historic Site
QTu Quaternary/Tertiary undivided		⑤ Missouri-Yellowstone Confluence Interpretive Center
Ts Sentinel Butte formation		⑥ Fairview Lift Bridge
Tb Bullion Creek formation		⑦ deposits of Cartwright gravels

meanders, oxbow lakes, sandbars, cottonwood stands, and other features that were characteristic of the valley two hundred years ago. Highway 1804 follows the edge of the Missouri River floodplain through most of this area.

Missouri River Floodplain

The floodplain of the Missouri River is 3 to 5 miles wide upstream from Williston, about twice the width of the floodplain downstream from there. The ancestral Yellowstone River carved this wide valley, which is much older than the Missouri River valley southeast of Williston. The ancestral Yellowstone flowed north at Williston, forming the valley that the modern Little Muddy River flows through. The wide meander loops of the Missouri River in this area require paddlers to travel 2 to 3 miles on the river in order to advance 1 mile up the valley, much as it did two hundred years ago. This is one of the reasons it took the expedition six days to travel only about 20 miles.

Aerial view to the west showing the broad Missouri River floodplain near the western end of Lake Sakakawea. Highway 85 is at the bottom of the photograph. Note the wide meander loops of the Missouri River similar to those encountered by the Lewis and Clark Expedition. From the Montana border to here, depending on the level of Lake Sakakawea, the Missouri River still flows as a river.

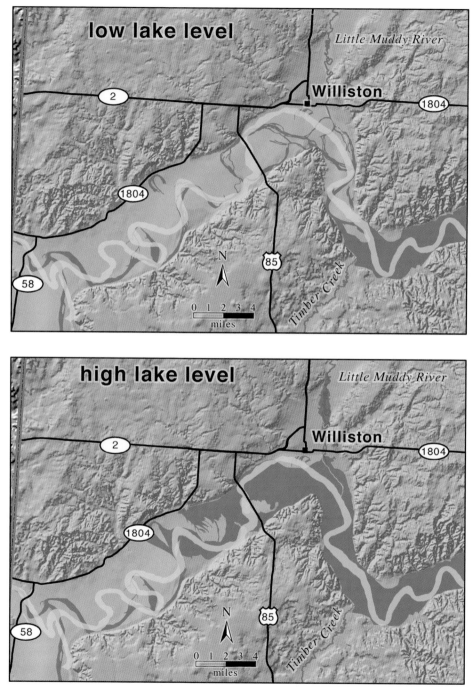

*Maps showing the location of the western edge of
Lake Sakakawea during low and high lake levels.*

Capt. Lewis assended a hill from the top of which he had a most inchanting prospect of the Countrey around & the meanderings of the two rivers, which is remarkable Crooked.

—CLARK, April 22, 1805

I ascended the hills from whence I had a most pleasing view of the country, perticularly of the wide and fertile vallies formed by the missouri and the yellowstone rivers, which occasionally unmasked by the wood on their borders disclose their meanderings for many miles in their passage through these delightfull tracts of country.

—LEWIS, April 25, 1805

High Winds and Sandstorms

In addition to the river's wide meander loops, strong April winds and sandstorms delayed the expedition as they traveled from what is now Williston to the Montana border. Boaters experience these same conditions today, especially in the spring. The prevailing north to north-westerly winds lift silt and sand from large sandbars and the broad floodplain, creating sandstorms. The wind seems to always blow across the treeless prairie. The weather patterns that create these winds can be particularly unstable in the spring, brought on by the interaction between fluctuating cold, dry air from the Arctic and warm, moist air from the Pacific or Gulf.

We proceeded on about 3 Miles, when the Wind blew so fresh, that we had to come too, it being a head Wind from the North west.

—WHITEHOUSE, April 23, 1805

This was a clear day, but the wind blew so hard down the river we could not proceed.

—GASS, April 24, 1805

Soar eyes is a common complaint among the party. I believe it origenates from the immence quantities of sand which is driven by the wind from the sandbars of the river in such clouds that you are unable to discover the opposite bank of the river in many instances. the particles of this sand are so fine and light that they are easily supported by the air, and are carried by the wind for many miles, and at a distance exhibiting every appearance of a collumn of thick smoke. so penitrating is this sand that we cannot keep any article free from it; in short we are compelled to eat, drink, and breath it freely. my pocket watch, is out of order, she will run only a few minutes without stoping. I can discover no radical defect in her works, and must therefore attribute it to the sand, with which, she seems plentifully charged, notwithstanding her cases are double and tight.

—LEWIS, April 24, 1805

We set out as usual and had a fine day; but about 11 were obliged to halt again the wind was so strong ahead.

—GASS, April 25, 1805

JOHNSRUD LEAF FOSSIL SITE

Widespread exposures of the Bullion Creek and Sentinel Butte formations occur in the bluffs along the Missouri and Yellowstone Rivers and in the uplands adjacent to the rivers in this area. Road, river, and ravine cuts in the badlands provide excellent views of these rocks. In 1987, road construction north of Trenton along Highway 1804 uncovered a fossiliferous bed in the Sentinel Butte formation containing abundant and beautifully preserved leaf fossils. A local sugar-beet farmer, the late Clarence Johnsrud, learned of this discovery from a neighbor and determined to collect and preserve the fossils. With a farm tractor and grain truck, Clarence collected over 20 tons of the cream-colored mudstone containing the fossils, transported the rocks to his barn, and began splitting the rocks with hammer and chisel. He recovered several hundred exquisite leaf-fossil specimens, representing more than twenty species of plants.

In 2000, the Johnsrud family donated most of this collection to the North Dakota State Fossil Collection at the North Dakota Heritage Center in Bismarck where many of the specimens are currently on display. Some of these fossils are also exhibited in Leonard Hall, the geology building at the University of North Dakota in Grand Forks, and at the student center of Williston State College. The North Dakota Geological Survey paleontology laboratory at the Heritage Center has been named the Johnsrud Paleontology Laboratory in honor of the Clarence Johnsrud family.

CONFLUENCE OF THE MISSOURI AND YELLOWSTONE RIVERS

Several of the expedition journalists commented on the beauty and fertility of the wide bottomlands near the confluence of the Missouri and Yellowstone Rivers. Lewis, in his April 26, 1805, journal entry, noted that there were more trees (principally cottonwoods) along this stretch

The late Clarence Johnsrud holding a plant fossil specimen at the entrance to a storage building on his farm near Trenton. Note the leaf fossils on shelves in the background.

This sycamore leaf fossil (Platanus), collected by Clarence Johnsrud from the Sentinel Butte formation, is 8 inches wide and is on exhibit at the North Dakota Heritage Center in Bismarck.
—North Dakota State Fossil Collection (ND 92–59.1)

of the river than the expedition had seen since leaving the "Chyenne river" in central South Dakota. Today, sugar beets are the primary crop grown in the fertile, irrigated floodplain from Trenton to Fairview, Montana. Garrison Dam has negatively impacted the agricultural potential of portions of this area, however.

> I went up the point about 9 miles, where there are the most beautiful rich plains, I ever beheld.
>
> —GASS, April 26, 1805

> So we made merry fidled and danced &.c. Camped for the night on the point between the 2 Rivers. a handsom place thinly covered with timber & a verry large bottom.
>
> —ORDWAY, April 26, 1805

Captain Lewis Sighting the Yellowstone—April 25, 1805, *by Charles Fritz. Meriwether Lewis and other members of the expedition looking at the Yellowstone River from a bluff on the south side of the Missouri River. In his April 25 journal entry Lewis recorded his impressions of the confluence area: "I ascended the hills from whence I had a most pleasing view of the country, perticularly the wide and fertile vallies formed by the missouri and yellowstone rivers, which occasionally unmasked by the wood on their borders disclose their meanderings for many miles in their passage through these delightfull tracts of country."*

The Country here is Priaries, and some thickets of Trees, the land appears very rich & fertile.

—WHITEHOUSE, April 26, 1805

In general, the faster a river flows, the more sediment it can transport. The current of the Missouri River slows quickly where it enters Lake Sakakawea, and the river deposits much of the sediment it is transporting, forming a delta of silt. The U.S. Army Corps of Engineers estimated that 26,000 acre-feet of silt was deposited in Lake Sakakawea, primarily at the upper end, during a twelve-month period in 1999 and 2000. This silt buildup has decreased channel depth, which in turn increases flooding because there is less room for water in the channels. The groundwater table has also risen because of silt buildup. Farmers have abandoned some farmsteads and fields because of the rise in the water table, and flooding has damaged many crops. In recent years the federal government has spent more than $15 million acquiring easements on land to mitigate flood damage in the Buford-Trenton area. Lewis noted in his April 26 journal entry that the confluence area was "subject to inundation." Fort Peck Dam in Montana helps reduce flooding in the confluence area because it controls spring flows in the Missouri River. The deposition of a nutrient-rich layer of sediment by spring floods enhances the fertility of floodplains. But the slow, year-round impacts of high water levels may not be beneficial.

Traveling slowly upstream into heavy head-winds, Lewis and Clark impatiently anticipated their arrival at the Yellowstone River, which Mandan and Hidatsa at the Knife River Indian villages had described to them. They had told Lewis and Clark that the river was navigable for pirogues and canoes to its source in the Rocky Mountains. Anxious to make astronomical observations to determine the position of the mouth of the Yellowstone River, Lewis traveled overland with four men to the eastern edge of the Yellowstone River valley on April 25.

> I determined, in order as mush as possible to avoid detention, to proceed by land with a few men to the entrance of that river and make the necessary observations to determine it's position, which I hoped to effect by the time that Capt. Clark could arrive with the party.
>
> —LEWIS, April 25, 1805

The name of the Yellowstone River is derived from the yellowish rocks of the Bullion Creek formation exposed along its valley. French trappers called the river, *Roche Jaune*, or "yellow rock," but it is likely that Native residents of the area named it initially. In his April 26, 1805, journal entry, Clark made the astute and accurate observation that the rocks along the Yellowstone were brighter than those downriver on the Missouri: "Clay of the bluffs appear much whiter than below." This is the main criteria geologists use today to differentiate the Bullion Creek formation from the overlying Sentinel Butte formation that crops out along the bluffs of Lake Sakakawea. Impressive exposures of the Bullion Creek formation occur along the east wall of the Yellowstone River valley. This rock formation generally contains yellowish to light-brown claystones and mudstones that contrast sharply with the dark gray mudstones of the overlying Sentinel Butte formation. You can see these exposures from the Highway 200 bridge over the Yellowstone River.

The Yellowstone River meanders across a 4- to 5-mile-wide floodplain before it joins with the Missouri River and helps create a floodplain of equal width for about 15 miles. Both upstream and downstream from the area between the confluence and the mouth of the Little Muddy River, the Missouri River valley is only about 2 to 3 miles wide. Clark commented on the narrowing of the Missouri River valley west of the confluence on April 28, 1805: "The bottoms are not So wide this afternoon as below." The dynamic interaction of the two rivers is complex

Yellow-colored strata of the Bullion Creek formation are exposed along the eastern side of the Yellowstone River valley south of the confluence of the Missouri and Yellowstone Rivers.

Aerial view of the Yellowstone River valley south of the confluence of the Missouri and Yellowstone Rivers. View is to the northeast. Yellow-colored strata of the Bullion Creek formation, from which the name of the river is derived, are exposed along the eastern side of the valley.

Aerial view of the confluence area of the Missouri and Yellowstone Rivers. View is to the northwest. Note the broad Missouri River valley with the Bullion Creek and Sentinel Butte formations exposed along the sides of the valley in the distance. The Missouri-Yellowstone Confluence Interpretive Center (arrow) is on the north side of the Missouri River across from the mouth of the Yellowstone River. Fort Buford State Historic Site is just northwest of the interpretive center.

and continually changing. The present position of the mouth of the Yellowstone River is about 1 mile to the northwest of where it was when Lewis and Clark saw it.

> The Missouri is 520 yards wide above the point of yellow Stone and the water covers 330 yards; the YellowStone River is 858 yards wide includeing its Sand bar, the water covers 297 yards and the deepest part is 12 feet water, it is at this time falling, the Missouri rising.
>
> —CLARK, April 26, 1805

The flow rates and turbidity of the Yellowstone and Missouri Rivers differed when Lewis and Clark passed the confluence. The expedition journalists compared the rivers and noted that the Yellowstone was shallower, the bed was sandier, the water more turbid, and the current, while fast, was slower than the Missouri. On the return trip, Clark estimated that the current speed of the Yellowstone River near its mouth was 2.5 miles per hour.

The confluence of the Missouri and Yellowstone Rivers in 1805–6 and now.

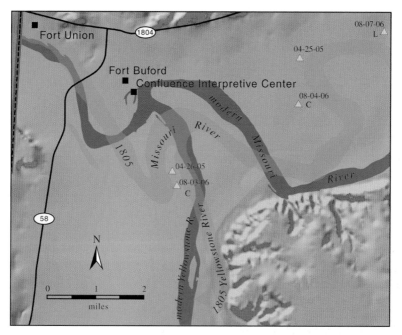

Today, dams on the Missouri River have changed its character. There are no dams on the Yellowstone, although some of its tributaries have dams. In April of 2000, gauging stations recorded that the rate of flow in the Missouri River was slightly higher than the Yellowstone River and that water in the Yellowstone was significantly more turbid (cloudy). Silt and mud settle out in reservoirs, so the Missouri River is quite clear below dams. You can readily see the difference between the two rivers' colors where the water mixes at the confluence.

> the corrent of the river gentle, and it's bed much interrupted and broken by sandbars . . . the bed of the yellowstone river is entirely composed of sand and mud, not a stone of any kind near it's entrance. . . . the water of the river is turbid, tho' dose not possess as much sediment as that of the Missouri.
>
> —LEWIS, April 26, 1805

> The river Jaune is shallow, and the Missouri deep and rapid.
>
> —GASS, April 26, 1805

> The River Roshjone is not quite as rapid as the missourie.
>
> —ORDWAY, April 26, 1805

> The River Roshjone is a Shallow River, the water in it is Clear and its current rapid.
>
> —WHITEHOUSE, April 26, 1805

> The Colour of the Water differs from that of the Missouri it being of a yellowish brown, whilst that of the Missouri[1] is of a deep drab Colour containing a greater portion of mud than the <Missouri> Rochejhone.
>
> —CLARK, August 3, 1806

FORTS AT THE CONFLUENCE

Lewis and Clark believed that the confluence would be a good place for a trading post. In their April 26 journal entries, they commented on the natural setting and available building materials at the confluence, including limestone. This rock type does not occur in the Paleocene-age rocks near the Missouri-Yellowstone confluence, so the limestone that Lewis referred to was probably glacial erratics transported from Canada to North Dakota during the Pleistocene Ice Age.

---

[1]Clark inadvertently wrote "Missouri" here but later corrected it with "Rochejhone" (Moulton, personal communication, 2002).

a suficient quantity of limestone may be readily procured for building near the junction of the Missouri and yellowstone rivers. I could observe no regular stratas of it, tho' it lies on the sides of the river hills in large irregular masses, in considerable quantities; it is of a light colour, and appears to be of an excellent quality.

—LEWIS, April 26, 1805

On April 27, with more precision, Lewis defined what he thought would be a good location for a post when he wrote, "on the point of the high plain at the lower extremity of this lake I think would be the most eligible site for an establishment." Clark disagreed and believed the best location would be on a lower terrace. Lewis eloquently and correctly suggested that Clark's location would be susceptible to flooding and that any fortification built there would be annihilated. This is one of the few cases where Lewis and Clark disagreed on an important issue. Clark plotted on his map "a handsome Situation for an establishment." Both the sites proposed by Lewis and Clark were located west of the confluence and on the south side of the Missouri River. In the years following the expedition, several fur trading companies and the United States military built forts in this area, all on a slightly higher terrace on the north side of the Missouri River.

about 1 mile from the point at which place the 2 rivers are near each other a butifull low leavel plain Commences, and extends up the Missourie & back, this plain is narrow at its commencement and widens as the Missouri bends north, and is bordered by an extencive wood land for many miles up the yellow Stone river, this low plain is not Subject to over flow, appear to be a few inches above high water mark and affords a butifull commanding Situation for a fort near the commencement of the Prarie.

—CLARK, April 26, 1805

Capt Clark thinks that the lower extremity of the low plane would be most eligible for this establishment; it is true that it is much nearer both rivers, and might answer very well, but I think it reather too low to venture a permanent establishment, particularly if built of brick or other durable materials, at any considerable expence; for so capricious, and versatile are these rivers, that it is difficult to say how long it will be, untill they direct the force of their currents against this narrow part of the low plain, which when they do, must shortly yeald to their influence; in such case a few years only would be necessary, for the annihilation of the plain, and with it the fortification.

—LEWIS, April 27, 1805

The Ashley fur expedition established the first fort at the confluence in 1822, a short-lived wintering station called Henry's Post. In 1828, Kenneth McKenzie of John Jacob Astor's American Fur Company established Fort Union along the north bank of the Missouri River near the confluence. This fort, an important fur trading post, operated until 1867. Notable explorers and artists such as George Catlin, Karl Bodmer, Prince Maximilian of Weid, James J. Audubon, and F. V. Hayden visited the fort. In the 1850s, F. V. Hayden did some of the earliest geological and paleontological research in the upper Missouri River area using Fort Union as a base. He made several trips to the upper Missouri country to collect fossils, and it has been reported that the Sioux gave him the name "The-man-who-picks-up-stones-running" (Foster, 1994). The National Park Service reconstructed the fort and manages the Fort Union Trading Post National Historic Site.

In 1864, the military used a rundown Fort Union as a storage depot to supply General Alfred Sully's campaign against the Sioux. Sully established an infantry post 3 miles east of Fort Union, directly overlooking the confluence of the Missouri and Yellowstone Rivers. Construction began on this post, called Fort Buford, in 1866. They used materials from the recently dismantled Fort Union for construction. Many soldiers considered Fort Buford the worst duty station in the army because of the extreme temperatures. It was abandoned in 1895 and became the Fort Buford State Historic Site in 1924.

The Missouri-Yellowstone Confluence Interpretive Center, a newly constructed facility managed by the State Historical Society of North Dakota, is on the north side of the Missouri River not far from Fort Buford. It includes interpretive exhibits of the history, geology, natural history, and cultural changes of the confluence area.

Bison Carcasses

On the broad floodplains in the confluence area of the Missouri and Yellowstone Rivers, Lewis and Clark marveled at the great numbers of antelope, elk, deer, bison, and beaver. For several days they observed great numbers of bison carcasses littering the shoreline and sandbars, some intact and some scavenged by wolves and bears. They speculated that these animals either drowned when trying to cross the river on ice in the winter or while trying to swim across the river. Today, you can find bison bones on the sandbars and shores adjacent to the Yellowstone and Missouri Rivers. Some of these remains may be from the bison and bison carcasses that Lewis and Clark observed two hundred years ago.

Fort Union on the Missouri *by Karl Bodmer. Exposures of the light-colored Bullion Creek formation are evident in the bluffs on the southern side of the Missouri River valley.* —Art courtesy of the Joslyn Art Museum, Omaha, Nebraska; gift of Enron Art Foundation

Aerial view to the south showing the broad Missouri River valley and sandbar development in the Fort Union area (bottom center). The Bullion Creek and Sentinel Butte formations are exposed in the bluffs on the southern side of the valley. When the fort was constructed the river channel was just south of the fort below the tree row.

for several days past we have observed a great number of buffaloe lying dead on the shore, some of them entire and others partly devoured by the wolves and bear. those anamals either drowned during the winter in attempting to pass the river on the ice during the winter or by swiming acrss at present to bluff banks which they are unable to ascend, and feeling themselves too weak to return remain and perish for the want of food; in this situation we met with several little parties of them.

—LEWIS, April 27, 1805

Fairview Lift Bridge

Highway 200 passes through the prime farmland of the Yellowstone floodplain, which is often planted with sugar beets. North of the Highway 200 Hjalmer Nelson Memorial Bridge, which spans the Yellowstone River, are noteworthy outcrops of the Bullion Creek formation. To the south is the Fairview Lift Bridge, an abandoned railroad bridge. It is the only lift bridge in North Dakota and is adjacent to the only railroad tunnel in North Dakota. In 1912 and 1913, when the 1,320-foot Fairview Lift Bridge was constructed, federal law required that an expensive lift bridge ($500,000) was built so as not to impede steamboat navigation on the Yellowstone River. However, other than a test lift in 1914, the center span has never been raised because commercial boat traffic on the river in this area had ceased by the time the bridge was completed. Planking was placed between the rails so automobiles could also use the bridge. Reportedly, a watchman was stationed at the bridge to prevent trains and automobiles from colliding. This unique car and train arrangement lasted until 1956 when the Highway 200 bridge was constructed. In 1997, the railroad bridge was listed on the National Register of Historic Places. A twin to this bridge, the Snowden Lift Bridge, crosses the Missouri River 10 miles to the northwest in Montana and is visible from Fort Union.

The 1,458-foot-long Cartwright Tunnel, 300 feet east of the Fairview Lift Bridge, was excavated, mostly by hand, through Bullion Creek strata. The tunnel was necessary in order to lessen the grade change on the east end of the railroad bridge. It was constructed through a hill that is 140 feet higher than the tracks on either side of the bridge. Had the tracks been laid over the hill top, it would have resulted in a short, steep grade that would have been difficult for trains to ascend. In 1986, the rail line, bridge, and tunnel were abandoned. Part of the tunnel has been walled off for safety reasons. There is interest in preserving at least part of the west end of the tunnel as a historic or recreational site.

Bison vertebra and horn core on the shore of Lake Sakakawea. Current action in the river and wave erosion along the reservoirs frequently expose bison bones that are entombed in the fluvial sediments. Some of these bones are possibly the remains of bison carcasses that Lewis and Clark noted in their journals.

Aerial view of the Fairview Lift Bridge, a railroad bridge built in 1912 that spans the Yellowstone River. View is to the northeast. The entrance to the Cartwright Tunnel, excavated by hand through the Bullion Creek formation, is 300 feet east of the bridge. The Highway 200 Hjalmer Nelson Memorial Bridge is north of the Fairview Lift Bridge.

CHARBONNEAU CREEK

On April 26, 1805, Lewis sent Joseph Fields to explore the Yellowstone River valley. Eight miles from the mouth of the Yellowstone River, Fields discovered a west-flowing creek, which Clark named Joseph Field's Creek on his map. Fields must have ascended the high ground on the eastern side of the Yellowstone Valley to view the area because the course of the creek for about 20 miles and two of the three branches of the creek are fairly accurate on Clark's map. It is now called Charbonneau Creek after another expedition member, Touissant Charbonneau.

When glaciers temporarily diverted the ancestral Yellowstone River to the east in this area, it carved the valley now occupied by Charbonneau Creek. Near the town of Charbonneau, the ancestral Yellowstone turned northeast, creating a broad, flat valley now occupied, in part, by Timber Creek. The channel contains up to 300 feet of sediment including sand and gravel, glacial till, and lake clay. The lake clay was deposited when glacial ice blocked the flow of water, causing it to pond in the channel. About 1 mile northwest of Charbonneau, where Highway 200 crosses the 2-mile-wide channel, gravel deposits from the ancestral Yellowstone River are exposed in a pit. The Yellowstone River abandoned this channel and returned to its present valley when the glacier receded. It is possible that the ancestral Yellowstone River occupied the Charbonneau Creek valley before glaciers descended into North Dakota.

> This morning I dispatched Joseph Fields up the yellowstone river with orders to examine it as far as he could conveniently and return the same evening. . . . in the evening, the man I had sent up the river this morning returned, and reported that he had ascended it about eight miles on a streight line; that he found it crooked, meandering from side to side of the valley formed by it; which is from four to five miles wide. the corrent of the river gentle, and its bed much interrupted and broken by sandbars; at the distance of five miles he passed a large Island well covered with timber, and three miles higher a large creek falls in on the S. E. side above a high bluff in which there are several stratas of coal.
>
> —LEWIS, April 26, 1805

UPLAND GRAVELS

Gravel deposits are present along the uplands bordering the Yellowstone River valley north of Cartwright. The ancestral Yellowstone and Missouri Rivers and their tributaries deposited these brownish, well-rounded, well-sorted gravels along their courses. The deposits, known as the Cartwright gravels, occur at elevations up to 300 feet above the present-day floodplains. Clark probably saw these gravels along the east edge of the Yellowstone River valley on April 26, 1805, when he noted in his journal, "on the Hill Sides I observe pebbles of different Size and Colour." The gravel consists of several rock types including reddish and yellowish quartzites, volcanic rock fragments, cherts, and lesser amounts of other igneous rocks, clinker, and silicified wood. Geologists have identified these same gravels in the Little Muddy River valley, another ancestral route of the Yellowstone River. Gravel deposits north of Cartwright are about 1 million years old and are overlain by glacial till.

7

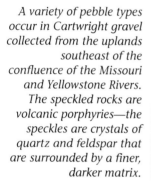

A variety of pebble types occur in Cartwright gravel collected from the uplands southeast of the confluence of the Missouri and Yellowstone Rivers. The speckled rocks are volcanic porphyries—the speckles are crystals of quartz and feldspar that are surrounded by a finer, darker matrix.

A layer of Cartwright gravel (medium brown layer in the upper part of the exposure) overlies the yellow- and white-colored Bullion Creek formation. Glacial till and windblown sediment occur above the gravel. The outcrop is along the eastern wall of the Yellowstone River valley, 5 miles south of the confluence of the Missouri and Yellowstone Rivers. View is to the northeast.

EPILOGUE

The expedition members received a hero's welcome when they returned to St. Louis following their two-and-a-half-year adventure. President Jefferson wanted a multivolume account of the expedition with maps completed as soon as possible and expected Lewis to write the account. Lewis intended to publish a detailed three-volume report of the expedition as outlined in his 1807 *Prospectus of the Lewis and Clark Tour to the Pacific Ocean through the Interior of the Continent of North America*. The first volume was to be a narrative of the expedition, the second would be concerned with geography and ethnography of the Native peoples, and the third would be "confined exclusively to scientific research, and principally to the natural history of these hitherto unknown regions. . . distributed under the heads of Botany, Mineralogy, and Zoology" (Jackson, 1978). Lewis had not begun the publication when he died in 1809, and Clark reluctantly became responsible for it.

Clark was uncomfortable with taking on the task of publishing the journals, so he and Jefferson commissioned Nicholas Biddle, an experienced writer and a Philadelphia lawyer, to publish the narrative account of the expedition. Biddle's version was published in 1814 under the title, *History of the Expedition under the Command of Captains Lewis and Clark, to the Sources of the Missouri, thence Across the Rocky Mountains and down the River Columbia to the Pacific Ocean. Performed During the Years 1804-5-6.* Clark's map of the expedition was published with it. During the intervening years, Clark continued to update his map with new geographical information that came from the explorations of men such as John Colter.

Unfortunately, it took many years to get the journals printed and much of the public's anticipation had waned; the narrative was met with less than an enthusiastic response. Biddle's account excluded most of the scientific information the expedition recorded and grossly understated the importance of the venture as a scientific expedition. University of Pennsylvania botanist Benjamin Smith Barton was commissioned to write a report on the scientific findings of the expedition but never completed it.

It was not until 1893 that the scientific accomplishments of the Lewis and Clark Expedition were recognized when Elliott Coues annotated

William Clark charted the course of the expedition with this compass, now in the Smithsonian Institution's Lewis and Clark Collection.
—Photograph courtesy of the Smithsonian Institution

Collage of Lewis and Clark's journals. Codex D, upper right corner, Lewis's journal from April 7, 1805, through May 23, 1805, recorded the expedition's journey from Fort Mandan to the Montana border.
—Photograph courtesy of the American Philosophical Society Library

and edited the expedition's documents. Coues organized the journals into a codex classification system that is still used today. Reuben Gold Thwaites provided the first comprehensive treatment of the Lewis and Clark journals in an eight-volume compendium published in 1904–5. Thwaites's work included a transcription and annotation of Lewis and Clark's original journals and newly discovered expedition documents including the journals of Charles Floyd, Jr. and Joseph Whitehouse. John Ordway's journal and Lewis and Clark's 1803 journal—the journals that detailed their trip from Pittsburgh to Camp Dubois (or Wood River camp) near the confluence of the Mississippi and Missouri Rivers, where the expedition stayed during the winter of 1803–4—were not discovered until 1913 by Biddle's grandson. Discovered in 1953 at the Minnesota Historical Society, the field notes made by Clark, at times with Lewis's comments, were particularly important to our understanding of the expedition's visit to North Dakota. Many of these notes, called the River Journal, were written from May 14, 1804, through April 3, 1805, including the time the expedition traveled through southern North Dakota and the winter they spent at Fort Mandan. The field notes were edited and published by Ernest Osgood in 1964.

At the Centennial Conference of the Missouri Historical Society in 1967, Donald Jackson suggested the need for a revised and comprehensive compilation and interpretation of the historical and scientific significance of documents from the Lewis and Clark Expedition. In 1979 the Center for Great Plains Studies at the University of Nebraska and the American Philosophical Society cosponsored a project to re-edit and reinterpret the expedition documents. Gary E. Moulton, history professor at the University of Nebraska, Lincoln, took on the task of editing the new edition. The Moulton edition is the first comprehensive account and annotation of all of the expedition journals and other documents. The journals are transcribed, as Moulton puts it, "verbatim et literatim et punctuatim," which provides the reader with insight into the personalities of the writers, a greater understanding of the observations they made, and the actual writing of the documents. Atlas of the Lewis and Clark Expedition, the first volume of the thirteen-volume work, was published in 1983. Volume 13, a comprehensive index, was published in 2001.

In 1948 the State Historical Society of North Dakota published a book titled Lewis and Clark in North Dakota, edited by Russel Reid and reprinted in 1988. The State Historical Society is updating and revising this important source for publication in 2003.

In compliance with army procedures, Lewis sold most of the equipment and instruments the expedition carried at public auction in St.

Louis; very few of the instruments the expedition used still exist. The Missouri Historical Society possesses an English telescope reportedly used by Lewis, Lewis's watch with a double—or hunting—case of silver (made in England in 1796–97), and a compass and magnet Clark used. One of the pocket compasses made by Thomas Whitney, believed to have been carried by Clark, is in the National Museum of American History at the Smithsonian Institution.

NORTH DAKOTA LEGACY

Perhaps the greatest contribution the Lewis and Clark Expedition made to knowledge of North Dakota geology were the descriptions and detailed land surveys of landforms and waterways. We can locate such features as the "flat-topped buttes," "barren hills," and "conical hills" south of Bismarck-Mandan because of Clark's comprehensive and accurate notes and maps. Americans have immortalized Lewis and Clark by naming parks, streets, towns, schools, and counties after them, so it is ironic that none of the names Lewis and Clark applied to landforms

LEWIS AND CLARK'S NAME	PRESENT NAME
Chien Creek	*Unnamed*
Barren Hills	Barren Butte
Shepherds River	Apple Creek
Myry Creek	Snake Creek
Turtle Hills	Killdeer Mountains
Goose Egg Lake	*inundated by Lake Sakakawea*
Small Creek	Skunk Creek
Charbonneau Creek	Bear Den Creek
Goat Pen Creek	Little Knife River
Grand Bend	*inundated by Lake Sakakawea*
Pumice Stone Creek	Tobacco Garden Creek
Halls Strand Creek	*inundated by Lake Sakakawea*
Halls Strand Lake	*inundated by Lake Sakakawea*
Burnt Hills	*unnamed*
Beaver Bends	*unnamed*
Joseph Field's Creek	Charbonneau Creek

Topographic features and waterways in North Dakota named by Lewis and Clark, and their names today.

and waterways in western North Dakota have survived. Only the names of the Missouri River's major tributaries that Native peoples or French fur-trappers had given them—the Cannonball, Heart, Knife, Little Missouri, and Yellowstone Rivers—are used today.

One of the expedition's missions, as stated in Thomas Jefferson's instruction letter to Lewis, was to record geological resources. Even though the expedition did not burn lignite coal for heat or cooking, they eventually came to realize that North Dakota lignite was not as inferior in quality as they had initially concluded. Today, lignite is one of North Dakota's leading economic resources. Another mission of the expedition was to identify potential areas for agricultural development. Expedition members often commented on the "beautiful," "handsome," "rich," and "fertile plains" in North Dakota, and, indeed, agriculture is the state's leading industry. Another mission, to discover if Ice Age animals existed in the Northwest, was dispelled because the expedition did not encounter them. Lewis and Clark were, however, the first people to record the occurrence of fossils—carbonized and petrified wood—in North Dakota.

Before leaving Fort Mandan on April 7, 1805, Lewis and Clark sent a keelboat loaded with several crates of biological, ethnological, and geological specimens to St. Louis, which were then shipped to Thomas Jefferson. Packing lists indicate that sixty-eight rock, mineral, and fossil specimens were included in box 4 of the shipment. Of these, at least seven specimens (Numbers 2, 24, 32, 55, 62, 66, 67) were collected in North Dakota and another seven (Numbers 5, 11, 25, 26, 47, 59, 63) may have been. The total list fairly represents the kinds of rocks and minerals the expedition would have encountered on their journey to Fort Mandan.

Jefferson sent the geological specimens to the American Philosophical Society in Philadelphia, and the November 16, 1805, minutes of the society indicate that the specimens were entered into the society's donation book. The society established a committee consisting of John Vaughan, librarian and treasurer of the American Philosophical Society, and Adam Seybert, a mineralogist, to examine the specimens. Seybert obtained at least thirty-four of the original specimens; he tentatively identified some of the specimens and recorded them in a record book of minerals on November 16, 1805. In 1812, the Academy of Natural Sciences in Philadelphia purchased Seybert's collection of more than two thousand specimens. To date, only four of the sixty-eight rock, mineral, and fossil specimens collected by Lewis and Clark have been found in this collection. Spamer and others (2000) note that these include crystals of the calcium sulfate mineral gypsum (Specimen

2. Found just above the entrance of the cannon Ball river, the butt[e] is principally composed of this sand & strongly impregnated with <a substance supposed to be blue vitriol> [*Sulphat of Iron in consequence of the decomposition of Pyrites.*] (This sand is from the Late Cretaceous Fox Hills formation that was deposited in a shallow marine environment about 68 million years ago.)

11. Generally met with on the Surface of the earth in the level plains & is very common from the calumet Bluff to Fort mandan [*Clay with aluminous impregnation derived from decomposed Shistus.*]

24. Carbonated wood found on the Std. side of Riv near fort Mandane 60 feet above high water mark in the Bank Strata 6 Inch thick. (The carbonated wood is from the Paleocene-age Bullion Creek or Sentinel Butte formations, about 60 million years old. This and Number 66 are the first fossils collected in North Dakota for scientific purposes.)

25. Precipitate of one pint of Missouri water weight 80:65 grs [*principally common Clay.*]

26. Pebbles common to the Sand Bars of the Missouri-[*Agatized flint & small quartzose pebbles.*]

32. Specimen of Globar Salts taken in Prairie of Std Shore 22 Octr. 1804 many bushels could have been obtained— [*a mixture of various kinds of Salt with alumine.*]

47. Specimen of the Earth of which the Hills of the Missouri are principally formed from the entrance of the river Sioux to fort mandan & if Indian information may be depended upon, for several hundred miles further up— It is in the tract of country that the Missouri acquires it coloring matter of which it abates but little to its junction to the Mississipi. This earth when saturated by the rains or melting snows becomes so Soft for many feet in depth, that being unable to support its own weight, it Seperates into large masses from the hills & Slipping down their Sides precipitates itself into the Missouri & mingles with its waters— great quantities of this earth are also thrown into the river by its Subsidiary Streams & rivulets which pass thro' or originate in this tract of open Country. M. L. [*Slate in a decomposed state*]. (It is likely that this specimen of clay, probably Paleocene in age, was collected in North Dakota perhaps at Fort Mandan, but there is no way to be certain.)

55. Incrustations of large round masses of rock which appear in a Sand bluff just above the entrance of the Cannonball river. This river derives its name from the appearance of these Stones many of them are a perfectly globular as art could form them. [*Carbonate of Lime be caustious that you do not confound*

A list of geological specimens collected, or possibly collected, by Lewis and Clark in North Dakota (modified from Moulton, 1987a). The number preceding the description of the specimen is the number assigned the specimen in the American Philosophical Society donation book. The description of the specimen is from

this with the globular Pyrites. See No. 58 below.] (Cannonball concretion from the Late Cretaceous Fox Hills formation. Perhaps the one that Ordway—October 18, 1804—noted that the expedition collected to be used as an anchor.)

59. A Specimen of calcareous rock, a thin Stratum of which is found overlaying a soft Sand rock which makes its appearance in many parts of the bluffs from the entrance of the River Platte to Fort Mandon. [*Mass of shells.*]

62.* Specimen of the pummice Stone found amongst the piles of drift wood on the Missouri, Sometimes found as low down as the mouth of the osage river. I can hear of no burning mountain in the neighborhood of the Missouri or its Branches, but the bluffs of the River are now on fire at Several places, particularly that part named in our chart of the Missouri *The Burning Bluffs.* The plains in many places, throughout this great extent of open country, exhibit abundant proofs of having been once on fire— Witness the Specimens of Lava and Pummicestone found in the Hills near fort mandon— [*Pumice.*] (Clinker formed by the baking of Paleocene-age sediments of the Bullion Creek or Sentinel Butte formations by the underground burning of lignite coal in a natural kiln environment.)

63.* Specimen of a Substance extremely common & found intermix'd with the loose Earth of all the Cliffs & Hills from the Calumet Bluff to Fort Mandon. [*crystallized Gypsum. Sulphated Lim*] (Gypsum is a soft, whitish to clear mineral composed of hydrous calcium sulfate.)

66 Found in the Bluffs near Fort mandan. [*Petrefied wood.*] (Petrified wood from the Bullion Creek or Sentinel Butte formations of Paleocene time, about 60 million years old.)

67.* A Specimen of Lava & pummice Stone found in great abundance on the Sides of the Hills in the Neighorhood of Fort Mandan 1609 miles above the mouth of the Missouri—exposed by the washing of the Hills from the rains & melting Snow.— These are merely the river Hills which are the banks only of a Valley formed by the Missouri, passing thro' a level plain— from the tops of these hills the country as far as the eye can reach is a level plain. The tract of Country which furnishes the Pummice Stone seen floating down the Missouri, is rather burning or burnt plains than burning mountains— [*Lavas*] (Clinker formed by the baking of Paleocene-age sediments of the Bullion Creek or Sentinel Butte formations by the underground burning of lignite coal in a natural kiln environment.)

* Specimens are in the Seybert collection of the
Academy of Natural Sciences in Philadelphia

the original donation book entry and was probably transcribed from Lewis's labels. The italicized comments in brackets are from Adam Seybert, a mineralogist at the society. Comments in parentheses are ours. See page 19 for a list of other abbreviations and editorial symbols.

Number 63), a fossilized fish jaw found in Iowa, and two pieces of clinker from North Dakota (Specimens Number 62 and 67). One of us (Ed) recently searched through the Seybert collection but was unable to identify any additional Lewis and Clark specimens collected in North Dakota. Thwaites (1904–5) and Moulton (1987a) listed the geologic specimens contained in the shipment from Fort Mandan.

Clinker specimens collected by Lewis and Clark and sent to Thomas Jefferson from Fort Mandan in April, 1805. These specimens are in the collection of the Academy of Natural Sciences of Philadelphia. Above, "Lava Stone" (Specimen Number 67), Academy of Natural Sciences of Philadelphia, Seybert Collection number 534 (3 inches x 2.72 inches). Below, "pummice Stone" (Specimen Number 62), Academy of Natural Sciences of Philadelphia, ANSP 3916, Petrologic Collection; Seybert Collection number 534 (2 inches x 1.5 inches). —Photographs courtesy of the Ewell Sale Stewart Library, the Academy of Natural Sciences of Philadelphia

Final Note

After the expedition, Jefferson appointed Lewis to be governor of the Louisiana Territory, a position he held until his death. Lewis suffered from depression and alcoholism after the expedition and was an inept governor and a poor businessman. He died, believed by most from self-inflicted gunshot wounds, at a place called Grinder's Stand along the Natchez Trace in Tennessee on October 11, 1809.

Clark remained in public service throughout most of his life and between 1807 and 1838 he served as brigadier general of the Louisiana militia, Louisiana Territory Indian agent, governor of the Missouri Territory, and superintendent of Indian affairs for the western region of the United States. Clark also established a natural history museum in St. Louis and was the cofounder, with Manual Lisa and others, of the Missouri Fur Trading Company. He died of an illness on September 1, 1838, at age sixty-eight.

Fur traders, mountain men, gold seekers, homesteaders, and other adventurous people followed the westward path blazed by these explorers. In fact, this expansion began even before Lewis and Clark had returned to the Knife River Indian villages. In August 1806, near present-day New Town, the expedition encountered two trappers heading west to trap along the Yellowstone River. Fort Union, a fur trading post, was built near the mouth of the Yellowstone River in 1828, and the first steamboat reached it in 1832.

Many Americans regard the Lewis and Clark Expedition as one of the greatest adventures of all time. The fact that they did not find an all-water route to the Pacific Ocean may have dampened some of the acclaim at the time, but the expedition is rightfully celebrated today as a daring, well-executed expedition into an unknown frontier. May we honor the Lewis and Clark Bicentennial by becoming better stewards of the Missouri River system that they so boldly explored.

GLOSSARY

Definitions are modified from the *Glossary of Geology: American Geological Institute* (1995) edited by Robert L. Bates and Julia A. Jackson, CD-ROM Folio Infobase, 3rd edition.

alkaline. Any strongly basic substance, such as a hydroxide or carbonate of an alkali metal (sodium, potassium). Water is alkaline if it has a pH higher than 7.0.

alluvium. A general term for clay, silt, sand, gravel, or similar unconsolidated material, deposited by running water during comparatively recent geologic time.

ammonite. A now-extinct marine (cephalopod) animal with a thick, strongly ornamented shell with sutures.

anthracite. Hard, black coal of the highest metamorphic rank.

anticline. A fold, generally convex upward, with a core that contains stratigraphically older rocks.

aquifer. A body of rock that is permeable enough to conduct groundwater and to yield economically significant quantities of water to wells and springs.

arid. A climate characterized by dryness, variously defined as rainfall insufficient for plant life or for crops without irrigation; less than 10 inches of annual rainfall; or a higher evaporation rate than precipitation rate.

artificial horizon. A device for indicating a horizontal position, such as a bubble, gyroscope, pendulum, or the flat surface of a liquid. It is sometimes simply called a horizon.

ash, volcanic. Fine material released during volcanic eruptions. The term usually refers to unconsolidated material but is sometimes also used for its consolidated counterpart, tuff.

badlands. Intricately stream-dissected topography. Badlands develop on surfaces with little or no vegetative cover, particularly in unconsolidated or poorly cemented clays or silts. The term was first applied to an area in western South Dakota that was called *mauvaises terres* by French fur-traders.

bar. A ridgelike accumulation of sand, gravel, or other alluvial material formed in the channel, along the banks, or at the mouth of a stream where a decrease in velocity induces deposition.

basin. A low area in the Earth's crust, of tectonic origin, in which sediments have accumulated, such as the Williston Basin.

bearing. The angular direction of any place or object at one fixed point in relation to another fixed point, usually given with reference to the cardinal points of the compass.

bed. The smallest formal stratigraphic unit of sedimentary rock. Coal beds and other beds of economic importance commonly are named, but such units and their names usually are not a part of formal stratigraphic nomenclature. The arrangement of beds or layers of varying thickness and character is called *bedding.*

bedrock. The rock, usually solid, that underlies soil or other unconsolidated, superficial material.

bituminous coal. Coal that ranks between subbituminous coal and anthracite in degree of metamorphism. It is dark brown to black and burns with a smoky flame.

bluff. A high bank or bold headland with a broad, precipitous, sometimes rounded cliff face overlooking a plain or a body of water, especially on the outside of a stream meander.

bottoms (bottomland). Low-lying, level land, usually highly fertile. In the Mississippi Valley region and farther west, the term signifies a grassy lowland formed by deposition of alluvium along the margin of a watercourse.

boulder. A rock larger than a cobble, having a diameter greater than 10 inches, or about the size of a volleyball. It is somewhat rounded from abrasion caused during water transport.

brackish. Said of water with a salinity intermediate between seawater and freshwater.

brontotheres. Elephant-sized, plant-eating, land-dwelling mammals that lived during Eocene time in North Dakota. They are also called *titanotheres,* or *thunder beasts.* They became extinct at the end of Oligocene time.

buried channel. An old river channel concealed by surficial deposits. It is often a preglacial channel filled with glacial drift.

butte. A conspicuous, usually isolated, generally flat-topped hill with relatively steep slopes or precipitous cliffs; often capped with a resistant layer of rock and bordered by talus. It usually represents an erosion remnant carved from flat-lying rocks.

calcareous. Said of a substance that contains calcium carbonate, $CaCO_3$.

Cambrian Period. The earliest period of the Paleozoic era, spanning between 570 and 500 million years ago. It is named after *Cambria*, the Roman name for Wales, where rocks of this age were first studied.

carbonate. A sedimentary rock, such as limestone, formed by the organic or inorganic precipitation from aqueous solution of carbonates of calcium, magnesium, or iron.

cementation. The process by which coarse sediments are consolidated into hard, compact rocks, usually through the deposition or precipitation of minerals, or cement, in the spaces between the individual grains of sediment. It may occur simultaneously with sedimentation or at a later time.

Cenozoic Era. An era of geologic time, from the beginning of the Tertiary period about 65 million years ago to the present. It is characterized paleontologically by the evolution and abundance of mammals, advanced mollusks, birds, and angiosperms. It is also called the Age of Mammals.

cephalopod. Any marine mollusk belonging to the class Cephalopoda, characterized by a definite head. Nautiloids and ammonoids are extinct cephalopods, generally valuable as index fossils; octopuses, squids, and cuttlefishes are common living cephalopods.

champsosaurs. Crocodile-like, fish-eating reptiles that lived in ponds and rivers during Cretaceous and Paleocene time and became extinct about 50 million years ago in Eocene time.

clay. A loose, earthy, extremely fine-grained, natural sediment or soft rock composed primarily of clay-sized particles, which are smaller than a very fine silt grain, having a diameter less than 1/256 millimeter.

claystone. An indurated clay that has the texture and composition of shale but lacks its fine lamination.

clinker. Sediment or sedimentary rock that has been baked by heat from buried, burning coal. Clinker may range from rock that has completely melted, to material with a glassy texture, to brick, to slightly colored and hardened material. The color may be pink, purple, black, brown, or other shades. Commonly called *scoria* in North Dakota.

coal. A readily combustible rock that contains carbonaceous material and formed from compaction and induration of variously altered plant remains similar to those in peat.

cobble. A rock fragment larger than a pebble and smaller than a boulder, having a diameter in the range of 2.5 to 10 inches.

concretion. A hard, compact mass or aggregate of mineral matter, ranging in size from a small, pelletlike object to a great spheroidal body as much as 10 feet in diameter. It is either a concentration of some minor constituent of the enclosing sedimentary rock or a concentration of cementing material, such as silica, calcite, dolomite, iron oxide, pyrite, or gypsum. The minerals precipitate from aqueous solution about a nucleus, such as a leaf, shell, fossil, or bone.

confluence. Where two or more streams meet; the point where a tributary joins the main stream.

contact. A plane or irregular surface between two types or ages of rock.

Cretaceous Period. The final period of the Mesozoic Era, spanning between 135 and 65 million years ago. It is named after *creta*, the Latin word for chalk, because of the English chalk beds of this age.

cutbank. A local term in the western United States for a steep, bare slope formed by the lateral erosion of a stream.

delta. The low, nearly flat, alluvial land at or near the mouth of a river, commonly forming a fan-shaped plain of considerable area. It forms through the accumulation of sediment supplied by the river.

deposit. Material of any type, either consolidated or unconsolidated, that has accumulated by some natural process.

deposition. The process of accumulation of loose rock material into beds, veins, or irregular masses by any natural agent such as water, wind, or ice.

dinosaurs. Small-sized to gigantic, land-living reptiles that became extinct at the end of Mesozoic time, about 65 million years ago.

discharge. The rate of stream flow at a given moment, usually expressed as cubic feet per second.

dissolved solids. The quantity of dissolved material in a sample of water.

drift, glacial. A general term applied to all rock material (clay, silt, sand, gravel, boulders) transported by a glacier and deposited directly from the ice or by running water emanating from a glacier.

dune. A low mound, ridge, bank, or hill of loose, windblown granular material (generally sand, sometimes volcanic ash). A dune may be bare or covered with vegetation, capable of movement from place to place but always retaining its characteristic shape.

embankment. A linear structure, usually of earth or gravel, constructed to rise above the natural ground surface. They are designed to prevent water from overflowing a level tract of land; to retain water in a reservoir, tailings in a pond, or a stream in its channel; or to carry a roadway or railroad.

Eocene Epoch. An epoch of geologic time, from 55 to 34 million years ago, in the Tertiary Period.

erosion. The general process or the group of processes whereby the materials of the surface of the land are loosened, dissolved, or worn away, and moved from one place to another.

erratic. A rock fragment carried by glacial ice from its place of origin to some distant location. Size ranges from a pebble to a house-sized block.

escarpment. A long, continuous cliff or relatively steep slope facing in one general direction, breaking the continuity of the land by separating two level or gently sloping surfaces. The term is often used synonymously with *fault scarp*, although escarpment is more often applied to a cliff formed by erosion.

esker. A long, narrow, sinuous, steep-sided ridge composed of irregularly stratified sand and gravel that was deposited by a stream flowing between ice walls or in an ice tunnel of a retreating glacier.

extinction. The total disappearance of a species so that it no longer exists anywhere.

fill. Any sediment deposited by any agent to fill or partly fill a valley, sink, or other depression.

flint. A widely used synonym for homogeneous, dark gray or black chert, which is microcrystalline quartz. The Knife River flint in North Dakota is silicified peat.

floodplain. The surface or strip of relatively smooth land adjacent to a river channel, constructed by the present river and covered with water when the river overflows its banks. It is built of alluvium carried by the river during floods and deposited in the sluggish water beyond the influence of the swiftest current. A river has one floodplain and may have one or more terraces representing former floodplains.

fluvial deposit. A sedimentary deposit consisting of material transported by, suspended in, or laid down by a stream.

formation. A body of rock, identifiable by certain characteristics and stratigraphic position, that is mappable at the Earth's surface or traceable in the subsurface. The formation is the fundamental unit in stratigraphic classification. Thickness is not a determining factor. Formations may be combined into groups or subdivided into members. A formation name normally consists of a geographic name followed by a descriptive geologic term (usually the dominant rock type) or by the word *formation* if the lithology is so variable that no single term is appropriate: Pierre shale, Cannonball formation.

fossil. Any remains, trace, or imprint of a plant or animal from some past geologic time that has been preserved in the earth.

gasification. Any process by which a combustible gas is made from coal or other solid hydrocarbons.

geologic age. The age of a fossil organism or of a particular geologic event or feature according to the geologic time scale.

glacial lake. A lake that derives much or all of its water from the melting of glaciers.

glaciation. The formation, movement, and recession of glaciers. A land surface that was formerly covered by a glacier—especially one that was modified by the action of a glacier—is said to be *glaciated*.

glacier. A large mass of ice formed, at least in part, on land by the compaction and recrystallization of snow, moving slowly downslope or outward in all directions due to the stress of its own weight and surviving from year to year.

Glauber's salt. Sodium sulfate, $Na_2SO_4.10H_2O$. Named after Johann R. Glauber (1604–1668), a German chemist.

granite. An igneous, crystalline rock in which quartz constitutes 10 to 50 percent of the light-colored minerals.

granule. A rock fragment larger than a very coarse sand grain and smaller than a pebble, having a diameter in the range of $\frac{1}{12}$ to $\frac{1}{6}$ inches.

gravel. An unconsolidated accumulation of rounded rock fragments resulting from erosion; predominantly consists of particles larger than sand (diameter greater than 2 millimeters) such as boulders, cobbles, pebbles, and granules.

groundwater. Subsurface water that is below the water table (in the zone of saturation).

group. The stratigraphic unit next in rank above formation, consisting partly or entirely of named formations.

ice age. A time of extensive glacial activity. The latest of the glacial epochs is known as the Pleistocene Epoch.

ice lobe. A large, rounded, tonguelike projection from the margin of an ice sheet.

ice sheet. A glacier of considerable thickness and more than 50,000 square kilometers (19,300 square miles) in area, forming a continuous cover of ice and snow over a land surface, spreading outward in all directions and not confined by the underlying topography. Ice sheets are now confined to polar regions (such as Greenland and Antarctica), but during the Pleistocene Epoch they covered large parts of North America and northern Europe.

igneous. Said of a rock or mineral that solidified from molten or partly molten material.

indurated. Said of a rock or soil hardened or consolidated by pressure, cementation, or heat.

interbedded. Said of beds lying between or alternating with others of different character.

invertebrate. An animal without a backbone, such as mollusks, arthropods, and coelenterates, including snails, clams, crabs, cephalopods, etc.

landslide. A general term covering a wide variety of mass-movement landforms and processes involving the downslope transport, under gravitational influence, of soil and rock material en masse.

latitude. Angular distance of a point on Earth's surface north or south of the equator, measured along a meridian through 90 degrees (the equator is latitude zero degrees and the North Pole is latitude 90 degrees north).

lava. A general term for rock that is solidified from magma.

lava stone. The term used by Lewis and Clark to describe clinker that showed evidence of having been melted.

layer. A general term for any bed or stratum of rock or unconsolidated material that lies parallel to the surface on or against which it formed.

lens. A geologic deposit bounded by converging surfaces (at least one of which is curved), thick in the middle and thinning out toward the edges.

leonardite. Weathered subbituminous coal or lignite. It is rich in humic and fulvic acids and soluble in alkaline water.

lignite. A brownish black coal that is intermediate between peat and subbituminous coal in the conversion of plant matter to coal.

limestone. A sedimentary rock consisting chiefly of calcium carbonate, primarily in the form of the mineral calcite.

loess. A widespread, homogeneous, fine-grained deposit of windblown silt of Pleistocene age. It is commonly nonstratified, porous, friable, slightly coherent, usually highly calcareous, and less than 100 feet thick. It consists predominantly of silt with subordinate grain sizes ranging from clay to fine sand. Loess is generally buff to light yellow or yellowish brown.

longitude. The length of the arc or portion of the Earth's equator, intersected between the meridian of a given place and the prime meridian, expressed either in time or in degrees east or west to a maximum value of 180 degrees.

main stem. The principal course of a stream.

mammoth. Extinct Pleistocene ancestor of the elephant, with hairy skin and long tusks curving upward. Mammoths were present nearly worldwide but became extinct in late Pleistocene time.

mastodon. One of a group of extinct, elephantlike mammals widely distributed in the Northern Hemisphere in Pleistocene time. It differs from mammoths and other true elephants in that teeth are low-crowned, with closed roots.

meander. One of a series of sinuous curves in the course of a stream. It is produced by a mature stream swinging from side to side as it flows across its floodplain or shifts its course laterally toward the outside bend of an existing curve.

meltwater. Water derived from the melting of snow or ice, especially the stream flowing in, under, or from melting glaciers.

member. A stratigraphic unit of subordinate rank, comprising some specially developed part of a formation. It may be formally defined and named, informally named, or unnamed. It is not necessarily mappable, and a named member may extend laterally from one formation into another.

Mesozoic Era. An era of geologic time, from the end of the Paleozoic Era to the beginning of the Cenozoic Era, or from about 250 to about 65 million years ago. It is known as the Age of Reptiles.

metamorphic rock. Any rock derived from pre-existing rocks by mineralogical, chemical, and/or structural changes, essentially in the solid state, in response to changes in temperature, pressure, shearing stress, and chemical environment, generally at depth in the Earth's crust.

mineral. A naturally occurring inorganic element or compound having an orderly internal structure and characteristic chemical composition, crystal form, and physical properties.

Miocene Epoch. An epoch of geologic time, from 24 to 5 million years ago, in the Tertiary Period.

mollusk. An invertebrate characterized by a nonsegmented body that is bilaterally symmetrical. Snails, clams, and cephalopods are mollusks.

mosasaurs. Marine lizards, related to the living monitor lizards, that inhabited the world's oceans during Late Cretaceous time. Many were huge, attaining lengths of 30 feet or more. Mosasaurs became extinct at the end of Cretaceous time, about 65 million years ago, with the last of the dinosaurs.

mud. An unconsolidated sediment consisting of clay and/or silt, together with material of other sizes such as sand, mixed with water.

mudstone. A blocky or massive, fine-grained sedimentary rock in which the proportions of clay and silt are approximately equal.

natural gas. Hydrocarbons such as methane, ethane, and propane that exist as a gas or vapor at ordinary pressures and temperatures.

Oligocene Epoch. An epoch of geologic time, from 34 to 24 million years ago, in the Tertiary Period.

outcrop. That part of a geologic formation or structure that appears at the surface of the land.

outwash. Stratified sand and gravel removed or "washed out" from a glacier by meltwater streams and deposited in front of or at the margin of an active glacier.

overburden. Rock material, either loose or consolidated, overlying a mineral deposit. It is removed prior to mining.

oxbow lake. The crescent-shaped, often ephemeral body of standing water situated by the side of a stream in the abandoned channel of a meander. It forms when a stream cuts through the neck of a meander and fills the ends of the original bend with silt.

Paleocene Epoch. An epoch of geologic time, from 65 to 55 million years ago, in the early Tertiary Period.

paleontology. The study of life in past geologic time, based on fossil plants and animals.

Paleozoic Era. An era of geologic time, from the end of the Precambrian Era to the beginning of the Mesozoic Era, or from about 570 to about 250 million years ago.

pebble. A small, roundish, waterworn stone that ranges in diameter from 1/6 (small-pea sized) to 2.5 inches (tennis-ball sized).

plain. An extensive region of comparatively smooth and level or gently undulating land, having few or no prominent surface irregularities but sometimes having a slope. A plain may be formed by deposition or by erosion.

Pleistocene Epoch. An epoch of geologic time in the Quaternary Period. It began 1.8 million years ago and lasted until the start of the Holocene Epoch, some 10,000 years ago.

plesiosaurs. Marine reptiles that lived in the world's oceans during Mesozoic time. Some were huge, attaining lengths of almost 50 feet. They inhabited oceans that covered North Dakota during Late Cretaceous time.

Pliocene Epoch. An epoch of geologic time, from 5 to 1.8 million years ago, in the Tertiary Period.

point bar. One of a series of low, arcuate ridges of sand and gravel developed on the inside of a meander by the slow addition of sediment accompanying migration of the channel toward the outer bank.

prairie. An extensive tract of level to rolling grassland, generally treeless, in the temperate latitudes of the interior of North America.

Precambrian. Geologic time before the beginning of the Paleozoic Era about 570 million years ago; it encompasses about 90 percent of geologic time (4.7 billion to 570 million years ago).

pumice. A light-colored, vesicular, glassy volcanic rock that can often float on water. Lewis and Clark referred to vesicular clinker as "pumice stone."

pumice stone. The term Lewis and Clark used to refer to the frothy variety of clinker.

quarry. Open workings, usually for the extraction of stone or gravel.

Quaternary Period. The second period of the Cenozoic Era, following Tertiary time. It began 1.8 million years ago and extends to the present. It consists of two epochs: the Pleistocene and the Holocene. The Holocene is the last 10,000 years.

radiocarbon dating. A method of determining an age in years by measuring the concentration of carbon-14, a radioactive isotope, remaining in organic material. The method is based on the assumption that an organism stops assimilating carbon-14 from the atmosphere upon death. Carbon-14 has a half-life of about 5,700 years, so the method is most useful to determine ages in the range of 500 to 40,000 years.

reach. A straight, continuous, or extended part of a stream, viewed without interruption (as between two bends), or a stretch between two specified points.

relief. The physical shape, configuration, or general unevenness of a part of the land surface. A region with a great variation in elevation has *high relief* and one with little variation has *low relief.*

reptile. Any cold-blooded vertebrate that is air-breathing at all stages of development.

reworked. Said of a sediment, fossil, rock fragment, or other geologic material that has been removed or displaced from its place of origin by natural agents such as water and then incorporated into a younger formation.

riparian. Pertaining to or situated on the bank of a body of water.

saline. Containing high concentrations of dissolved salts.

sand. A rock particle smaller than a granule and larger than a coarse silt grain, having a diameter in the range of 1/16 to 2 millimeters.

sandbar. A bar or low ridge of sand built by currents or wave action that borders the shore and is as high, or nearly as high, as the water surface.

sand dune. An accumulation of loose sand heaped up by the wind; commonly found along low-lying seashores above high-tide level, more rarely on the border of large lakes or river valleys, as well as in various desert regions where there is abundant dry surface sand during some part of the year.

sandstone. A medium-grained sedimentary rock composed of abundant rounded or angular fragments of sand set in a fine-grained matrix (silt or clay) and more or less firmly united by a cementing material (commonly silica, iron oxide, or calcium carbonate).

savanna. An open, grassy, essentially treeless plain. Usually there is a distinct wet and dry season; trees and shrubs are drought resistant.

sediment. Material that originates from weathering of rocks and is transported or deposited by air, water, or ice; forms in layers on the land at ordinary temperatures in a loose, unconsolidated form.

sedimentary rock. A rock resulting from the consolidation of accumulated layers of loose sediment, a chemical rock formed by precipitation from a solution, or a rock such as limestone that consists of the remains or secretions of plants and animals.

sedimentation. The act or process of sediment forming or accumulating in layers.

semiarid. A climate with slightly more precipitation (10 to 20 inches) than an arid climate and in which sparse grasses are the characteristic vegetation.

sextant. A hand instrument used to measure angular distances. It is also called a *quadrant*.

shale. A fine-grained sedimentary rock, formed by the consolidation of clay, silt, or mud. It is characterized by a finely laminated structure, which imparts a fissility approximately parallel to the bedding and along which the rock breaks readily into thin layers. It may be red, brown, black, or gray.

siliceous. Said of a rock containing abundant silica.

silicified wood (petrified wood). A material formed by mineralization of wood by silica in such a manner that the original form and structure of the wood is preserved. The silica is generally in the form of opal or chalcedony.

silt. A rock particle smaller than a very fine sand grain and larger than coarse clay; has a diameter in the range of 1/256 to 1/16 millimeter; the upper size limit is approximately the smallest size that can be distinguished with the unaided eye.

siltstone. Indurated silt that has the texture and composition of shale but lacks its fine lamination or fissility. The composition of siltstone is intermediate between those of sandstone and shale. It tends to contain hard, durable, generally thin layers.

slump. A landslide characterized by a shearing and rotary movement of a generally independent mass of rock or earth along a curved slip surface.

soil creep. The gradual, downhill movement of soil and loose rock material on a slope that may be very gentle but is usually steep.

soil horizon. A layer of soil that is distinguishable from adjacent layers by physical properties such as structure, color, texture, or by chemical composition, including content of organic matter or degree of acidity or alkalinity.

spoils. An accumulation of mining waste.

stratified (sedimentology). The formation, accumulation, or deposition of materials, such as sediment, in layers.

stratigraphy. The science concerned with the original succession and age relations of rock strata and with their form, distribution, composition, fossil content, geophysical and geochemical properties.

stratum (pl. strata). A tabular or sheetlike body or layer of sedimentary rock, visually separable from other layers.

swelling clay (bentonite). Clay that is capable of absorbing large quantities of water, which increases its volume. It shrinks and cracks when drying.

tectonics. The forces involved in the regional structural or deformational features on the outer surface of Earth.

terrace (river). Any long, narrow, relatively level or gently inclined surface above the level of the river; marks a former water level.

Tertiary Period. The first period of geologic time in the Cenozoic Era. It spans the time between 65 and 1.8 million years ago. It is divided into five epochs: the Paleocene, Eocene, Oligocene, Miocene, and Pliocene.

till. Dominantly unsorted and unstratified glacial drift, generally unconsolidated, deposited directly by and underneath a glacier without subsequent reworking by meltwater. It consists of a heterogeneous mixture of clay, silt, sand, gravel, and boulders ranging widely in size and shape.

trap. Any subsurface barrier, such as an impermeable rock layer, that blocks the upward movement of oil or gas and causes either or both to accumulate.

turbidity. The reduced clarity of a fluid due to the presence of suspended matter such as silt and clay.

vertebrate. An animal characterized by an internal skeleton of cartilage or bone.

weathering. The physical disintegration and chemical decomposition of rock by atmospheric agents at or near the Earth's surface. The process may change a rock's color, texture, composition, firmness, or form, with little or no transport of the loosened or altered material.

whetstone. Any hard, fine-grained, naturally occurring rock, usually siliceous, that is suitable for sharpening tools such as razors and knives.

Wisconsinan. Pertaining to the classical fourth glacial stage of the Pleistocene Epoch in North America.

Selected References and Suggested Reading

History

Ahler, S. A., T. D. Thiessen, and M. K. Trimble. 1991. *People of the Willows*. Grand Forks: University of North Dakota Press.

Allen, J. L. 1975. *Passage through the Garden: Lewis and Clark and the Image of the American Northwest*. Urbana: University of Illinois Press.

———. 1998. Geographical knowledge and American images of the Louisiana Territory. In *Voyages of Discovery: Essays on the Lewis and Clark Expedition*. Ed. J. P. Ronda, 39–58. Helena: Montana Historical Society Press.

Ambrose, S. E. 1996. *Undaunted Courage: Meriwether Lewis, Thomas Jefferson, and the Opening of the American West*. New York: Simon and Schuster.

———. 1998. *Lewis and Clark: A Voyage of Discovery*. Washington, D.C.: National Geographic Society.

Bakeless, John. 1964. *The Journals of Lewis and Clark*. New York: New American Library.

Bedini, S. A. 1990. *Thomas Jefferson: Statesman of Science*. New York: Macmillan.

———. 1998. The scientific instruments of the Lewis and Clark Expedition. In *Voyages of Discovery: Essays on the Lewis and Clark Expedition*. Ed. J. P. Ronda, 143–65. Helena: Montana Historical Society Press.

Bergantino, R. N. 1990. A moon to light the way. *We Proceeded On* (August), 19–22.

———. 2001. Revisiting Fort Mandan's longitude. *We Proceeded On* (November), 19–30.

Betts, R. B. 1980. "We commenced wrighting & c": A Salute to the Ingenious Spelling and Grammar of William Clark. *We Proceeded On* (November), 10–12.

———. 1981. "The writingest explorers of their time": new estimates of the number of words in the published journals of the Lewis and Clark Expedition: *We Proceeded On* (August) 4–9.

Biddle, Nicholas, ed. 1814. *The Journals of the Expedition under the Command of Capts. Lewis and Clark*. 2 vols. (Reprinted in 1962) New York: The Heritage Press.

Brown, R. W. 1943. Jefferson's contribution to paleontology. *Journal of the Washington Academy of Sciences* 33(9):257–59.

Browne, C. A. 1944. Thomas Jefferson and the scientific trends of his time. *Chronica Botanica* 8:363–423.

Burroughs, R. D. 1961. *The Natural History of the Lewis and Clark Expedition*. East Lansing: Michigan State University Press.

Chuinard, E. G. 1979. *Only One Man Died: The Medical Aspects of the Lewis and Clark Expedition*. Glendale, California: A. H. Clark.

Coues, Elliot, ed. 1893. *History of the Expedition under the Command of Lewis and Clark*. 3 vols. (Reprinted in 1965) New York: Dover Publications.

Cutright, P. R. 1969. *Lewis and Clark: Pioneering Naturalists*. Urbana: University of Illinois Press.

Dillon, R. 1965. *Meriwether Lewis*. New York: Coward-McCann.

Duncan, Dayton. 1997. *Lewis & Clark: An Illustrated History*. New York: Alfred A. Knopf.

———. 1999. The chimneys of Fort Mandan. *We Proceeded On* (August), 13–18.

Duncan, Dayton, and K. Burns. 1997. *Lewis and Clark—the Journey of the Corps of Discovery*. New York: Alfred A. Knopf.

Gilman, C., and M. J. Schneider. 1987. *The Way to Independence: Memories of a Hidatsa Indian Family, 1840–1920*. St. Paul: Minnesota Historical Society.

Greene, J. C. 1984. *American Science in the Age of Jefferson*. Ames: The Iowa State University Press.

Hart, H. C. 1957. *The Dark Missouri*. Madison: The University of Wisconsin Press.

Holland, L. 2001. Preserving food on the Lewis and Clark Expedition. *We Proceeded On* (August), 6–11.

Howard, R. W. 1975. *The Dawnseekers: the First History of American Paleontology.* New York: Harcourt Brace Jovanovich.

Hunt, R. R. 1992a. The blood meal, mosquitoes and agues on the Lewis & Clark Expedition, Part I. *We Proceeded On* (May), 4–10.

———. 1992b. The blood meal, mosquitoes and agues on the Lewis & Clark Expedition, Part II. *We Proceeded On* (August) 4–10.

———. 1999. Luck or providence? Narrow escapes on the Lewis and Clark Expedition. *We Proceeded On* (August), 6–11.

Jackson, D. D., ed. 1962. *Letters of the Lewis and Clark Expedition with Related Documents, 1783–1854.* Urbana: University of Illinois Press.

———, ed. 1978. *Letters of the Lewis and Clark Expedition, with Related Documents, 1783–1854.* 2nd Edition. Urbana: University of Illinois Press.

Jones, L. Y. ed. 2000. *The Essential Lewis and Clark.* New York: ECCO Press.

Karsmizki, K. W. 1995a. Searching for the invisible: some efforts to find expedition camps, Part I of II. *We Proceeded On* (August), 4–11.

———. 1995b. Searching for the invisible: some efforts to find expedition camps, Part II of II. *We Proceeded On* (November), 4–12.

———. 1997. The lost wintering post of 1804–05. *We Proceeded On* (May), 21–24.

Large, A. J. 1994. Expedition specialists, the talented helpers of Lewis and Clark. *We Proceeded On* (February), 4–10.

Lentz, Gary. 2000. Meriwether Lewis's medicine chests. *We Proceeded On* (May), 10–17.

Lewis, T. D., J. A. Leitch, and A. J. Meyer. 1998. Characteristics, expenditures, and economic impact of resident and nonresident hunters and anglers in North Dakota, 1996–1997: Season and trends. *North Dakota State University, Agricultural Economics Report* No. 389.

Moore, Bob. 2000. Corps of Discovery gravesites. *We Proceeded On* (May), 5–9.

Morris, L. E. 2001. Dependable John Ordway. *We Proceeded On* (May), 28–33.

Moulton, G. E. 1983a. Another look at William Clark's map of 1805. *We Proceeded On* (March), 19–25.

———. 1983b. *The Journals of the Lewis and Clark Expedition, vol. 1. Atlas of the Lewis & Clark Expedition.* Lincoln: University of Nebraska Press.

———. 1986. *The Journals of the Lewis and Clark Expedition, vol. 2. August 30, 1803–August 24, 1804.* Lincoln: University of Nebraska Press.

———. 1987a. *The Journals of the Lewis and Clark Expedition, vol. 3. August 25, 1804–April 6, 1805.* Lincoln: University of Nebraska Press.

———. 1987b. *The Journals of the Lewis and Clark Expedition, vol. 4. April 7–July 27, 1805.* Lincoln: University of Nebraska Press.

———. 1993. *The Journals of the Lewis and Clark Expedition, vol. 8. June 10–September 26, 1806.* Lincoln: University of Nebraska Press.

———. 1995. *The Journals of the Lewis and Clark Expedition, vol. 9. The Journals of John Ordway, May 14, 1804–September 23, 1806, and Charles Floyd, May 14–August 18, 1804.* Lincoln: University of Nebraska Press.

———. 1997a. *The Journals of the Lewis and Clark Expedition, vol. 10. The Journal of Patrick Gass, May 14, 1804–September 23, 1806.* Lincoln: University of Nebraska Press.

———. 1997b. *The Journals of the Lewis and Clark Expedition, vol. 11. The Journals of Joseph Whitehouse, May 14, 1804–April 2, 1806.* Lincoln: University of Nebraska Press.

———. 1998. On reading Lewis and Clark: the last twenty years. In *Voyages of Discovery: Essays on the Lewis and Clark Expedition.* Ed. J. P. Ronda, 281–98. Helena: Montana Historical Society Press.

———. 1999. *The Journals of the Lewis and Clark Expedition, vol. 12. Herbarium of the Lewis & Clark Expedition.* Lincoln: University of Nebraska Press.

———. 2001. *The Journals of the Lewis and Clark Expedition, vol. 13. Index.* Lincoln: University of Nebraska Press.

Murphy, E. C. 1995. The Northern Pacific Railway Bridge at Bismarck. *North Dakota History—Journal of the Northern Plains* 62(2):2–19.

National Climatic Data Center, 2002, website address, <http://lwf.ncdc.noaa.gov/oa/ncdc.html>.

Osborn, H. F. 1935. Thomas Jefferson as a paleontologist. *Science* 82(2136):533–38.

Osgood, E. S., ed. 1964. *The Field Notes of Captain William Clark, 1803–1805.* New Haven, Conn.: Yale University Press.

Paton, B. C. 2001. *Lewis & Clark: Doctors in the Wilderness.* Golden, Colo.: Fulcrum Publishing.

Peck, T. R. 2002. Archaeologically recovered ammonites: Evidence for Long-term Continuity in Nitsitapii Ritual. *Plains Anthropologist* 47(181):147–64.

Plamondon, M., II. 1991. The instruments of Lewis and Clark. *We Proceeded On* (February), 7–18.

———. 2000. *Lewis and Clark Trail Maps: A Cartographic Reconstruction*, Vol. I. Pullman: Washington State University Press.

———. 2001. *Lewis and Clark Trail Maps: A Cartographic Reconstruction*, Vol. II. Pullman: Washington State University Press.

Preston, R. S. 2000. The accuracy of the astronomical observations of Lewis and Clark. *American Philosophical Society* 144(2):168–191.

Robinson, S. 1993. *Along the Lewis and Clark Trail in North Dakota*. Garrison: North Dakota, BHG, Inc.

Ronda, J. P., ed. 1998a. *Voyages of Discovery: Essays on the Lewis and Clark Expedition*. Helena: Montana Historical Society Press.

Ronda, J. P. 1998b. "So vast an enterprise": thoughts on the Lewis and Clark Expedition. In *Voyages of Discovery: Essays on the Lewis and Clark Expedition*. Ed. J. P. Ronda, 1–25. Helena: Montana Historical Society Press.

———. 1998c. "A most perfect harmony": The Lewis and Clark Expedition as an exploration community. In *Voyages of Discovery: Essays on the Lewis and Clark Expedition*. Ed. J. P. Ronda, 77–88. Helena: Montana Historical Society Press.

Reid, Russell, ed. 1948. *Lewis and Clark in North Dakota*. (Second printing 1988) Bismarck: State Historical Society of North Dakota.

Reid, R. 1986. *Sakakawea: the Bird Woman*. Bismarck: State Historical Society of North Dakota.

Saindon, B. 1987. Old Menard. *We Proceeded On* (May,) 4–10.

Satchell, M. 1998. Historian's Corps of Discovery. *U.S. and World Report* (December 7), 57.

Scarnecchia, D., S. Everett, T. Welker, and R. Rychman. 2002. Missouri River fishes: big changes in Big Muddy. *North Dakota Outdoors* (March), 10–13.

Schmidt, T., and J. Schmidt. 1999. *The Saga of Lewis and Clark: Into the Uncharted West*. New York: DK Publishing Company.

Schultz, C. B. 1943. Thomas Jefferson, pioneer paleontologist. *The Compass of Sigma Gamma Epsilon* 23(4):264–67.

Starr, E. 2001. Celestial navigation basics. *We Proceeded On* (November), 12–18.

Steffen, J. O. 1977. *William Clark: Jeffersonian Man on the Frontier*. Norman: University of Oklahoma Press.

Thwaites, R. G., ed. 1904–1905. *Original Journals of the Lewis and Clark Expedition, 1804–1806.* 8 vols. New York: Dodd, Mead, and Company.

———. 1905. *Travels in the Interior of North America.* Cleveland, Ohio: The Arthur H. Clark Company. Volumes 22 and 23 contain Maximillian's accounts of his travels through North Dakota.

White, H. (McCann). 1966. *Ho! for the Gold Fields.* St. Paul: Minnesota Historical Society.

Wick, D. A. 1988. *North Dakota Place Names.* Bismarck, N. Dak.: Hedemarken Collectibles.

Wood, W. R. 1983a. John Thomas Evans and William Clark: two early western explorers' maps re-examined. *We Proceeded On* (March), 10–16.

———. 1983b. *An atlas of early maps of the American Midwest.* Springfield, Illinois, State Museum, Scientific Papers, vol. 18.

———. 2001. John Thomas Evans: an overlooked precursor to Lewis and Clark. *North Dakota History* 68(2):27–37.

Wood, W. R., and T. D. Thiessen, eds. 1985. *Early Fur Trade on the Northern Plains: Canadian Traders among the Mandan and Hidatsa Indians, 1738–1818.* Norman: University of Oklahoma Press.

Woolworth, A. R. 1988. New light on Fort Mandan: a wintering post of the Lewis and Clark Expedition to the Pacific, 1804–1806. *North Dakota History* 55(3):3–14.

GEOLOGY

Ahler, S. A. 1988. The Knife River Quarries. *We Proceeded On* (May), 4–7.

Bluemle, J. P. 1971. Geology of McLean County, North Dakota. *North Dakota Geological Survey Bulletin* 60(pt. 1).

———. 1977. *Surface geology of North Dakota.* North Dakota Geological Survey Miscellaneous Map 18.

———. 1984. Geology of Emmons County, North Dakota. *North Dakota Geological Survey Bulletin* 66(pt. 1).

———. 1988a. *North Dakota Geological Highway Map.* North Dakota Geological Survey Miscellaneous Map 29.

———. 1988b. Drainage development in North Dakota. *North Dakota Geological Survey Newsletter* (June).

———. 2000. *The Face of North Dakota.* North Dakota Geological Survey Educational Series 21, Third Edition.

————. 2001. *The 50ᵗʰ Anniversary of the Discovery of Oil in North Dakota.* North Dakota Geological Survey Miscellaneous Series 89.

Bluemle, J. P., and Lee Clayton. 1982. *Geologic Time in North Dakota.* North Dakota Geological Survey Educational Series 14.

Brostuen, E. A. 1981. *Petroleum—A Primer for North Dakota.* North Dakota Geological Survey Educational Series 13, p.34.

Carlson, C. G. 1973. *Geology of Mercer and Oliver Counties, North Dakota.* North Dakota Geological Survey Bulletin 56(pt. 1).

————. 1982. *Geology of Grant and Sioux Counties, North Dakota.* North Dakota Geological Survey Bulletin 67(pt. 1).

————. 1983a. *Geology of Morton County, North Dakota.* North Dakota Geological Survey Bulletin 72(pt. 1).

————. 1983b. *Geology of Billings, Golden Valley, and Slope Counties, North Dakota.* North Dakota Geological Survey Bulletin 76(pt. 1).

————. 1985. *Geology of McKenzie County, North Dakota.* North Dakota Geological Survey Bulletin 80(pt. 1).

Carlson, C. G., and S. B. Anderson. 1966. *Sedimentary and Tectonic History of the North Dakota Part of the Williston Basin.* North Dakota Geological Survey Miscellaneous Series 28.

Clayton, Lee. 1966. *Notes on Pleistocene Stratigraphy of North Dakota.* North Dakota Geological Survey Report of Investigation 59.

————. 1975. Bison trails and their geologic significance. *Geology* 3:498–500.

Clayton, Lee, W. B. Bickley Jr., and W. J. Stone. 1970. Knife River Flint. *Plains Anthropologist* 15(50):282–90.

Clayton, L., S. R. Moran, J. P. Bluemle, and C. G. Carlson. 1980. *Geologic Map of North Dakota.* United States Geological Survey, 1:500,000 scale.

————. 1980. *Explanatory Text to Accompany the Geologic Map of North Dakota.* North Dakota Geological Survey Report of Investigation 69.

Clayton, Lee, W. J. Stone, and W. B. Bickley, Jr. 1970. Knife River Flint. *North Dakota Quarterly* 38(2):43–55.

Cvancara, A. M. 1976. *Geology of the Cannonball Formation (Paleocene) in the Williston Basin, with Reference to Uranium Potential.* North Dakota Geological Survey Report of Investigation 57.

Cvancara, A. M., and J. W. Hoganson. 1993. Vertebrates of the Cannonball Formation (Paleocene) in North and South Dakota. *Journal of Vertebrate Paleontology* 13(1):1–21.

Davis, N. M. 2000. The gentle-souled Caspar Wistar taught Meriwether Lewis about fossils and straightened out Jefferson on *Megalonyx*. *We Proceeded On* (February), 24–27.

Erickson, B. R. 1999. *Fossil Lake Wannagan (Paleocene: Tiffanian) Billings County, North Dakota*. North Dakota Geological Survey Miscellaneous Series 87.

Erickson, J. M. 1992. Subsurface stratigraphy, lithofacies and paleoenvironments of the Fox Hills Formation (Maastrichtian: Late Cretaceous) adjacent to the type area, North Dakota and South Dakota—toward a more holistic view. In *Proceedings of the F. D. Holland, Jr., Geological Symposium*. Eds. J. M. Erickson and J. W. Hoganson, 199–241. North Dakota Geological Survey Miscellaneous Series 76.

Erickson, J. M. 1999. The Dakota Isthmus—closing the Late Cretaceous Western Interior Seaway. *Proceedings of the North Dakota Academy of Science* 53:124–29.

Feldmann, R. M. 1972. *Stratigraphy and Paleoecology of the Fox Hills Formation (Upper Cretaceous) of North Dakota*. North Dakota Geological Survey Bulletin 61.

Foster, Mike. 1994. *The Life of Ferdinand Vandeveer Hayden*. Niwot, Colo.: Roberts Rinehart Publishers.

Freers, T. F. 1970. *Geology and Ground Water Resources of Williams County, North Dakota*. North Dakota Geological Survey Bulletin 48(pt. 1).

Gerhard, L. C., S. B. Anderson, J. A. LeFever, and C. G. Carlson. 1982. *Geological Development, Origin, and Energy Mineral Resources of the Williston Basin, North Dakota*. North Dakota Geological Survey Miscellaneous Series 63.

Groenewold, G. H., L. A. Hemish, J. A. Cherry, B. W. Rehm, G. N. Meyer, and L. M. Winczewski. 1979. *Geology and Geohydrology of the Knife River Basin and Adjacent Areas of West-central North Dakota*. North Dakota Geological Survey Report of Investigation 64.

Heck, T. J., 2000. *Oil Exploration and Development in North Dakota Williston Basin: 1998–1999 Update*. North Dakota Geological Survey Miscellaneous Series 88.

Hoganson, J. W., E. C. Murphy, and N. F. Forsman. 1998. Lithostratigraphy, paleontology, and biochronology of the Chadron, Brule, and Arikaree Formations in North Dakota. In *Depositional environments, lithostratigraphy, and biostratigraphy of the White River and Arikaree Groups (late Eocene to early Miocene, North America)*. eds. D. O. Terry, H. E. LaGarry, and R. M. Hunt Jr. Geological Society of America Special Paper 325, pp. 185–96.

Hoganson, J. W., J. M. Campbell, M. Hanson, and D. L. Halvorson. 1999. *Plioplatecarpus* (Reptilia, Mosasauridae) and associated vertebrate and invertebrate fossils from the Pierre Shale (Campanian), Cooperstown Site, Griggs County, North Dakota. *Proceedings of the North Dakota Academy of Science* 53:119–23.

Holland, F. D. Jr. 1961. *The Status of Paleontology in North Dakota.* North Dakota Geological Survey Miscellaneous Series 14.

Howard, A. D. 1960. *Cenozoic History of Northeastern Montana and Northwestern North Dakota.* United States Geological Survey Professional Paper 326.

Jefferson, Thomas. 1782. *Notes on the State of Virginia: written in the year 1781, somewhat corrected and enlarged in the winter of 1782, for the use of a foreigner of distinction.* Paris (actual date of publication 1784).

———. 1799. A memoir on the discovery of certain bones of a quadruped of the clawed kind in the western parts of Virginia. *Transactions of the American Philosophical Society* 4:246–60.

———. 1964. *Notes on the State of Virginia* (reprint). New York: Harper and Row.

Kume, Jack, and D. E. Hansen. 1965. *Geology and Ground Water Resources of Burleigh County, North Dakota.* North Dakota Geological Survey Bulletin 42(pt. 1).

Large, A. J. 1995. Lewis & Clark meet the "American Incognitum." *We Proceeded On* (August), 12–18.

Moore, Robert. 1998a. Lewis & Clark and dinosaurs. *We Proceeded On* (May), 26–28.

———. 1998b. More of fossils. *We Proceeded On* (November), 15.

Moran, S. R., M. Arndt, J. P. Bluemle, M. Camara, L. Clayton, M. M. Fenton, K. L. Harris, H. C. Hobbs, R. Keatinge, D. K. Sackreiter, N. L. Salomon, and J. Teller. 1976. Quaternary stratigraphy and history of North Dakota, southern Manitoba, and northwestern Minnesota. In *Quaternary Stratigraphy of North America.* Ed. W. C. Mahaney. Stroudsburg, Penn.: Dowden, Hutchinson, and Ross.

Murphy, E. C. 1995. *North Dakota Clays—A Historical Review of Clay Utilization in North Dakota.* North Dakota Geological Survey Miscellaneous Series 79.

———. 1996. *The Sodium Sulfate Deposits of Northwestern North Dakota.* North Dakota Geological Survey Report of Investigation 99.

————. 2001. *Geology of Dunn County, North Dakota.* North Dakota Geological Survey Bulletin.

Murphy, E. C., J. W. Hoganson, and N. F. Forsman. 1993. *The Chadron, Brule, and Arikaree Formations in North Dakota—the Buttes of Southwestern North Dakota.* North Dakota Geological Survey Report of Investigation 96.

Murphy, E. C., D. J. Nichols, J. W. Hoganson, and N. F. Forsman. 1995. *The Cretaceous/Tertiary Boundary in South-central North Dakota.* North Dakota Geological Survey Report of Investigation 98.

Oihus, C. A. 1983. *A History of Coal Mining in North Dakota.* North Dakota Geological Survey Educational Series 15.

Roberts, L. N. R., and M. A. Kirshbaum. 1995. *Paleogeography of the Late Cretaceous of the Western Interior of middle North America: Coal distribution and sediment accumulation.* U. S. Geological Survey Professional Paper 1561.

Root, M. J., S. A. Ahler, C. R. Falk, J. E. Foss, H. Haas, and J. A. Artz. 1986. *Archaeological Investigations in the Knife River Flint Primary Source Area, Dunn County, North Dakota: 1982–1986 Program.* University of North Dakota Department of Anthropology Contribution 234.

Royse, C. F. 1967. *The Tongue River-Sentinel Butte Contact in Western North Dakota.* North Dakota Geological Survey Report of Investigation 45.

Spamer, E. E., R. M. McCourt, R. Middleton, E. Gilmore, and S. B. Duran. 2000. A national treasure: accounting for the natural history specimens from the Lewis and Clark Expedition (western North America, 1803–1806) in the Academy of Natural Sciences of Philadelphia. *Proceedings of the Academy of Natural Sciences of Philadelphia* 150:47–58.

United States Army Corps of Engineers. 2002. *Ice Engineering.* Manual Number 1110-2-1612.

INDEX

This photo of Ed (left) and John was taken at the mouth of the Cannonball River. The name of this river was derived from the numerous round concretions in this area, such as the one at their feet. A smaller specimen was collected by the Lewis and Clark Expedition to be used as an anchor and then sent to President Jefferson.

About the Authors

From West Fargo, North Dakota, **John W. Hoganson** is the paleontologist for the North Dakota Geological Survey and the curator of the state fossil collection at the North Dakota Heritage Center in Bismarck. He graduated from North Dakota State University with a degree in earth science. He then obtained a master's in geology from the University of Florida and a doctorate in geology from the University of North Dakota. He has authored numerous scientific and popular articles about North Dakota geology and paleontology. In 1993 he received the Governor's Award for Excellence in Public Service and in 2001 was honored as a master alumnus by the College of Science and Mathematics at North Dakota State University.

Edward C. Murphy was raised in Bismarck, North Dakota, and grew up hunting, fishing, hiking, and camping along the Missouri River. He obtained an associate of arts degree from Bismarck State College and bachelor's and master's degrees in geology from the University of North Dakota. He is an assistant director of the North Dakota Geological Survey and has been with that agency for twenty-three years. In addition to numerous articles and maps he has authored on various aspects of North Dakota geology, he has also written an historical account of the Northern Pacific Railway Bridge at Bismarck.

We encourage you to patronize your local bookstore. Most stores will order any title they do not stock. You may also order directly from Mountain Press, using the order form provided below or by calling our toll-free, 24-hour number and using your VISA, MasterCard, Discover or American Express.

Some geology titles of interest:

____AGENTS OF CHAOS	14.00
____CHASING LAVA	16.00
____DINOSAURS UNDER THE BIG SKY	20.00
____FIRE MOUNTAINS OF THE WEST	18.00
____GEOLOGY OF THE LEWIS AND CLARK TRAIL IN NORTH DAKOTA	18.00
____GEOLOGY UNDERFOOT IN CENTRAL NEVADA	16.00
____GEOLOGY UNDERFOOT IN DEATH VALLEY AND OWENS VALLEY	16.00
____GEOLOGY UNDERFOOT IN ILLINOIS	15.00
____GEOLOGY UNDERFOOT IN SOUTHERN CALIFORNIA	14.00
____GLACIAL LAKE MISSOULA AND ITS HUMONGOUS FLOODS	15.00
____ICE AGE MAMMALS OF NORTH AMERICA	20.00
____NORTHWEST EXPOSURES	24.00
____ROADSIDE GEOLOGY OF ALASKA	18.00
____ROADSIDE GEOLOGY OF ARIZONA	18.00
____ROADSIDE GEOLOGY OF COLORADO, 2nd Edition	20.00
____ROADSIDE GEOLOGY OF HAWAII	20.00
____ROADSIDE GEOLOGY OF IDAHO	20.00
____ROADSIDE GEOLOGY OF INDIANA	18.00
____ROADSIDE GEOLOGY OF MAINE	18.00
____ROADSIDE GEOLOGY OF MASSACHUSETTS	20.00
____ROADSIDE GEOLOGY OF MONTANA	20.00
____ROADSIDE GEOLOGY OF NEBRASKA	18.00
____ROADSIDE GEOLOGY OF NEW MEXICO	18.00
____ROADSIDE GEOLOGY OF NEW YORK	20.00
____ROADSIDE GEOLOGY OF NORTHERN and CENTRAL CALIFORNIA	20.00
____ROADSIDE GEOLOGY OF OREGON	16.00
____ROADSIDE GEOLOGY OF PENNSYLVANIA	20.00
____ROADSIDE GEOLOGY OF SOUTH DAKOTA	20.00
____ROADSIDE GEOLOGY OF TEXAS	20.00
____ROADSIDE GEOLOGY OF UTAH	20.00
____ROADSIDE GEOLOGY OF VERMONT & NEW HAMPSHIRE	14.00
____ROADSIDE GEOLOGY OF VIRGINIA	16.00
____ROADSIDE GEOLOGY OF WASHINGTON	18.00
____ROADSIDE GEOLOGY OF WYOMING	18.00
____ROADSIDE GEOLOGY OF THE YELLOWSTONE COUNTRY	12.00

Please include $3.00 per order to cover postage and handling.

Send the books marked above. I enclose $_____

Name_____

Address _____

City/State/Zip _____

☐ Payment enclosed (check or money order in U.S. funds) **OR** Bill my:

☐ VISA ☐ MC ☐ Discover ☐ A   Daytime Phone _____

Card No. _____ Expiration Date:————

Signature _____

MOUNTAIN PRESS PUBLISHING COMPANY
P.O. Box 2399 • Missoula, MT 59806 • Order Toll-Free 1-800-234-5308
E-mail: info@mtnpress.com • Web: www.mountain-press.com